WINDS *of* SKILAK

WINDS *of*
SKILAK

The Continuing Saga

BONNIE ROSE WARD

SAMUEL TREE
PUBLISHING

CONTENTS

CHAPTER ONE

Return to Skilak

The day I left Minnesota, by most people's standards, should have been full of heartache, but while heaviness over leaving my family indeed filled my heart, excitement filled my head as I headed back to the place that had become *home* to me: Skilak Lake in Alaska.

At first, the three months I'd been away (February to May of 1983) seemed like a vacation. But the longer I stayed away from Sam, who'd been working on the North Slope, and away from our cabin on the lake, the sadder I became. Who would ever believe that I'd fallen so deeply in love with being a wilderness wife?

The morning we boarded our new boat, an eighteen-foot, v-haul Alaskan Smoker Craft with a thirty-five-horsepower Evinrude outboard motor, a shiver ran through me. But it wasn't from the cold. Anticipation made me smile so broadly

1

that my face hurt. Sam's grin stretched as widely as mine, and the sparkle in his blue eyes matched that of the sunlight glinting off the water.

"I can't wait to see it, Sam." I stretched out my hand to him, and he reached from his seat to take my hand and squeeze. He knew I spoke of our cabin without asking. He returned to steering our boat, and I held on as he accelerated and we began our trip across Skilak Lake.

As anxious as I was to reach the shore of Caribou Island, I enjoyed every minute of our cruise across the lake. Even the occasional chop and splash of waves against our boat didn't bother me, and the icy wind cooled my flaming cheeks. As the island grew larger in front of me, my heart beat faster. Hawks soared overhead, and in the distance I saw two trumpeter swans swimming together on the water, gracing the lake with their beauty. Even the lake-scented air seemed to wrap around me like a blanket, welcoming me home.

Before Sam cut the motor and drifted the boat onto the shore, I stood. No longer able to contain myself, I leapt onto the beach and let out a shout.

Sam laughed. "It's good to be back, all right." He secured the boat, and hand-in-hand, we started through the woods on the water trail up the hill toward our cabin home.

It was all I could do not to turn loose of his hand and run up the hill, but a big part of me wanted us to see the cabin we'd built together—our first glimpse of it in months.

I'm not sure what I was expecting to see, but when we topped the hill, the utter loneliness of our little cabin sitting among sky-scraping birch and spruce surprised me. Please don't misunderstand me—Sam and I were thrilled to be there, and neither of us could stop smiling—but the lively sounds we'd grown used to hearing around our mountain abode were now silent. The rowdy chicken coop built of logs, as well as its fishnet-covered pen, stood empty. Petunia the pig no longer grunted the welcome I was used to hearing when I'd climb the water trail, water jugs in each hand, and walk into this clearing. I missed seeing Billy the goat, our turkey, General Lee, and, of course, my darling Ester, our milk goat, and little Heidi. Samson no longer stood atop the chicken pen and crowed to announce our arrival. A few of our animals were killed before we left, and we gave the rest to our friend Ted, who stayed in our cabin from time to time, whenever he could get away from the store.

Sam must have sensed my sadness at the loss of our furred-and-feathered family, and he wrapped an arm around my shoulders and pulled me close. "We'll get us some chickens and goats as soon as we settle in." He smiled. "Make this place a little livelier."

"Thank you, Sam." I sniffed and swiped a tear from my face as Sam pressed his hand against my back and guided me toward the door. *Home!* I couldn't wait to step inside the cabin we had built together—both literally and figuratively.

Other than perhaps being a little bit dusty, nothing had changed since the day we'd left. The curtains I'd made still hung at the windows, and even the beaver-fur hat I'd sewn for Sam still hung on the hook by the door. I clapped my hands like a schoolgirl. "I'm so glad to be home, Sam!"

His grin matched mine, and he quickly walked through the living room and into the kitchen, then back through to the bedroom. "All's good," he said as he passed back through the living room and headed toward the door.

I turned to watch him. "Where are you going?"

He answered without looking back. "We've got a boat to unload and luggage to unpack. It might be May, but it'll get mighty cold when the sun goes down. Need firewood to start a fire before dark, too."

That's my Sam. Always the first to do what needs doing. I chuckled and followed behind him toward the door. I hesitated before I walked out, turned and looked around our pretty little home one more time. Though the cabin felt cold and looked lonely, every cell in my body seemed to beam my happiness about being there. *Thank you, Lord, for bringing us safely home,* I prayed.

And then I bounded out the door and across the yard to catch up to my hard-working husband.

Sam's face still shone with joy, even though his arms were already laden with firewood from the stack that stood outside our front door. "Need some help?" I asked, anxious to do something useful.

He nodded toward the front door. "You can light the propane lamp."

I hustled inside right behind him, and was quickly reminded how quickly dusk approaches in the woods.

When I touched the match to the propane lamp's mantle, the sizzling sound pleased me in a surprising way. I breathed in a deep, satisfying breath as I watched the lamplight play along the logs inside the cabin.

Home.

I happily bustled about, lighting candles, and preparing the old-fashioned drip coffee pot. As if reading my mind, Sam appeared with fresh water, and I filled our coffee pot with water and placed it on the stove. As quickly as Sam returned with our belongings, I'd unpack each box, bag, or bundle. By the time the aroma of fresh-brewed coffee and the warmth of the woodstove filled our cabin, Sam and I were moved in and ready to relax.

We settled into our seats across from each other at the kitchen table, and I smoothed the tablecloth with my palm. Sam held up his mug as if in toast, then sipped the steaming brew and let out a deep, satisfied sigh. "It's good to be home, Bonnie."

"Yes, it is, Sam." I felt the stretch of my cheeks as I smiled and raised my mug. "I'll drink to that."

He reached across the table for my hand, and my love for him filled me to the point of nearly spilling out my eyes. *God, how I had missed him these last three months!* I watched him as he looked around, surveying the cabin, and when his face lit up, I knew he was already planning what he'd do next. I pressed my lips together to keep from chuckling. That's my Sam, always ready for the next adventure.

"You know that beach property at the end of our road?" He leaned forward, excitement causing his eyes to sparkle in the lamplight.

"Mm-hmm," I murmured as I swallowed a mouthful of hot coffee.

"I want to find out who owns it." He nodded, agreeing with himself as he talked. "I'm going to buy it, and then I'm going to build you a bigger home right on the beach. No more walking up and down this hill for your water. No more carrying load after load of anything and everything up this hill." He spread an arm toward the far wall. "We'll eventually get a pump and pump our water from the lake to our new beach home."

I sat down my coffee mug and opened my mouth to speak, but Sam was on a roll.

"We've got the money now to make more money. What I mean is, we'll buy more lots, and we'll build getaway cabins. I think I've already got a couple buyers who want this cabin—

two bachelors I worked with up on the slope—they told me if I ever want to sell, they're first in line. In fact—"

"You're selling our cabin!" I'd just settled in again, thrilled to be here, and he was going to sell it? "Really? You'd sell it?"

Sam again reached for my hand, and this time he patted it. "It's more money for us to build our new home. Our *new* home. And Bonnie, it's money for our future here."

I let out the breath I'd been holding, realizing that what he said made sense. Besides, a cabin on the beach sounded dreamy. And the thought of not having to climb that hill toting heavy water jugs . . . "Okay," I said, grinning at him. "I'm in."

Sam hopped from his seat and planted a kiss on my mouth, nose, and forehead. "That's great!"

While I poured us a second cup of coffee, Sam lit a Camel and eased back on his chair, tapping on the table with his finger as he laid out his plans. "First thing we need to do is restore our food supply. We need meat!"

I looked toward the shelves where I stored our canned goods, realizing just how bare those shelves were. We'd encouraged Ted to help himself while we were gone, knowing that whatever remained might not be safe to eat after we were gone so long. Our dry goods remained plenteous, but Sam was right; we needed more food.

"Tomorrow I'll pack up a tent and supplies and head to the upper end of the lake, maybe find us a black bear or a marmot or two," Sam said.

"Tomorrow! We just got here, and you're going to leave tomorrow?"

A devilish look flashed across Sam's face. "Welllll," he drawled out, "I was hoping you'd join me. That is, if you're up to it. What d'ya say?"

"Yes! I'd love to go!" Having a whole day or two to explore Caribou Island after being away so long sounded heavenly to me. And to be truthful, so did having that time on the land with Sam again. "It'll be nice to stock up on meat again. I hope we get a bear."

"Me, too. Be nice to have our food stock replenished before we start building."

My mind rushed ahead to the beach, and our new house Sam would build. "At least we won't have to cut a road to the beach house."

"That's true. But I'll cut roads to the other cabins we'll build. We have to follow the routes laid out on the plot map, of course, but we can do it." He sipped the last from his cup and sat it back on the table. "We've done it before."

I nodded. "I'm so proud of you, Sam."

He cocked his head. "What do you mean?"

"You're the first man on Caribou Island to cut any of the designated right-aways. That's impressive! In fact, you're the *only* man who's done it. Others have just made pathways through the forest wherever they could. You've built *roads,* Sam. Roads! With your own hands!" I leaned in closer toward him. "You know, I remember that first winter we were here, when Skilak Lake was frozen so completely solid that we drove our Jeep all the way across it and right up to our cabin site on the road you cut out with a chainsaw. I was terrified, and I was amazed. We drove right on top of one of the most dangerous lakes in the country! And now, here we are, happy to be living on Caribou Island, getting ready to build another cabin, and then others after that. All because of you!"

Sam took my hand and ran his thumb across my knuckles. "And because of you. I couldn't have done it without you, Bonnie." He tried to smile, but a yawn interrupted him.

I squeezed his hand, then pulled away and picked up our mugs and stood. "I could stay up all night talking with you, Mr. Ward, but my husband has big plans for me tomorrow." I winked at him. "We're going hunting in the morning, so he and I need to get some shut eye."

"Got that right," Sam said. "I'd like to head out before daylight."

"What! Sam, we'd have to leave by four in the morning!" The summer solstice was over a month away, but still, the daylight hours quickly grew longer and longer each day.

"Yep!" Sam nodded. "That's why we need to turn in early."

As I padded toward the kitchen to rinse out our mugs with the water Sam had carried in, the first lonesome howl of a nearby coyote filled the clear night air. As I dried my hands, Sam crept up behind me and slid his arm around my waist, pulling me toward our bedroom. I knew we'd rest soundly this night, drifting off to sleep to a coyote serenade.

CHAPTER TWO

Cycle of Life

While the morning was still blue-black, Sam and I packed our pup tent and supplies into our boat. I snuggled my head backward into my fur-trimmed hood, protecting my face from the wind as I settled into the boat for the ride to the upper end of the lake. With drowsy eyes, I watched water trickle from my hip waders and puddle into the boat's floor—until the moment Sam took off. Then, with newfound wonder, I watched the world come alive as the rising sun's glow began to highlight the dark objects around me, and trees, shrubs, and even the shape of a moose appeared in the awakening dawn on the distant shore.

Morning brightness began burning off the fog as we reached the edge of the glacier flats. We worked for a few hours setting up our camp, clearing a smooth spot, pitching the tent, gathering firewood, building a fire pit, and unpacking our supplies. Once we were satisfied that we'd created a comfortable camp, we headed out to find a bear.

All day, and late into the evening, we tramped over the mountains, both of us searching and peering as far as we could see, but as the sun began to set, we headed back to camp empty handed. After we'd eaten, we sat close to the fire and sipped a final cup of coffee together, and even though the coffee was caffeinated, I think I might have momentarily dozed with my cold hands wrapped around the steaming mug. I blinked rapidly and sat upright, peering hard into the darkness around us. Yes, my muscles had grown soft over the last few months, and yes, weariness invaded them through to my bones, but my not-at-all-irrational fear of brown bears invading and ripping into our camp—or us—caused me to at least attempt to remain alert to our surroundings.

Still, by the time I'd swallowed the last dregs in my mug, I no longer cared about our safety. I no longer cared about aggressive brown bears. I only cared about climbing into our tent, snuggling deep into our down-filled sleeping bag next to Sam's warm body, and sleeping like Rip Van Winkle for *at least* a hundred years.

The soothing sounds of calling loons on the lake woke Sam and me the next morning, and we turned to each other and grinned. I stretched lazily, then curled up tightly, thinking I might doze again, but then the excitement of a new day on Skilak nudged me wide awake. We got up and dressed, and we agreed that, instead of preparing breakfast, we'd head back up the mountain to hunt, in case the bears were more active in the morning hours.

As our luck would have it, we didn't get a bear on that trip, either. Fortunately, we spotted a marmot above the tree line, and Sam's shot was true. I'd soon be dining on marmot.

The next morning, we broke camp and packed up our belongings. As we balanced our backpacks and walked across the glacier flats, Sam shifted his gun on his shoulder and turned to me.

"Want to take one more look?"

"Climb the mountain again?" I asked.

He shrugged. "If you're up for it."

Of course I was up for it. The view never grew old, and another chance at bringing home a bear was well worth the hike.

As we crested a bluff, Sam stopped and pointed. I followed his direction, and I stared hard, until I gasped when I made out the herd of Dall sheep a good distance away, high up from where we stood. I lifted my binoculars from my neck for a better look, and I wasn't disappointed. The ewes stood, almost majestically, against the backdrop of a rocky cliff. Lambs were scattered around them, some lying, some standing, and a few scampering about. I panned across the herd and watched as a ram turned and looked upward, the profile of his full curl glowing bronze against the white of his coat. "Ohhh, Sam," I said. "Have you ever seen anything so wonderful?"

I kept panning the sheep, adjusting the focus on my binoculars, and I'm pretty sure Sam and I spotted the eagle at the same time. "Look!" we said simultaneously.

"An eagle!" I said.

"Two," Sam said. "Golden eagles."

I searched and found the second one. "I see—" and then I gasped.

Sam and I watched, horrified, as one of the eagles swooped low, it's razor-like talons fully extended, and clutched one of the lambs. He half-dragged, half-carried, the large lamb in his talons and knocked it off the cliff. "Oh, no!" I squealed. "Did you see that?"

Sam lowered his binoculars. "I saw it."

"That poor baby!"

"There's nothing we can do about it, Bonnie. Cycle of life."

"I know. It's still so—so *sad.*"

Sam patted my shoulder. "That's the breaks." He jerked his head toward the lake. "We need to get home while the getting's good." He grinned and chucked my chin. "I'm hankering for some fried marmot."

I coughed out a laugh. Sam has always been able to make me smile.

He shifted his big pack until he had its weight comfortably distributed on his back. My pack was small, by comparison, and certainly much lighter. For Sam's sake, I was glad we didn't have to walk far back to the boat. We always packed more than we needed, but in the Alaskan wilderness, it paid to be prepared. The weather could turn nasty on a moment's notice, and we'd need the extra food and supplies in case we couldn't make it home as planned.

Fortunately for Sam and me, the weather remained nice. Skilak Lake looked like an azure-tinted mirror, smooth and glassy as it reflected the cloud-free blue sky. Still, we took nothing for granted, as we'd seen both the lake and sky grow violent in a few short minutes.

CHAPTER THREE

Breaking New Ground

The days that followed my unsuccessful hunting trip with Sam were filled with merriment. Rare were the visitors to our backwoods cabin, so when our friends Harry and Foster and their wives arrived on the island, our house overflowed with pleasant conversation, laughter, and occasional happy mayhem. The camaraderie we all developed caused the days to fly past.

I'd rushed to prepare not only Sam's and my cabin, but also the little cabin at the back of our lot, which we fondly called our "guest cabin." We always wanted the few visitors we had to enjoy their privacy—one of the main attractions of living in the wilderness is solitude—but it pleased both Sam and me that our guests spent much of their time—when they weren't hunting, fishing or sleeping—in our cabin with us.

The men spent their days hunting, and all the ladies would come over to Sam's and my cabin, where we'd play cards, cook big meals together for the hungry men, and swap stories, recipes, and tips for homesteading in the wilderness.

Jane and I unpacked, washed, and put away the large box of nice dishes, pots, and pans that I'd brought back from Minnesota, and the ladies oohed and ahhhed over them when I set the table with them that first evening we all had dinner together. We'd decided that living in the wilderness didn't mean I couldn't have nice things to make my cabin feel special and homey.

As I looked around our cabin that evening, with our friends gathered around a table overflowing with bear stew, venison steaks with gravy, and freshly baked bread, I paused to thank God for this little paradise He'd allowed Sam and me to help create there on the island. The friends He'd brought into our lives here enriched us, entertained us, and made us better people.

Only a few days after our friends left, Nels and Anna arrived. Nels and I had long since gotten over our quarrel, and even if I hadn't come to appreciate the reason he killed my pet goat, I understood it. He was only defending his property, and a garden in the Alaskan wilderness is truly a life-giving force that must be protected.

I counted down the minutes completing the two-hour span of time I'd allowed Anna to settle in before I half-sprinted down the path to their cabin. She'd already anticipated my arrival, and she'd made a chocolate cake topped with ganache and raspberries she'd purchased in town, and her cabin was filled with the fragrance of hot vanilla coffee. Oh, how I'd missed my friend!

Now that Anna had arrived "home," our little island once again felt like a tiny neighborhood, even though we were flung a fair distance apart. The single-digit population of Caribou Island was growing and would continue to grow, thanks in no small part to Sam Ward. In addition to purchasing the beach lot at the end of our road, where we planned to build our own new cabin, Sam also bought a few other inland lots on the island, where we hoped one day to build more cabins that we'd sell.

We spent the next few weeks clearing our new property. Sam worked up a sweat cutting down trees with his chainsaw, while I'd drag the brush down to the beach. In the evenings, we'd light fire to those brush piles, and sometimes they'd burn until well past midnight.

Once we'd cleared the trees and brush away, we'd both chop at the ground and dig up ground cover and roots, working until the soil was loose. Then Sam would level the land and move into place huge rocks he'd dug up, which would serve as foundation cornerstones.

When we'd accomplished those sweat-popping chores, we'd begin hauling 4" X 6" timbers (logs cut flat on all four sides) from a sawmill on the mainland in Sterling. We cut and shaved down our own timber for the first cabin we'd built, and it was a pleasure to purchase it now already cut and ready for use.

Many mornings, Sam would head across Skilak Lake in our new boat. On the other side, he and the sawmill owner, a kindhearted older man with the same snow-white hair and beard as Santa Claus—and cheeks just as red and jolly—would load down our boat with timbers. Some days I'd ride along with Sam, but many times I stayed on the island, as Sam could haul more lumber if I wasn't in the boat. I'd meet him on the beach as he came ashore, and together we'd unload the timbers and carry them to our new homesite.

At first, I tried to help Sam carry those heavy timbers, each of which were sixteen to eighteen feet long. I tried carrying them like I'd carry a log, but they were too long for me to hold and balance to move them more than a few feet at a time. Then I tried dragging them, which did more to carve up the beach and make walking more difficult than it did to move the timbers.

After a few more failed attempts at "helping," Sam fired me from the job.

"Bonnie, stop lifting that thing," he said as he watched me struggle to get an eighteen-foot timber off the beach. His mischievous grin disarmed me. "You're gonna strain something you might need."

Relegated to less-cumbersome chores, I carried bundles of insulation and other building supplies, plus more rocks. And on occasion, when the boat load of lumber contained shorter timbers—eight and ten foot—I helped unload those. More than once, with my upper back and shoulders aching, I'd pause to stretch my muscles and my heart, giving thanks to God for the fact that our new cabin would be on the beach, not up the hill where we currently lived. When I grew tired, I'd remind myself how wonderful it would be to no longer carry our groceries and supplies up that hill, once our new cabin was built. Then I'd smile and grab another load.

While Sam was crossing Skilak for a load of timbers, I'd continue arranging the rocks. We'd decided that we'd create the foundation of our cabin from rocks, so I scoured the beach for the biggest and smoothest, and I'd carry them and carefully placed them in the 20' X 24' space we'd cleared for our cabin. We planned our new cabin to be two stories, with the second floor being half the size as the first at 12' X 20', creating a large, upstairs bedroom overlooking the lake. I dreamed about the view from that bedroom, even while awake.

When the sun bore down around the spot we'd cleared, the heady scent of the spruce and birch Sam had cut filled the air as if it were Mother Nature's own perfume. I'd breathe deeply, inhaling that natural air freshener, feeling it open my head and lungs. We were truly blessed.

Eventually, I'd take a break and hike back up the hill to our little cabin. I'd kick off my shoes at the door, pad across the smooth wooden floor toward my cozy kitchen, and I'd make a fresh pot of coffee to enjoy with our lunch. I'd prepare sandwiches for Sam and me, and sometimes I'd get our dinner started, enjoying the peaceful feeling of basking in a ray of warm sun that shone through our largest window. Then I'd fill our Thermos and pack our sandwiches into a basket for easy carrying, and I'd hustle back down the hill to our beach worksite, where Sam and I would enjoy our lunch break together.

Does it sound too idyllic to be true? Much of the time, it certainly seemed like it, and I often wondered how we'd become so fortunate—*how I had become so fortunate*—because not only did I live in a peaceful Alaskan wonderland, I had (and still have) an amazing, hard-working, God-fearing husband to share it with.

My Wilderness Kitchen

CHAPTER FOUR

The Cowboy & the Lady

"I met a cowboy," Sam said.

I stared at him. He'd hoisted a couple of eighteen foot 4" X 6" timbers onto his shoulders, and I wondered if the weight caused him to talk nutty. "What?"

"I met a cowboy." He grinned. "A real cowboy. Oh, and his friend. A woman—not a girlfriend, just his friend."

I hefted a bag of supplies and followed Sam, still not sure what he was talking about. "A cowboy?" I said. "In Alaska?"

Sam dropped the timbers to the ground near our building site. "Uh-huh."

As we walked up the hill toward home, Sam teased me, making me drag the story out of him, knowing my curiosity would cause me to probe him for every detail, which he relished sharing one tasty morsel at a time.

After some long minutes of our Q & A game, I learned the man was indeed a real cowboy named Winston—who wore a cowboy hat, cowboy boots, leather chaps and a vest—visiting from Wyoming. His friend, Valerie, was several years older than Winston, and she'd come along to help Winston find and establish a home in Alaska before she headed back to Wyoming.

"Winston reminds me of us, Bonnie," Sam said.

"How do you mean?"

The sincerity in Sam's eyes touched me. "He's been looking for a place in the Alaskan wilderness. He wants to build a cabin, live off the land. You know . . . like us."

I nodded, but this time, I didn't ask questions. Sam had more to say without my prompting, and I knew it was coming from his heart.

"He's about to give up on his dream." Sam looked away for a moment, staring into the trees as if remembering his own past. He spoke in a solemn, quiet voice. "He's searched for a place all over Alaska, but he hasn't found a homesite. He said if he doesn't find something soon, he plans on returning to Wyoming." He turned back to me. "You remember how difficult it was for us to find a place?"

"Sure do!" I answered.

"Bonnie, I want to sell him a lot here. On our island." He waved a hand toward our cabin and the tree-canopied land beyond, then his earnest gaze found mine. "He'd be our neighbor."

I stepped toward Sam and placed my hand on his chest. "You're a good man, Sam Ward. If you approve of this cowboy, then I know he'll make a fine neighbor."

Two days later, Sam guided our boat into shore at the lower landing and jumped into the water—wearing his waders, of course—and held out a hand to steady me. I stepped out of the boat and looked up, surprised to see a tall, well-built man striding toward us. He grinned and tipped his hat. Sam's cowboy.

"Hello, Sam."

The man had a bit of a five o'clock shadow around his chin and cheeks, but it did nothing to hide his broad smile. "You must be Bonnie," he said, thrusting his hand toward me. "I'm Winston."

When I offered my hand, Winston's engulfed it, his fingers wrapping all the way up my wrist. I had to tilt back my head to smile at him—he was well over six feet tall. Just beyond Winston, a woman with shoulder-length gray hair approached us, her smile equally bright. Of course, that woman was Valerie.

The men tied up the boat, and the four of us walked toward the Jeep, where we chatted for a short time. It took no time before I understood why Sam wanted to offer Winston a lot on our land. The man was openly serious about his desire to homestead in Alaska, and he had the experience to do it. He'd spent his life doing hard work on ranches, much of that time on the back of a horse.

Conversation came easy with Winston and Valerie, and I learned that once Winston had settled in Alaska, Valerie planned to drive back to Wyoming on her own. She talked easily of her own dreams, and while she loved visiting Alaska, she was anxious to get back to her own ranch in Wyoming.

After lunch, Sam and I caught up on the local news—which didn't take long—at the post office, where we picked up our mail before heading back to the boat with groceries and supplies from our whirlwind visit to town. When we arrived, Winston and Valerie stood waiting for us.

"Say, Sam?" Winston removed his cowboy hat and nodded at me. "What say I take a ride to the island with you and Bonnie? Check out your land? That is, if you don't mind."

Sam glanced at me, and I nodded. "Sure!" I turned to face Valerie. "We'd love to have you two visit with us."

Valerie tilted her head. "Thanks, Bonnie, but Winston would come alone. Someone's gotta stay here and tend to our camp. Maybe I can come visit you another time."

"Yeah," said Winston, his drawl making the word two-syllables.

I'll admit I was a bit saddened that Valerie wouldn't be there to visit with me—I always enjoyed the company of another female in what seemed to be a largely male-inhabited region—but Sam and I had a great time during Winston's visit.

While Sam showed Winston around our homestead, I prepared egg salad using the eggs I picked up in town (only briefly mourning the loss of our chickens), and sliced the fresh bread I'd made the day before. I had also bought some sunny-looking lemons, so I squeezed their juice, added a generous scoop of sugar, and made fresh lemonade.

Over lunch, the two grown men acted like excited young boys. Winston's cheeks flamed red as he and Sam discussed the lot they'd chosen together for the cabin Winston would build. At one point, Winston clapped Sam on the shoulder and stared at him earnestly.

"I'm grateful, Sam. I truly am grateful. This is exactly what I've been looking for, for months—heck, for all my life! You've offered me a place to start, and I'm thankful for the chance you've given me."

Sam beamed. "Hey, I haven't given you anything. You've still got to pay for it."

The two men laughed, and I couldn't help but join in. Though the piece of land that Winston had chosen was a good distance from our cabin, Sam and I would soon have a new neighbor—a neighbor we had chosen.

I often wonder at the blessings Sam and I received, and I can't help but believe that some of it wasn't because of my husband's kind and generous heart. He'd made an amazingly good offer to Winston for a large piece of land, and as I later learned, he'd even given the man a huge stack of really nice logs that he'd been cutting over the course of a couple years. Winston now had material to begin building his own cabin.

Soon afterward, Winston and Valerie broke camp and moved all their gear to the island. They set up Winston's wall tent a few yards away from where he'd build his new home. We visited often; Valerie and I frequently baking or cooking together, the men working together on our cabin and clearing Winston's property, and all of us commiserating over aching muscles, Skilak's moody weather, and the general nuisances of bruises and the occasional mashed thumb. Even stormy weather didn't dampen our spirits for long, as we all enjoyed the company and camaraderie of kindred spirits—folks who loved the outdoors enough to build a homelife among spruce, sunshine, and snow.

Spring passed like the whirlwind that frequently accompanied its storms. Mid-July arrived, and with it came sockeye salmon season. This year, it was Sam who first spotted them—a frothing red tidal pool churning in Skilak Lake.

"Time to go fishing!" Sam pumped a fist into the air.

He didn't have to say it twice. I rushed to join him when I heard him shout.

Though we were busy with the business of building, all work stopped for sockeye salmon season. The Alaskan state law allowed us only three fish per day, per person, so we had to make the most of the season so I could can our catches to last throughout the long winter to come.

"How long will they stay here?" Winston asked, his face red and glowing with excitement.

Sam shoved his hat back on his head, suddenly serious. "Not long enough. We might get four or five days of fishing out of it, if we're lucky. See, they're on the way upriver to spawn, so they don't stick around long."

"Ohhh," Valerie breathed out. She ticked her fingers with her thumb, counting. "So . . . we can only catch four or five dozen fish? That's not much. How will that carry you all through the winter?"

Sam grinned and winked at me, then stuck out his arm. "Up close, these salmon are at least as long as my arm, and twice as round. That's a whole lot of meat. Besides, we'll get us a bear or two, plus moose and maybe a Dall sheep. Don't worry. We won't starve."

I draped an arm around Valerie's back, turning her toward Sam's and my cabin. "Come on, Valerie. We've got work to do to get ready to can the fish we'll catch today."

The first time I'd canned sockeye, I'd worked with Anna and Nels—well, mostly Anna, as the men fished while the two of us ladies canned. I'd learned from her how to tend her cookstove, keeping the temperature steady, so the jars would heat correctly, and they'd properly seal, so we'd have salmon that would taste fresh into next spring.

This year, would be my second year using my own wood cookstove, and I couldn't wait to use it for canning again. I went to the bedroom and pulled out boxes of empty canning jars from under the bed, causing Valerie to laugh.

"Well, I'd never have thought of that! A bedroom pantry. You've thought of everything, Bonnie."

The two of us quickly washed and scalded the jars to get them ready, then we carried five-gallon buckets of water to salt, so we could soak the sockeye after Sam and Winston filleted them. In a matter of minutes, all four of us stood on the shore of Skilak Lake, ready to throw our lines into the water.

"Wow!" Valerie shielded her eyes with her hand as we watched the small red volcano of fish. "They're even bigger than I thought!" She turned to Sam. "No wonder you weren't worried about catching only a few dozen of these little whales."

We laughed at her description, and I wondered what kind of fish she'd pictured them to be when she saw them from farther away.

We returned to the cabin with our first day's haul shortly after noon, and when we carried the fish to our outdoor worktable for filleting and placed them in a pile, I was astounded anew at the amount of meat we'd soon be canning.

Sam must have read my mind, as he so often does, because he grinned when he slapped one of the fish with his broad hand. "Don't worry, Bonnie. We'll grill one of these babies over the fire for dinner tonight, so you'll only have eleven to can this afternoon."

My mouth actually watered at the mention of freshly caught, grilled salmon. When I'd first tasted the red salmon, its rich flavor seemed a little too strong for my tastes, but in no time, I'd grown to love it, and sockeye became a valuable staple of our Alaskan diet.

"Want to do it over the fire, or in the cabin?" I asked.

Sam tilted his head toward the fire pit we'd made from beach rocks. "Let's grill it outdoors. Nothing like the wood smoke and salmon to tingle the taste buds."

"You won't believe me," Winston said, rubbing his belly, "but my stomach just growled."

Sam dragged a fish into place in front of him, and he pulled out his fillet knife. "Grab you a fish then, Winston. The sooner we get these big boys filleted, the sooner we can eat."

The two men worked on the fish. I'd never seen anyone who could fillet a fish as swiftly and cleanly as Sam, and I remembered watching Nels and Bill step aside in the past to leave the filleting to Sam. He had turned it into an art, and I wondered if he shouldn't teach that skill to a roomful of the world's greatest chefs.

In the cabin, Valerie and I cut the fish the men filleted into chunks that would fit into jars. In no time at all, we had two canners full of jars of red salmon.

Next, we sliced bread and fried potato wedges to go with our fish. Valerie cut a lemon into paper-thin slices to place on the salmon while it grilled, and then we set the table, taking care to keep an eye on the pressure of my canners. I steeped a pitcher of fresh tea. Valerie and I joined the men by the fire with an empty platter, ready to receive the grilled fish.

If you'd have asked any of us as we sat around the table that evening, I'm sure we'd have said that we'd just enjoyed the most delicious dinner of our lives. I bemoaned the fact that in my haste to go fishing, I hadn't made dessert, but all three told me I was silly, as no one had room for one more bite.

After nightfall, we each took a turn in the wood-heated sauna Sam had built for us last year. I recalled the first time I'd bathed on the island—in a galvanized metal washtub filled with water we'd heated over the fire—and I realized just how very far Sam and I had come in making a comfortable home on Caribou Island.

I slept like a baby that night.

CHAPTER FIVE

The Big Bust

If I've learned anything at all, it should be that boasting about how perfect things are is a sure sign that something is going to go wrong. And yet, as Valerie and I stood in my kitchen in our new cabin later that summer, chatting as I varnished my cupboards—I chanced to brag about how Caribou Island was a wilderness paradise where only the best of people ventured to live and visit.

No sooner had the words left my mouth than Valerie and I turned our heads toward the window, toward the sound of a boat motor pulling up at our beach. We looked at one another, puzzled. Sam and Winston had gone to town for mail and supplies and shouldn't be back until the evening, and besides, that didn't sound like our boat's motor.

I placed my paintbrush across the top of the can, turned to the wash basin and quickly scrubbed and dried my hands.

"It's a whole bunch of men," Valerie said as she peered out the window. "Looks like police."

My stomach clenched. I headed toward the living room, Valerie behind me, just as the men arrived at the door—or should I say, the cutout for where a door would one day be. I swallowed hard. "Yes?"

The kind smile of our friend Al Thompson immediately calmed me. He knew Sam well, and if something had happened to my husband, his face would no doubt have registered deep concern.

"Bonnie," he said, extending his hand.

In my relief, I probably shook it like I was priming a pump, but if he noticed, he didn't let on.

Sam and I had met Al our first winter on the lake, when he'd made a dramatic entrance into our lives by flying his bush plane low over our heads as we were crossing frozen Skilak Lake in our Jeep. Al circled around us, then landed the plane directly on the ice in front of us, stepped out, and introduced himself as the Alaska State Fish and Wildlife Trooper.

The three of us stood right there in the middle of Skilak Lake, talking between the plane and our Jeep, like it was a perfectly normal thing to do. To this day, I recall the memory as surreal—all that weight resting on what, in a few months' time, would be a turbid, churning, vicious lake known for taking lives.

That day Al asked us about ourselves, how we'd come to be on the lake, where we lived, what we planned to do. In turn, he shared his own story, and it left me breathless. He and his wife had been on a moose-hunting trip in the Kenai National Moose Range in the early fall of 1972, hiking a little over eight hours into the wilderness. They set up camp in the high country, commonly known as the bench lands near the headwaters of the Funny River—roughly ten or so miles from where the three of us now stood on Skilak Lake.

Their third night at camp, a brown bear crashed through their Visqueen covered lean-to in the early morning hours before sunrise. Al, like Sam, always camped with a gun within reach, and though he grabbed his rifle, the impact from the surprise attack knocked it out of his hand.

The bear dropped down onto Al's wife, Joyce.

I held my breath as Al told the story of how he grabbed the bear's head and punched it with his fist to get it away from Joyce.

This only angered the bear, which turned his vicious attack on Al. The bear bit down on Al's left arm and flung him into the air. He attacked Al again and again, ripping into his right side, then biting into Al's skull. The angry animal picked up Al by the head, shaking him as it carried him out of the clearing and into the woods.

Fortunately—if one can call the horrific incident fortunate—Al's scalp gave way, and the bear dropped Al while retaining a chunk of the man's scalp in his mouth. Al still had enough presence about him to lie flat on his stomach and play dead. The bear continued clawing and biting into Al's back. In spite of the excruciating pain, Al didn't move. The bear pawed and stalked around him for a few long, grueling minutes, and then ambled off in the direction of a lake near the campsite.

Al stood, dizzy from pain, and ran as best and fast as he could back to his annihilated campsite to find Joyce frightened and worried, but unscathed. Al must have looked frightful, covered in blood, his clothes ripped and hanging from his bleeding body, and a chunk of his scalp gone.

The first thing they did was to find their guns and start a fire. Then they spent the longest three hours of their lives waiting for daylight in the 25-degree temperature, watching for the bear to return while tending to Al's wounds. Joyce tore strips of muslin from the game bags she had sewn together for this trip, and bandaged Al the best she could. As soon as they could see to walk out, they headed back toward the main road.

Al shared that the same hike that took them over eight hours to arrive at camp took them less than six to get back. Still, six hours of hiking with a mangled body must have seemed like days.

At this point, Al removed his game warden's cap, and try as I might, I couldn't look away from the damage I saw. Al's scalp looked like a roadmap of scars.

He told us how the surgeon had tried to reattach his scalp, after Joyce and some Alaskan State Troopers had helicoptered back to the campsite to search for and locate the missing chunk, but the reattached piece didn't live, so Al had to have skin grafts to cover his skull.

When he shared that part of the story, I recalled that I'd heard it before.

"Al, I think I read about you!" I said. "Did someone write an article about you in a magazine?"

Al's cheeks flushed from wind-chaffed pink to red, and he grinned shyly. "Yeah. Quite a few articles came out about it, including one that Joyce wrote."

I put a hand on Sam's arm. "Remember, Sam? You and I both read it and talked about how awful that must have been."

Sam nodded. "I do." He stuck out his hand. "Let me shake your hand again, Mr. Thompson. It's an honor to meet someone who lived through an ordeal like that, then returns to the woods to protect animals like the one who attacked him."

Al chuckled. "Well, I can't say I'd protect *that* one. In fact, they never did find that bear, though a guy did get a shot in him." He gazed out over the frozen lake toward the south shore. "We believe he might have tromped somewhere into the woods and died."

A shiver raced up my back that had nothing to do with the cold.

"And please," the game warden said, "call me *Al.*" He smiled at Sam and me. "You can even call me *Bear Bait.*"

The three of us laughed.

"That's what my friends call me."

Sam and I had never referred to Al as Bear Bait, though each time I saw him, the name popped into my mind, just as it did as I introduced Al to Valerie.

In return, Al introduced Valerie and me to the men with him—Alaska Wildlife Troopers and Fish and Wildlife officers.

"Gentlemen," I asked once the five men stood inside my living room and all introductions had been made, "how can I help you?"

"Bonnie," Al began, "have you noticed anything out of the ordinary around the lake recently?"

The question caught me off guard, and I ran images of the lake and surrounding area through my mind, and came up with an honest answer. "No, sir."

He looked at Valerie, and she shook her head. "No."

"Have you heard about the big bust we made?" Al asked.

Drugs were the first thing that entered my mind, but Al wasn't a DEA officer. "No!"

"We just made one of the biggest busts for illegal possession of sport fish, and they were caught right here on Skilak Lake." He jerked a thumb over his shoulder toward the lake.

One of the young officers with Al hooked his thumbs in his belt, thrust back his shoulders, and puffed out his chest. I looked at the difference between the two officers—Al, a competent, older gentleman who'd seen a little bit of everything, knew his job extremely well, and had nothing to prove, and these young guns who walked with artificial swagger and were out only to make a name for themselves. I shifted my body in a quarter turn, angling myself toward Al, mentally shutting out these other men who stared at me with distrust and suspicion in their eyes.

"You know, Al, I do recall seeing a white boat over on the south shore quite a few times when I'd walk down the water trail to the lake to fetch water." I chewed my lip for a moment, remembering. "It seemed small to me, but I guess in the distance, it could have been a lot bigger."

"Did you do any sport fishing this summer?" asked one of the other officers.

Before I could answer his accusatory question, Al pressed his lips into a line and nodded toward my newly built kitchen, where the smell of varnish permeated the air and mingled with the scent of freshly sawn wood. "I think it's easy to see what these ladies have been up to all summer." He extended his hand for a shake. "Bonnie." He offered his hand toward my friend. "Valerie." Then he touched a finger to his cap. "Ladies, we won't take up any more of your time."

It might have been my imagination, but I thought I saw a stern look from Al to the young officer who'd snapped his question at me, and Al motioned toward the doorway and ushered out the officers.

I stood, a bit confused, as one of the men stood to the side of the door and didn't leave. Unlike the uniformed officers, this man wore quilted flannel and Carhartt pants. He lifted a hand and took off the dark sunglasses he wore, and a grin broke across his face.

"Lucas!" I said. "What in the world! Sam is going to be surprised to see you!"

His black eyes sparkled merriment in the way I remembered from the first time I'd met him. I hadn't recognized him, since he'd shaved his beard and wasn't wearing his trademark red-plaid mackinaw and matching pants.

Sam had met Lucas while working on the slope, and the two of them became hunting buddies. Lucas had visited us every spring and fall, driving down from Anchorage to hunt and fish on Skilak.

"It's amazing, Bonnie," he said, looking around the cabin.

Lucas was built like a bear, and though it's hard to imagine a barrel-chested man pushing out his chest any farther, Lucas did just then, puffing it out in pride. "You and Sam have done a fantastic job with this cabin. Well, with *all* the cabins you've built! You really have created a little piece of wilderness heaven here."

Valerie agreed, and I believe my pride matched Lucas's in that moment.

"Are you planning to stay awhile?" I asked.

"I'd like to stay a coupla days, and do some sheep hunting." He shrugged. "That is, if you don't mind me using the guest cabin."

I waved his question away. "Of course not! You know you're always welcome here."

We chatted briefly, and then Lucas left to do some fishing at the upper end of the lake, promising to return in a couple of hours.

Early evening arrived, and with it, Sam and Winston, followed a short while later by Lucas. When we told Sam about Al and the accompanying troopers' visit, he wasn't surprised.

"Winston and I heard about it in town. Everyone's talking about it. Said it's the biggest over-the-limit illegal possession in the state's history."

"Wow, Sam. What were they catching?"

"Hundreds of salmon, dolly, rainbow trout."

"Yeah," Winston said in his Wyoming drawl. "They caught their fish at the upper end of the lake, where the Kenai River dumps into the lake. Then they went up the river a-ways to fish. They camped on the other side of the island from us."

"How did they keep all that fish fresh?" Valerie asked. "Wouldn't it spoil? It's not cold enough out to keep it on ice for very long."

"Canned it," Sam said.

Valerie and I looked at each other, mentally communicating about what a lot of work that must have been. She and I had spent many long hours canning the legal-limit catch the four of us had caught during sockeye season. To can several hundred of the big fish that come out of Skilak would have been exhausting.

Sam chuckled as he watched us. "Commercial canner." He waved his hand toward the kitchen. "Nothing like what you two used here to can."

"Ohhh," Valerie and I chorused together, then laughed.

"Only my Bonnie," Sam said. "Feeling sorry for the hard labor that those poor criminals had to go through to can all that fish."

We all laughed, and Sam pecked a kiss on my forehead.

Though we laughed about it in the moment, that incident was a wake-up call for all of us. We'd learned that Nels and Anna were also unaware of the poachers. We thought we knew everything that went on around us in our wilderness paradise, but that summer we'd been so hard at work on our own beach property that we'd missed the largest illegal sport fishing operation in Alaska's history—right under our noses!

That night, as we sipped coffee in front of the stove before Winston and Valerie headed back to their wall tent and Lucas left for the guest cabin, we all vowed to be more alert to our surroundings. I thought of Al Thompson's scarred head, Sam's accident a few years back when he broke his back and pelvis, and even Anna's deeply cut finger when a bowl broke. Out here on Caribou Island, we were far away from police, hospitals, and fire departments. *We were* the police, doctors, and firemen—we were our own first line of defense.

"Folks, y'all stay up and talk as late as you like." Sam stretched and covered his mouth as he stifled a yawn. "This old feller needs his beauty rest."

Valerie retrieved hers and Winston's coffee mugs and carried them to the kitchen.

Winston's yawn followed Sam's. "I'm bushed," he said. "All that shopping wears me out worse than a hard day's labor."

I laughed, and Sam and I hugged our friends goodnight, then they headed out the door and up the little trail to their campsite. Lucas lingered with us in front of the fire, and the three of us drank hot chocolate as we listened to North Wind Messages.

"Here's one for Sam on Caribou," the announcer said, and Lucas, Sam, and I exchanged surprised glances. "Ted writes, 'Sam, please pick me up at the lower landing. I'd like to come stay a couple of days and hunt.'"

Sam and Lucas grinned at each other. "Perfect timing," Sam said. "Let's go get us some sheep!"

Half an hour later, Lucas and Sam stood outside the cabin discussing their hunting plans, while I tidied the kitchen.

As I lay in bed that night and listened to the regular rhythm of Sam's breathing, I felt safe; safer than I'd felt a few hours ago, when I worried about all that could happen out here on our isolated island.

Accidents and crime can happen anywhere, but I'm sure big-city crime occurs more often and more dramatically than what happens on Skilak Lake. For that, I gave thanks. I wasn't naïve enough to believe we were completely safe, but I rested easy knowing that nothing could happen to Sam and me or our friends without God's knowledge.

CHAPTER SIX

Another Kind of Trophy

The next morning, Sam and Lucas took the boat to the landing to pick up Ted, and the three men headed to the upper end of the lake to hunt sheep. Winston stayed behind with Valerie— she'd be leaving for Wyoming in a week, so I'm sure the two had to plan and prepare for that day. None of us were looking forward to her departure. She was a great sport and a joy to be around. I would definitely miss my new friend—*very much!*

I worked around the house while the men were gone, and I spent much of that time baking and preparing dinner for what I knew would be three hungry men upon their return.

They were starving all right—and cold, because the mighty hunters didn't return until the following day. As the men regaled me with their hunting tale, they had seconds, thirds, and then second helpings of dessert, and for a moment, I wondered if I'd prepared enough food. Fortunately, they pushed away their plates and continued with their story just as I ran out of spice cake. They did, however, accept refills of coffee.

"Bonnie, do you remember when we saw the eagle jerking the lamb off that narrow ledge?" Sam asked.

I nodded, and a shudder rippled across the back of my neck.

"Well, we came across the bones of dozens of Dall sheep up there. Not just lambs, either. Grown sheep, too."

"How on earth did you men get up in there?" They would've had to cross Bear Mountain's little creek multiple times, as it zigzagged down the mountain.

"Crossed the creek a bunch," Sam said.

"Blazed a trail the rest of the time." Lucas rubbed his bicep. "Had to cut through all kinds of brush, alder patches, you name it."

Ted chimed in. "We climbed up onto a big plateau—we were still a long way from the top. Had to climb a bunch of rock shelves that we couldn't go around. Now and then we'd find a flat plateau that might be, oh, fifty to a hundred feet across, and we'd rest a spell. The rest of it," he shook his head, "was rough going. Rocks slip out from under you, crags cutting into your hands, you name it." Ted held up his hands, which were covered in cuts and abrasions and scrubbed raw.

"We climbed for hours," Sam said. "Got about three-quarters of the way up Bear Mountain, and that's when we spotted them."

"Rams," Lucas said.

Ted jabbed Lucas's arm with a finger. "Not that you could do anything about them."

Ted and Sam laughed, and Lucas found sudden interest in his coffee.

"What?" I asked.

Sam leaned toward me. "We were getting closer to the top—and let me tell you, Bonnie," he said, leveling his hand out, describing a scene from his mind, "the view of the glacier flats and lake from up there was incredible. You can see for miles and miles.

"Anyway, Lucas here takes off his gun strap and puts it around his waist, and he's carrying his gun." Sam grins at his friend. "Guess he wanted to be the first one ready to shoot, in case a big Dall ram sneaked up on us."

Ted coughed out a laugh, and Lucas's face turned crimson.

"He's holding on to that Colt Sauer .375 H & H rifle in one hand, and he grabs this rock with his other to pull himself up, and his hand slips. He starts to fall backward—"

At this, I gasped, envisioning those sheep falling down those deep, rocky crevices.

"—and ol' Lucas has no choice but to grab that rock with both hands to keep from tumbling to his demise. That pretty new sporting rifle of his goes bouncing and bumping down the mountainside, and all Lucas can do is watch."

Ted is laughing hard at this point, pushing against his friend Lucas, who pushes him back, like two tussling boys. "Lucas has to climb down about thirty feet to get his gun," Ted says, "and it's all dinged up, scratched, scarred, that Leopold scope missing—ruined it, he did."

Sam grinned and pointed at Lucas. "And you know what this man has the nerve to do?"

I shook my head and smiled sympathetically at poor Lucas.

"He asks me for *my* gun! Wanted my Model 70 Winchester! I looked him square in the eye, never cracked a smile, and said, 'You think I'm going to trust you with *my gun,* after you dropped *yours?* I don't think so!"

At this, even Lucas had to laugh. "Sam said, 'Maybe Ted will let you use his,' so I turned to my good buddy here, and Ted says, 'Oh, no! You ain't getting mine, either!'"

"Poor Lucas!" I said. "So you didn't get to hunt at all?"

Lucas, whose face was now burgundy, tilted his head toward Sam. "Aw, your hubby took pity on me and let me use his gun."

Sam grinned. "By that time it was getting too dark to hunt, so we set up camp and spent a cold night on that mountain. Planned on hitting it again in the morning, but woke to a storm brewing in the distance and decided we needed to get off the mountain."

Lucas swallowed the last of his coffee and set down his cup. "Well, lady and gentlemen, I hate to be a party pooper, but if I'm going to get home tonight, I better get myself across the lake before it gets any worse." He scooted his chair back from the table and stood. "It's a long drive home and I have to go to work in the morning."

Sam pointed out the window. "Looks like that storm has caught up with us, fellas. You better get a move on, Lucas!"

It was true! Dark clouds had gathered as we ate, and the wind was beginning to pick up. We couldn't see the lake from our little cabin on the hill, but we could hear it.

"Don't have to tell me twice. C'mon, Ted, I'll take you across the lake with me and give you a ride to your vehicle."

Though the men didn't have Dall ram horns to show for their hunting efforts, they had indeed bagged another kind of trophy—they had a humdinger of a story to tell.

A couple days later, Valerie and Winston went across the lake with Sam and into town. While there, Winston sold Valerie his truck, then he used the money to buy himself an 18-foot boat and motor. The three returned to the island happy with their purchases, and—to make sure I didn't feel left out—Valerie presented me with a cookbook—a sourdough recipe book she'd inscribed *Summer of 1983, Bonnie & Sam, Happy New Home! Valerie.*

Oftentimes after she left, I'd use the cookbook not just for baking, but to run my fingers over her inscription. The company of a female was rare on Caribou Island, and the company of one I'd grown to love was extremely special.

CHAPTER SEVEN

Move-In Day!

I woke up the morning of August 24th, and for a split-second, I stretched lazily.

Then it hit me.

It's move-in day!

Months of planning, of refining those plans, of lifting and hauling and falling into bed exhausted, only to wake up and lift and haul some more . . . this was the day it would all pay off. Sam and I were moving into our gorgeous new cabin!

I bounded out of bed, dressed in a rush, and sprang out to the kitchen to start a pot of coffee. When I got there, coffee already awaited me. Sam had already made a pot, drank about half of it, and started working without me. It was just like him to get an early start on a big day like today.

I gulped down a cup, wolfed down a few bites of breakfast, then headed out the door to catch up to him.

"Sam!" I called out. "Sam!"

Where was he?

I headed down the hill and into our new cabin, and just inside the door, I stopped and gasped. Sam had already moved in the new furniture we'd bought, and it sat askew in the center of the living room floor, awaiting my arrangement. Overhead, I heard a thump, and I took the stairs, two at a time, toward our bedroom.

Sam must have heard my approach, because he stepped to the top of the stairs and held out his hand, palm toward me. "Stop. Not yet, Bonnie."

I paused on the stairway. "What? What do you mean, 'Not yet'?"

His grin challenged me. "I have a surprise for you, and it's not quite ready." He nodded toward the living room below. "Why don't you figure out how you want to arrange the furniture down there? Or better yet, you can carry over some of the kitchen boxes from our old cabin, and start putting that stuff where you want it. I know better than to try to arrange your kitchen."

I laughed, remembering the time when I'd caught the flu, and after recovering, returned to my kitchen to discover I couldn't find a pot, a skillet, or even my favorite knife without minutes of searching. Sam—in an effort to help me—had cooked, washed dishes, and put away everything in odd places that took days for me to discover. I'd even found a neatly folded stack of dishtowels in the pantry!

"You've got that right." I winked at my husband, then turned and headed down the stairs and out the door to retrieve my boxed kitchen supplies.

Once I was back in our old cabin—yes, I'd already come to think of it as our *old* cabin, even though I'd just spent the night there—Romeo, the cat Sam and I had adopted in town, danced figure eights around my legs. I'd named him *Romeo* because he was such a little lover, forever on my heels like a puppy or hopping into my lap—even crawling up to curl onto my shoulder. He had an affinity for cardboard boxes, and more than once he'd hop onto the box I was picking up to tote, and I'd carry him, along with the box, down the hill to our *new* beach cabin.

"Better on the box than in my arms, Romeo," I said to him. "Especially after your last meltdown over Moose."

Romeo turned his nose upward and sniffed the air, as if checking to see if the huge Malamute were anywhere around.

"You're safe," I said. "But just in case, keep riding on top of the boxes instead of on top of me."

Moose was the humongous dog of a nice young couple who owned a small A-frame cabin a little way down the beach from ours, and they occasionally visited the island during the summer months. Once they visited me in our cabin on the hill, and I'd been holding Romeo in my arms when I answered the door.

My happy surprise of seeing our friends quickly turned into a not-so-happy screech when Romeo spotted the enormous Malamute and tried to spring from my arms, using his claws to gain traction on my bare skin. Romeo quite literally soared through the air, landing halfway across the cabin before scurrying to hide behind the wood stove, where he stayed for hours after the big dog left. I'd yanked down my sleeves so that our friends wouldn't see the damage Romeo had done, but by the time they'd left, tiny red dots of blood spotted my shirt, and I wore those welted scratches for weeks to come.

Now Romeo sat atop the box I carried until I came within a few yards of the new cabin, when he politely hopped down and sat outside the door, keeping an appraising eye on our new chickens while I dropped off the box and headed back up the hill for another load.

Sam had made great use of the leftover 4" x 6" timbers, building an elegant-looking outhouse (yes, it's possible!).

A couple hours later, I'd carried the last of the kitchen boxes and set up my lovely, efficient kitchen. I stood in the living room to appraise my work, beaming as Sam came down the stairs.

"You look happy," he said.

"Oh, Sam! I'm beyond happy. This cabin looks like it belongs on the cover of a magazine. You've done such a great job!"

"*We've* done a great job, Bonnie. I couldn't have done it without you." He pulled me into his arms, and we hugged and rocked, savoring the moment as we looked around at all we'd accomplished. Then Sam pulled away. "We've still got more to do, but first, I need your opinion on something."

"Oh?"

"Come with me." Sam took my hand and led me toward the stairs, and I eagerly followed him to see what surprise awaited me in our bedroom.

He stopped me just before we reached the upper level, and he slipped around behind me and covered my eyes with his hands.

My heart beat faster in anticipation, my senses heightened by lack of vision. The heady fragrance of freshly-sawed lumber mingled with that of rich wood oil, and I inhaled the scent deep into my lungs. Yet, when Sam removed his hands, I sucked in an extra breath. I couldn't have imagined the room that lay before me—it stunned me!

Sam had varnished the walls until they glowed with a golden sheen around a large window that framed a view of the lake and surrounding trees. Below the window stood a gorgeous, hand-hewn bed, made by Sam's very own hands. Atop it lay a patchwork quilt, a gift made by Sam's mother especially for our new home.

"What do you think?" Sam asked.

I opened my mouth, but I couldn't speak. I felt breathless, almost weightless, and a shiver ran across my skin. I put my hand over my mouth, an effort to quiet the squeal I couldn't contain. Then I spread my arms wide, as if I could hug the entire room and everything in it. "Oh, Sam!" I turned in a circle, arms still outstretched. Then I turned back and wrapped my arms around my husband.

"So, you like it?" Sam's grin filled his entire face and lit up his blue eyes.

I nodded, still unable to speak. I sniffed deeply, then turned back to survey the room. I ran a hand over the carefully stitched quilt, knowing firsthand the many hours—many *weeks*—that went into its creation. I stepped to the window, and my eyes filled again, blurring the sunlit view that spread before me.

Finally, I found my voice. "It's heaven. It's heaven on earth, Sam." I turned to smile at my husband, who stood with his thumbs hooked into his belt loop, his chest thrust forward in pride. "I can't believe you did all this for me." I traced my fingertips along the bed's polished footboard. "How did you hide this from me? It must have taken weeks to make!"

Sam pulled a smug smile and nodded. "Wasn't easy. Good thing you were busy packing up the house. Gave me a little time to slip it in without you knowing."

"It's bigger, too!" I said. Our bed on the hill was three-quarter sized, and this new one was a double.

He patted the bed. "Try it out."

I walked around the bed, sat down, and bounced lightly. "It's wonderful, Sam. You did a beautiful job." I reached for my husband's hand, pulling him toward the bed. "Let's lie down; try it out."

Sam's eyebrows raised. "You want to nap *now*?" He glanced out the big picture window overlooking the lake. "Shouldn't we finish moving the boxes while the weather is still nice?"

I smiled knowingly at the man whose love filled every cell in my body, whose love sustained me through every good or bad day. "Sam," I said as I lay back and patted the space beside me. "I never said anything about a nap."

Our new home on the beach

Move-In Day!

Kitchen

Kitchen. I have no clue what I'm doing there!

51

Sam's gun & reloading room. Every wilderness man needs one!

CHAPTER EIGHT

Settling In

One might envision a beach cabin as sitting right on the sand, but the beach at Skilak Lake wasn't sand and seashells like many coastal regions. Instead, it was rocky, and we'd built the cabin just far enough from the water's edge to protect us during storm surges and ice breaks. The one-and-a-half story cabin nestled among widely spaced trees, and just beyond the animal pens and chicken coops we'd built, we had a broad space tufted with grass that passed for a yard between the cabin and the beach.

We'd settled comfortably into our new cabin, so I turned my attention toward digging out a spot for the garden. Early September was too late in the season to plant a full vegetable garden, and besides, we had a decent garden on the hill by our old cabin, from which I could still harvest carrots, cabbage, potatoes, onions, and greens. Still, I knew—if I worked hard enough and fast enough—Sam and I could split and transplant some rhubarb from the garden on the hill into this new one, and with luck, they could be harvested next year.

Digging a garden on Caribou Island required more than simply hoeing up a patch of dirt and planting seeds. First, I had to take an axe to the soil, chopping up chunks of surface roots that spread out for several feet under the hard earth. The heavy snows and deep winter freezes compacted the ground into something not far removed from concrete.

I'd chop at the ground with my axe for a while, then tug up great chunks of roots and sod, beating them with the heel of my hand to bust off any loose dirt, which I could then hoe and rake into fine-enough soil to use for planting. I would then mulch in large handfuls of rotten leaves to use as natural fertilizer.

Chopping out a garden spot

I stood to arch and stretch my back after planting a long row of rhubarb. The ground rumbled beneath me. I spread my feet apart to steady myself from the awkward shift I felt—as if someone had shaken a rug as I stood on it.

I looked at the cabin and could actually see the timber walls moving, more like *rolling*. A ridiculous thought went through my mind in that split-second of confusion: *the house must be settling*. I realize how silly that sounds now, but when the solid ground beneath you feels like a rolling wave on the ocean, your mind grasps at any bit of reasoning it can muster.

In the next second, logic found its grip on my brain, and I eeked out the word I never liked to say. *"Earthquake!"*

I bolted toward the house as the ground continued to vibrate, flew through the open front door, and took the stairs two at a time, yelling for my husband, who was building a closet in the corner of our bedroom. "Sam! Did you feel that? Saaaaaam!"

When I burst into our bedroom, Sam's bemused smile dissolved into a chuckle. "I'm on the second floor, Bonnie. You bet I felt it."

"That was a big—"

"Earthquake," he finished for me. "Yeah, it was a humdinger." He motioned toward the doorway behind me. "Let's go down and turn on the radio."

Downstairs, Sam flipped on the battery-powered radio that stayed tuned to KHAR, where we listened each night at 7:00 p.m. to the local news and North Wind Messages, where anyone could call in and leave messages for those living in the bush.

" . . . . felt it," the announcer said. "Reports just in that the center of the 'quake is some forty miles southwest of Valdez, Alaska."

Sam and I sat on our new couch and listened for another twenty minutes or so as reports came in from seismologists who determined that the earthquake registered a 6.0 on the Richter Scale.

Such is the life in this great land some call Alaska and we call *home*. Earthquakes are commonplace, but some, like this one, shake, rattle, and roll a little more than others.

I stood, realizing for the first time that my hands were covered in dirt and I'd transferred some of that dirt to Sam's hand as I'd held it. I pointed and laughed. "You'd better get cleaned up, and I'd better get back to my rhubarb."

Sam stood beside me and dusted his hands together. "I'll check out the cabin's foundation, though I'm pretty sure we didn't suffer any damage." He smacked his big hand against the wall. "She's pretty sturdy, this ol' gal." He playfully thumped a hand against my backside. "And so is this one."

In addition to gardening, September brought with it moose season. Each morning, I'd stand at our kitchen's big picture window and look out at the kaleidoscope of fall colors—sunny golds, piney greens, and majestic purples contrasting against the deep blue of Skilak and the glorious turquoise of the sky—and I'd peer into the woods to search for the unmistakable movement of moose antlers emerging from the forest. Unless a moose came out into the open, it was nearly impossible to see them in the dense woods, as their bodies were tall enough to blend with foliage.

Many times, during our Skilak years, a curious moose on stilt-like legs would make its way onto our homestead, and sometimes they'd gaze right into one of our windows. It was thrilling and disconcerting at the same time, having an animal that size staring right at me. It was odd, however, that the giant beasts seemed to know instinctively when moose season arrived, as they'd stay deeper in the forests instead of venturing into a clearing, where they'd surely end up as someone's dinner.

Since, yet again, no moose came to visit, Sam and Winston planned a hunting trip to find one. While they were gone, I harvested armloads of rhubarb stalks from the upper cabin garden to make into sauce, butter, and a pie. I'd just canned the last jars of rhubarb butter and was rolling out a pie crust (I used my grandmother Mary Rose's pie crust recipe, which makes the tastiest, most tender and flaky crust I've ever tasted), when I heard Sam's shout. I turned to look out the big picture window and gasped when I saw him and Winston each burdened by a quarter of a moose slung onto their backs, heading my way across the beach. I don't know how I missed hearing our boat approaching our beach, but I did.

The men had already skinned, gutted, and quartered the moose, and they carried three of those huge quarters to the shed, where they'd hang in the chilly darkness until I could can them. The fourth quarter, Sam carried into the cabin and slung it off his back onto the table with a heavy thump. "Thought you might want some moose for dinner, Bonnie."

"You mean, for a lot of dinners!" I said, and we all had a good laugh.

Winston placed the cooler he'd been carrying onto the countertop. "I'm betting you know what to do with this."

I cautiously opened the cooler and peered inside. "Moose liver! Yeah, you betcha! I know exactly what to do with this. I'll go get some onions from the garden, and gentlemen," I said, turning to the men, "we'll have ourselves a feast tonight."

"Now that's what I'm talking about," Sam said.

Winston rubbed his belly. "Me, too!"

Later that evening, after Sam helped cut some of the meat from the moose quarter he'd brought in, I started a big pan of homemade biscuits. As soon as the biscuits came out of the oven, my rhubarb pie went in, and before I could shut the oven door, in walked Sam and Winston just in time for dinner.

I brewed a pot of coffee and set the big tray of liver and onions and a bowl of brown gravy on the table. Within minutes, our happy chatter dissolved into silence broken only by the occasional sound of silverware meeting stoneware, or a satisfied, "Mmmm," as we enjoyed an incredibly good dinner together.

After we'd cleared the table, the men told me the story of the hunt. Sam had dropped Winston about half a mile down the beach from where he'd planned to hunt, and the two had searched the woods for a moose. Winston said he'd had no luck at all and was about to give up when he heard the crack of Sam's gun, and he broke into a run in the direction of the sound, only to find Sam standing atop the big moose, waving his gun in the air.

"It was the darndest thing you ever saw," Winston drawled in his Wyoming accent. "Like he was playing King of the Hill and winning."

Sam laughed and stroked his chin. "You didn't have to tell that part, Winston. Some things a man ought to keep to himself."

I received a lot of personal joy from observing Sam and Winston's friendship. The two men had so many things in common, despite that they were from different parts of the country and had experienced life in such different ways. They'd bonded like brothers, and the two of them share a close kinship to this very day.

In the days that followed, I prepared and canned the moose, and felt blessed as I worked, watching Skilak's ever-changing moods from my kitchen window.

By the end of the week, I'd canned moose barbeque, moose meatballs, moose Swiss steak, moose pepper steak, moose burger, and moose stew. While it sounds like a lot of work—and I suppose it was—it was enjoyable work, and I knew that the work I did now would help sustain Winston, Sam, and me through the harsh winter ahead.

CHAPTER NINE

A Surprise Visitor

October brought with her plenty of overcast, chilly days. While it wasn't uncommon for snow in October, none had fallen yet this year, though it seemed daily the sky threatened it. Sam and I were outside working to establish another large cord of wood for winter, and he'd chop the logs into pieces and stack them into my arms, and I'd carry them to our cord pile and carefully stack them where they'd be accessible on the coldest of days.

I peered hard into the woods—all trees except the spruce were bald—and in spite of working up a bit of a sweat, I felt a chill when the tall, bare branches creaked and scraped against one another as the wind whistled through.

I'd just returned for Sam to pile another load into my arms, when he and I looked skyward. I cocked my ear toward the sky, straining to hear over the wind. "Is that a—"

"Plane," Sam finished for me. He held a hand to shield his eyes, then pointed off into the sky. "Float plane," he said.

"Harry and Foster!" I clapped my hands and bounced where I stood, thrilled to have company.

"I believe you're right." Sam pushed his hat back on his head, and we ambled down toward the shoreline as the float plane landed and taxied close to the shore. When the plane stopped, the doors on both sides opened, and out stepped Harry and a woman. "Marie!" I squealed. Not only would I have company, I'd have *female* companionship again! I could hardly wait for Harry's wife to see our new cabin and all Sam and I had accomplished since her last visit to the island.

As I waited for them to unload their belongings and wade ashore, I saw a third person disembark—could it be? Yes, it was another woman! She was too tall to be Foster's wife Jane, and besides, I'd never seen Jane in a coat that zipped all the way up to her eyeballs. This woman, whomever she was, was definitely not used to wilderness living—yes, I'd become quite good at knowing such things at a glance.

I watched the woman awkwardly move onto the float, and I realized she must be quite young. Harry was already on his second trip for more luggage, and it was curious to me why there was so much.

Sam waded right out into the frigid water, despite not having on his waders, and—shocking to me!—he picked up the young woman, slung her over his shoulder like a large sack of potatoes, and carried her toward the shore, where he sat her down gently and said playfully, "Hello, you little shit."

My mouth fell open.

Who? Why on earth? What would provoke Sam to—

And then the young woman turned to me and unzipped her hood to reveal her face.

"Dawn!" I ran to my younger sister and wrapped my arms around her, laughing and crying and squealing and dancing all at once. I pushed her away to get a better look, then hugged her closely and tightly once more. I never wanted to let go of my baby sister again.

Dawn was the first person in either of our families to come visit us on Skilak Lake, and I could hardly wait to share with my sister this wilderness life that we'd made.

She must have been as anxious as I was, because she looked around, then grabbed my hand, and pulled me toward the house. "Let's go get something to eat. I'm starving!"

I laughed and looked back over my shoulder, watching as Sam and Harry carried the last of Dawn's luggage onto the beach. "Wait," I said, pulling to slow my sister's hustle toward the cabin. "Let me say hello to Harry and Marie."

I offered quick hugs and briefly chatted with the couple, and I learned they weren't staying, but had only brought Dawn down from Anchorage for her visit with us.

"Your folks put Dawn on a plane from Minnesota to Alaska," Marie said, "and I picked her up. She had to spend a few days with me while we waited for Harry to get back from the slope, so he could fly her out here."

"Marie has been a peach," Dawn gushed. "I arrived sick as a dog—some virus or something turned into an upper respiratory infection—but Marie nursed me right back to health. She made some kind of special hot toddy, and if they bottled that stuff, no one would ever be sick again!" She laughed, and Marie rubbed her back.

"Thanks for your vote of confidence," Marie said. "Stay well, you hear?"

Our goodbyes said, Dawn again tugged me toward the cabin. "I can't believe you call this place a 'cabin,'" she said as we neared the front door. "It's gorgeous! I'd pictured *Little House on the Prairie,* but this is more like *Architectural Digest!*"

My face warmed, but I loved her gushing. Inside, Dawn prowled every nook of our home, opening cabinet doors, drawers, and closets. Some might consider that nosiness, but I loved it! We were sisters, after all, and I realized she was just like a little puppy, happily sniffing out its new home.

While Dawn explored, I put on a fresh pot of coffee and sliced up large pieces of cranberry bread for a snack before lunch. When Sam came in, I sent him to the shed to cut off a slab of moose ribs, which I'd prepare for a special dinner to welcome my sister to our home.

"Hey, Sam," I said just as he reached for the doorknob, "why don't you head over to Winston's first? Ask him to join us for dinner. I'd love for him and Dawn to meet."

After a hearty lunch of creamed salmon and biscuits, Sam went back to chopping wood, and Dawn and I set to work putting together a dinner feast. That evening, just after dusk, the four of us sat down at the table in front of our big picture window. We chattered happily as we devoured second helpings of moose ribs, potatoes, and homemade yeast rolls.

"I can't believe you all eat like this," Dawn said.

Sam, Winston, and I laughed.

"Did you think we roasted skunk skewers over the fire?" Winston asked and winked. "Dug up some grubs for dessert before settling into our teepee for a long winter's nap?"

Dawn giggled, and her face colored. "No. I just—well, I don't know what I thought. But I sure didn't think I'd be sitting here with this unbelievable view eating a scrumptious dinner fit for a king." She shook her head. "And y'all call this 'roughing it.'"

We chuckled again, though this time our laughter was a bit softer, and I wondered if the men, like me, recalled some of the more treacherous events that had challenged us, frightened us, even threatened our lives since moving onto Skilak Lake.

"She's disappearing," Dawn said, motioning toward the lake, as it seemingly dissolved along with the sunset. Already, my sister spoke of the lake as though *she* were human, tempering her voice with a tone of reverence and respect.

Sam nodded. "Wait until tomorrow. Her sunrises are spectacular."

"Hear, hear," Winston said, lifting his cup toward the picture window in toast. We all followed suit, our happy chatter momentarily quieting into peaceful reverie.

The next morning, Dawn slept in about an hour beyond the time when Sam awoke and went for water, while I made another batch of fresh dough for cinnamon rolls. It must have been the heavenly scent from my oven that roused her. She padded across the floor, covering her yawn with the back of her arm to feign a complaint.

"How on earth do you expect anyone to sleep with that kind of smell coming from your kitchen?" She crept up behind me and wrapped her arms around me, and it surprised me when tears sprang into my eyes.

"I'm so glad you're here, little sister," I said.

"Me, too."

Sam came in through the door, a whoosh of cold air gusting around him. "About time, sleepy head," he said, grinning. "You up for some rabbit hunting, little girl?"

Dawn jerked her head up, wide awake now. "Seriously? You betcha!"

"You have to skin what you catch," Sam warned, his eyebrows lifting in a challenge.

Dawn pawed at the air. "No problem. You show me what to do, and I'll do it."

I loved that my little sister was game for trying new things, and I wished—not for the first time in the less-than-twenty-four-hours that she'd been on the island—that she'd fall in love with Caribou and wouldn't leave.

Shortly after lunchtime, I went outside to bring in another armload of wood to stoke the fire, and I saw my little sister holding the hind legs of a large snowshoe rabbit while Sam skinned it.

"Look, Bonnie!" she called. "We got three of them! I got one all by myself!"

Sam turned toward me and grinned. "She's a natural-born rabbit hunter." He looked up at Dawn. "We'll make a wilderness woman out of you yet." Sam turned back to the rabbit, knife in hand and started gutting it, then paused, and pointed to the internal organs. "Look here, Dawn."

Dawn leaned down and peered closer at the rabbit they were working on. "What's that?" she said, as I drew closer to them.

"Tularemia," he said. "We won't be eating this rabbit." He took the rabbit and its fur and placed it to the side. "I'll need to dig a hole and bury it."

"What's tularemia?" Dawn asked.

I moved over to where Sam had tossed the rabbit to examine it for myself. Sure enough, little yellow spots dotted the entire surface of its liver.

"Sometimes it's called 'rabbit fever.'" Sam looked up at Dawn. "Nasty disease."

Dawn pressed her lips into a thin line, but didn't say anything.

"Be sure to wash your hands really well," Sam said. "That's important any time you deal with rabbit meat, but especially after handling this ol' boy."

I noticed the other two rabbits lying on a nearby log, already skinned and cleaned. "I take it these two are okay to eat?"

"Yeah." Sam nodded. "Fortunately, we cleaned them first."

"Good!" I picked up the rabbits. "C'mon, Dawn, we have some rabbit to fry."

Once indoors, we washed up with soap and hot water, then rinsed and patted dry the rabbit meat.

I pulled down my large iron skillet from the nail where it hung on the wall and filled it with cooking oil, then set it over the heat.

"What does rabbit taste like?" Dawn asked.

A memory from our childhood flashed through my head, and I grinned. "Tastes a whole lot like that fried chicken you made for Mom and Dad that time."

Dawn and I both broke into laughter, and she playfully punched my shoulder. "It's going to be delicious, then!"

When Dawn was sixteen, she came to stay with Sam and me for a short while when we lived in Ohio. When she returned to Minnesota, Dawn wanted to surprise my parents by cooking a family dinner on her own. She wanted no help from Mom, though I imagine my mother occasionally rounded through the kitchen, pretending to need one thing or the other, just to watch what her daughter was doing. Overall, I'm sure Mom was impressed with how well Dawn was putting together an entire family dinner.

Dad arrived home from work, and the story has it that when he came in, Dawn had just finished placing the last pieces of golden fried chicken onto a platter she'd placed on top of the stove.

Dad walked into the kitchen and deeply sniffed the aroma of fried chicken. "Sure smells good in here!" he said. He nodded toward the platter. "Looks good, too. Mind if I snatch a bite before dinner?"

Dawn shooed him away. "No, because you'll eat it all! It's that good, Dad." She playfully pushed him toward the dining table. "Go sit down, and I'll bring it out in a minute."

To say that Dawn was pleased with the meal she'd worked so hard on would be an understatement, as Mom said that Dawn was fairly bursting with pride when she placed the large platter, heaped and heavy with fried chicken, at the head of the table in front of our father.

Her face was expectant as she watched him pick up a piece, smile at her, and take a big bite. Mom said that, from where she sat, she could hear the perfectly crisp crunch, and she fully expected Dad to crow in delight.

Instead, he froze. He'd stopped chewing, and he looked around the table as if seeking a way out. He placed the big piece of chicken onto his plate, and he slowly, almost painfully, chewed a few more times, then grabbed his glass and took a big gulp, then swallowed hard.

"What do you think, Dad?" Dawn asked, her eyes round and sparkling.

"Dawn, honey, how did you make this chicken?" he asked.

She beamed as she recited how she dipped each piece in buttermilk blended with egg, then dredged it in flour, and carefully placed it in a pan of hot oil.

"Flour, you say?" Dad asked. "Um, what kind of flour might that be?"

Mom said that she looked from her husband, to Dawn, and back to her husband, and she quickly put her hand in front of her mouth to keep from laughing.

"You know. Flour-flour. The kind you bake with." Dawn waved toward the kitchen. "In Mom's green Tupperware canister."

At this, my mother could contain herself no longer, and though she'd tried not to laugh, Dawn said Mom's shoulders jiggled until a giggle finally slipped out, and her parents erupted in laughter.

"What!" Dawn said, confused and somewhat offended by their reaction.

"Sweetie," Mom said, swiping at her eyes. "That's not flour. It's powdered sugar."

Now Dawn and I giggled as we recalled the story and rolled pieces of rabbit through seasoned flour before placing into the sizzling skillet. "We could try it again," she said. "Make Sam some sugar-bunny for dinner."

I laughed until I snorted, envisioning what Sam's face would do if he bit into powdered-sugar-covered fried rabbit smothered in brown gravy, and I'm not even sure my own father's stunned expression would come close to what Sam's would be.

Sam and Dawn skinning the rabbits they shot.

My little sister, Dawn, is turning into quite a rabbit hunter!

Dawn's going all out wilderness woman!

Dawn removing freeze-dried socks off the clothesline.

Dawn adapted beautifully to our wilderness lifestyle. She not only went rabbit hunting and skinned her own dinner, but she helped with our daily chores such as hauling water, carrying firewood, and fishing, and she helped me with baking and cooking our meals. We fell into an easy, peaceful routine, even though what she was doing was far from any routine she'd ever experienced. In the evenings, we'd sit together in front of the stove and read, or we'd work together on a puzzle, and sometimes we'd coax Sam and Winston into joining us for a game of cards or Scrabble.

One such lazy evening, we decided to call it an early night and get some much-needed rest. It had been dark for a few hours already, and the brisk outdoor temperature combined with the warmth of our cozy cabin put all of us in the mood for an early bedtime.

"Before we turn in," Dawn said, "I'm going to make another quick trip to the outhouse." She pulled on her heavy coat and wrapped a scarf around her face against the chilly wind off the lake.

I put out all but one of our propane lights, and I prepared the coffee pot for the next morning's brew. I'd just headed for the stairs when my sister's shriek pierced the night. "Dawn!"

I bolted for the door, and the second I swung it open, Dawn burst into the cabin, nearly pile-driving me. Her eyes were wild, and when she slammed the door behind her, half her scarf still trailed outside.

"What on earth?" Sam said, coming down the stairs three at a time. "What happened?"

"There's—there's a woman! A woman screamed!" Dawn briskly rubbed her arms, still clad in her heavy coat. "Somewhere out there, there's a woman screaming. It's the most—the *most terrible* scream you've ever heard!"

I pushed past my sister to open the door, and she immediately slammed it closed.

"Don't go out there!"

I touched her arm. "I'm just getting your scarf, before you choke on it." I tried not to smile and make light of what I could tell was very real fear on her part.

Sam smiled and slipped into his boots. "I'll check it out."

Dawn stepped aside, still rubbing her arms.

Sam later teased Dawn about how she wouldn't let her sister step outside, but she quickly offered him up to whatever beast might be assaulting a woman in our woods. I stepped out on the porch behind him, and I couldn't help but laugh when I saw Dawn's face peering out the window. She wanted no part of whatever caused that woman to scream.

But of course, it wasn't a woman, and Sam and I instantly knew what she'd heard. When a rabbit is caught by a predator, they'll let out a very feminine-sounding howl that can curdle your blood—especially the first time you hear it. Sam walked around the cabin, trekked to the outhouse and back, and when he came back inside, he assured us it was, indeed, a caught rabbit had made that sound.

We tried to laugh it off, but Dawn found no humor at all in what had happened. Every night for the next week or so, Sam and I took turns escorting Dawn to the outhouse, so no screaming rabbit—and certainly no sugar-bunny—would ever terrorize her again.

Not all our days during Dawn's visit were cold. We woke one morning to sunshine reflecting off Skilak and streaming through the windows, and when we went out to do our morning chores, we realized we were having a rare warm November day. We celebrated with a fishing trip! Winston joined the three of us, and we all took out the boat, cruising all the way up the river, where we caught a nice string of large lake and rainbow trout.

Back at the cabin afterward, the men cleaned the fish while Dawn and I made side dishes, and we decided to enjoy the afternoon weather with an outdoor cookout. We ate seconds and thirds of the freshly grilled fish until we could hardly move.

Even as the sun went down and the temperatures began to plummet, we weren't ready to put an end to the wonderful day, so we each bundled up, and Sam built a bigger campfire, and we sat around the fire telling stories.

Winston's stories were about herding cattle from atop his horse and sleeping under the stars in Wyoming—he was a *real* cowboy, after all, and he spent many nights guarding his herd from wolves and other predators—even the occasional two-legged kind. He made Wyoming sound so good that Dawn tells me still today that sometimes she dreams of moving there and sleeping under those same glowing stars.

Soon the fire began to die, and we decided to head indoors in time to catch the North Wind Messages on the evening radio news. Sam cranked up our generator—we used it only for charging the radio battery—and we removed our coats and cozied up near the stove to listen for any word from back home.

As luck would have it, during her visit with us, Dawn received her very first North Wind Message, and it thrilled her so much she crowed about it for days. Her boyfriend (who later became her husband and father to their three children!) sent a message to her. Though she'd been thrilled to visit with us, she missed him dearly, and after three weeks without him, hearing a message from him brought tears to her eyes.

"To Dawn on Caribou Island," the announcer read, causing Dawn to lurch to the edge of her seat, "I got a kick starter for my bike, so you don't have to push me anymore. From *A*."

We all had a good laugh, as only earlier that evening at the campfire Dawn had told us about having to push her boyfriend on his motorcycle so he could jumpstart it. Even over the thousands of miles between us and our families, the timing of North Wind Messages always seemed to be perfect, especially when one was for you.

Dawn had planned to leave in only a few days, but the williwaw winds were determined to keep her a little longer. Those fierce winds pounded the island and lake with such force that boating across would be impossible—and deadly. While she was anxious to return home, we were happy to have her stay a little longer, and in truth, she greatly enjoyed her time with us.

Thanks to our cousin who worked for Northwest Airlines, Dawn had an open, round-trip ticket, so she could leave whenever she wanted. When williwaw winds finally calmed, we crossed the lake and drove my sister to the Kenai Airport. I did my best not to cry in front of her, and though my eyes were moist, I succeeded.

She'd not made it through her gate, however, until my face was wet with tears. Before she was even out of sight, I missed her terribly. I knew she'd miss me, too, but I also knew how happy she'd be to return home.

Though my heart was heavy on the return trip to our cabin, once I was there and I'd settled into my kitchen with a cup of hot tea and my view of Skilak Lake, I realized that, while happiness might be fleeting, true joy is long-lasting. I'd been happy with Dawn by my side, and I was saddened to see her go. Yet cocooned inside the cabin my husband had built with his own hands, looking out over one of the most gorgeous places in our universe, my heart—and my eyes—overfilled with joy. Real, honest-to-goodness, spirit-filling *joy*.

CHAPTER TEN

A Little Accident

Early December arrived, and soon we'd again be locked on our island. The williwaw winds kept Skilak from freezing (she was always the last lake to freeze), but once those winds settled, the lake would freeze—not deeply enough to drive across—then the winds would pick up again and break up the ice, and the cycle would repeat until shortly after Christmas, when the wind would still long enough for a deep freeze to occur.

Prior to Christmas and the deep freeze that followed, Sam and I took our night walks on the beach. Now, these were not leisurely walks—we had a mission. Fishing! Before the freeze, whitefish swim close to the shore to spawn in the shallow water.

Sam had cut and limbed a small spruce tree, and peeled its bark. Into one end, he'd inserted a 6" spike left over from our cabin-building. He pounded it out into a sharp spear-point.

We'd walk along the shore, and Sam would shine a flashlight into the water and spear whitefish. I carried the bucket, and in under an hour, it would be full of fish. Some of these fish, we ate right away. Others, we smoked and canned for later in the winter.

A few days later, on a day we'd call "fairly calm," Sam and Winston decided to go into town. We'd left our Jeep on the mainland, and after they'd docked the boat and climbed into the Jeep, they drove along the graveled Skilak Loop Road toward the errands that lay ahead. Skilak Loop Road was seldom maintained by the State of Alaska—seldom-traveled as it was—though sometimes the state-road workers would plow as far as the road to the lower landing, which is why we kept our Jeep parked there all winter instead of the upper landing.

Though sometimes I felt lonely while Sam was away, on this particular day, I enjoyed my time alone. I puttered around the house, cleaning, redecorating for winter, and I finally ended up in my usual haunt—my kitchen. I decided I would bake a couple of loaves of sourdough bread, and then I set aside some of the dough to make fried doughnuts for dessert. After considering moose casserole, rabbit potpie, and creamed bear, I decided I'd make a hot and hearty dish for the men's return, predicting that they'd be chilly and hungry. I pulled out a jar of moose stew and retrieved an armload of the stored potatoes I'd harvested from the garden in late October before the ground risked an early freeze.

Before long, the house was filled with the fragrance of yeasty bread and tangy stew. I used an extra chunk of butter in the mashed potatoes, feeling decadent as I plopped it into the bowl of steaming potatoes.

I checked the time, realizing I'd better get the doughnuts started so they'd have time to rise before the men returned. I expected them any minute now, so I rushed to put on a pot of coffee, and soon the scent of cinnamon and coffee added to the cabin's winter fragrance. I inhaled deeply, smiling at all I'd accomplished while the men were away. Cooking was my gift to my husband, and I loved preparing special surprises for him, especially after he'd been away—even if only for a day.

As I set the table, I peered out, wondering what was holding up the men. I expected I'd see them rounding Frying Pan Island by now, but there was no sign of our boat. No matter, I told myself. I'd have time to spruce up a bit before they arrived.

I hurried upstairs and put on a clean blouse (I'm notorious for dusting myself with flour when I'm baking) and smoothed back my hair, and then I returned to the kitchen. *Rose hip jam.* Yes, that would be another perfect treat to slather on the still-warm sourdough I had resting in a cloth-covered basket on top of the stove. I spooned the jam into a dish and added a small spoon, and placed it near the center of the table.

There. I looked around, pleased with all I'd done. I returned to the window. Where were the men? I checked the stew, tasting it to make sure it was still hot, and after I dried and put away the last of my cooking dishes, I decided I'd need to warm the stew up again.

I went ahead and put on the oil to start warming for fried doughnuts, wanting them to be as hot as possible when I served them. And then I checked the window again. *No Sam.*

Another thirty minutes passed, and I started to worry. I told myself that Sam and Winston had probably ran into someone they knew, or had come across someone who needed their help, or perhaps they'd stopped to chat with Ted and Susan in town, but either way, they'd be here any minute.

And then another half hour went by.

I'd started wringing my hands, but then I realized my worry was useless. I needed to pray.

Lord, whatever is holding up my husband and Winston, give them Your strength and wisdom to handle whatever task is ahead of them, and please, Father, bring them home safely.

I wish I could say that my worry completely dissipated, but like many women I know, I sometimes hand over my burdens to the Lord, only to selfishly snatch them back and hold onto them.

Back in the kitchen, I began frying the raised donuts. I lowered the flame under the moose stew, but I kept it low, trusting that soon the men would be home.

And then I heard the boat motor. While I know thankfulness should have been my first emotion—and somewhere within me, I felt greatly relieved—I nevertheless simmered with anger. I'd worked hard to prepare a special hot meal for Sam and Winston, and here they were, almost two hours later than expected! As the sound of the boat's motor grew louder, then stopped, I chastised myself for being so selfish. Only minutes before, I'd been almost sick with worry, and now I was feeling petty. *Father, forgive me. Thank you for answering my prayer and bringing the men home safely.*

Outside the door, the tromping and stomping of boots told me the men were coming in, but when the door opened, I knew they had a fine reason for being late. Sam's pants were crinkled and frozen stiff from the knees down, and Winston's were frozen and caked with chunks of snow. The two of them looked haggard; their faces red with windburn, and my first thought was *frostbite*. Thank God, I was wrong.

"Sam! Oh, my goodness! You two look terrible!" I rushed toward him. "What happened? Are you okay? I've been worried sick!"

He smiled and nodded. "We're fine. Sorry we're late." He peeled off his gloves and took off his hat. "Sure smells good in here."

"Winston, you two look a mess. What in the world have you guys been into?"

He struggled out of his coat and hung it by the door, then nodded toward Sam. "I'd better let him tell it," he drawled. "Some things best come from the husband."

Sam's grin was sheepish, and he headed toward the dinner table as Winston picked chunks of snow from his outer trousers, then stepped out of them and hung them on a hook to melt. "Sure looks good!" he said. "Let me get something warm in my belly, and then I'll tell you all about it."

I let out a huff, then hurried to the coffee pot to pour the men a steaming cup. Hustling as fast as I could, I brought the pot of stew to the table, followed by the mashed potatoes that had been warming in the oven. It was all I could do not to yell at my husband to tell me what had happened as the two men shoveled heaping forkfuls of food into their mouths, as if famished.

Soon—but not soon enough for my impatience—Sam put down his fork and eased back on his chair. "Well, first off, we stopped and visited Ted a while—stayed a little longer than we planned. You know how that goes." Sam cleared his throat. "And then, we had a little accident," he said nonchalantly

I leaned forward. "What kind of accident?"

"Might have flipped the Jeep," Sam said.

"Might have—*might have!* Sam!"

He raised his still-reddened hands. "They must have plowed the loop road when the snow was deep and slushy, and then it snowed some more, and then it froze again, so there were solid ridges frozen on each side of the road."

Winston nodded and chimed in. "Must have been a good two feet high. Frozen solid as a stone wall."

"The road itself was nothing but ice, with deep ruts," Sam said, "so even though it might sound easy to stay in those tracks, it wasn't. We'd slide up on those frozen walls at every curve." He pulled a sip of coffee and swallowed as I held my breath.

"I hit that frozen ridge in one curve with enough force to send us airborne, and the Jeep flipped over on its side." He smacked the back of one hand against the palm of his other. "Wham! All of the mail and supplies and five gas jugs bouncing helter-skelter all around us. It's a wonder we didn't get badly hurt."

"Oh, Sam!" I briefly covered my face with my hands; a weak effort to hide from the horrific scene I envisioned. "What did you do?"

Winston, fork still in his hand, cocked his arms in the air and made muscles. He looked at Sam, and the two of them laughed.

Laughed!

They could have been badly hurt *or killed*, and here they sat laughing!

Sam nodded. "Yeah. We climbed out the window, and we pushed her back up on her wheels." He winked at me. "Brute strength, baby." He chuckled again.

I forced a tight-feeling smile and pushed up from the table. "That heroic effort just earned you boys some hot, fried donuts. Let me get you another cup of coffee, and y'all settle in front of the stove to warm up, and I'll bring them out in a minute."

I dusted the fried donuts with cinnamon, and then I gave them an extra-generous sprinkling of sugar, all the while thanking my Heavenly Father for the extra-generous sweetness He'd shown me in bringing the men safely home.

CHAPTER ELEVEN

A Christmas to Remember

Among the packet of mail Sam had picked up were nestled several colored envelopes of red and green; Christmas cards our family and friends had had the foresight to send out early, knowing our mail took extra weeks to arrive and be picked up. I opened the cards, and Sam and I read them in front of the fire as we sipped from large mugs of steaming hot chocolate sprinkled with cinnamon. We admired the lovely scenes on each card, read the verses within, and read and re-read the handwritten notes inside.

I set aside the wrapped gifts—we'd decided to save and open them Christmas Day, less than two weeks away—our way of celebrating the holiday with our far-away families. The festive cards put me in the spirit of Christmas.

"Sam," I said, "I'd like to put up a Christmas tree this year." Our new cabin, larger than our last, held enough room for a small tree.

He rolled his eyes. "You want to kill a perfectly good tree, just to celebrate Christmas?" He held up a finger. "One day?" He twisted his lips and shook his head. My environmentalist husband couldn't for the life of him grasp why anyone would want to slaughter a perfectly good, growing, young pine tree for mere decorative purposes. "You'll throw it out a few days later."

"Yes." My reply was simple, and I saw no reason to plead my case.

A few days later, while Sam was out traipsing the wild Alaskan forest, I donned my warm winter garb, shouldered an ax, and went in search of a Christmas tree. I hummed carols as I walked the woods, pausing now and then to finger the needles of a small spruce, stepping back to appraise its height or girth.

Despite winter's chill, the sun shone down, and I occasionally walked into a clearing to let sunshine warm my bones. What a gorgeous day! I sniffed deeply, inhaling the piney fragrance and the clean, crisp smell of winter. Ah, how I love Caribou Island!

I wandered back into the woods, feeling the temperature drop a good ten or twenty degrees under the heavy tree canopy. My eyes adjusted to the shade, and I looked up to see it—my Christmas tree! She was perfect in every way; a classic triangular shape, frothy with needles and flawlessly straight. I wanted to hug her!

Instead, I pushed my face into her branches, inhaled her scent, and giggled. Yes, alone in the middle of the woods, I sniffed my Christmas tree and giggled like a schoolgirl.

Several minutes later, I walked out of the woods, dragging my tree by her trunk, and I brought her into the cabin and stood her in the corner. Then I made a steaming cup of tea and curled into my comfy chair, awaiting Sam's return with a giant grin on my face.

I sipped my tea, imagining his face when he saw her. We'd make a stand for her, and then we'd decorate her, and— *decorations!* I needed decorations!

I hopped up from my chair and hustled to the kitchen. I rummaged through my kitchen drawers until I found my Christmas cookie cutters, and then ran upstairs to empty a cardboard box from my closet.

Half an hour later, when Sam walked through the door, he found me sitting at the kitchen table, still humming Christmas carols as I traced cookie cutter shapes onto cardboard. I gave him my sweetest smile, and—after he feigned a frown and shook his head—he returned a crooked smile of his own.

"Guess I'd better find a stand, huh?"

Sam fashioned a lovely, rustic, Christmas-tree stand out of an old wheel. I wrapped my cardboard shapes—Santa Clauses, Christmas trees, candy canes, wreaths, and bells—in aluminum foil. While Sam adjusted and re-adjusted the tree in its stand, I baked gingerbread cookies shaped like hearts in hands and gingerbread men, and I hung those on the tree, as well.

That night, as the silvery ornaments sparkled with reflected firelight, I threaded popcorn onto strings. The house not only looked like Christmas, it *smelled* like Christmas . . . pine and gingerbread and cinnamon and burning logs. A long wedge of light lay across the floor where moonlight splayed through the window.

I looked at my husband, and when I saw the pure joy emanating from his face, my eyes welled. Mr. Bah-humbug-

No-Tree had indeed caught the spirit of Christmas, and in that moment, he looked as much like a little boy as he must have as a child.

Christmas Day soon arrived, and though Nels and Anna had left Caribou Island until spring, Winston still planned to join Sam and me later that afternoon to celebrate the day our Jesus was born. We'd managed to make one last trip into town before Christmas—williwaw winds had kept us island bound since the men's last trip to town—and I spent the early morning hours of Christmas Day stuffing and baking a turkey and preparing all the trimmings—mashed potatoes, gravy, homemade cranberry sauce, vegetable casseroles from food I'd canned over the summer, and freshly baked sourdough rolls.

Just before Winston arrived, Sam and I opened the huge box of gifts my parents had sent to us. Our faces lit with happiness as we bragged and preened over the thoughtful treasures my family had given us. Cigarettes and a shirt for Sam, a nightgown and slippers for me, books, homemade treats, and even a canned ham and canned bacon. And then there were batteries, yarn and sewing paraphernalia, and so much more.

As Sam cleared away the wrappings, Winston knocked at the door and entered with a big "Ho! Ho! Ho! Merrrrrrrrry Christmas!" He leaned back and rubbed his non-existent jelly-belly, causing me to cackle.

Some hours later, after the three of us had eaten until we could hardly move, I repeated his move, rubbing my swollen tummy as I ho-hoed through the living room. "Who has room for dessert?"

As I expected, none of us had room for even a tiny bite more, so we lounged in front of the fire and told stories until early evening came, along with a renewed appetite. Sam turned on our radio—a treat we saved for daily messages and emergent warnings—and we listened to Christmas carols until nightfall.

Winston decided he needed a long winter's nap, so Sam and I walked outside to see him off. In the near distance, the Northern Lights danced overhead, and the three of us stood there for quite a while watching Mother Nature's light show. Ahhh, the beauty of an Alaskan wilderness Christmas!

While Winston made his way home on foot to his tent encampment, Sam and I stood and watched the dancing colors reflecting on the lake and listened to the waves lap against the ice shelf that had formed along the shoreline.

Minutes later, the lapping turned to tinkling, then crackling, then clanking as the ice began to break up.

"Skilak doesn't give up easily, does she?" Sam wrapped his arm around my waist to pull me closer.

I leaned my head against him. "No, she sure doesn't."

We turned to go inside, and just as I put my hand on the door, a loud blast pierced the night.

Sam laughed when I jumped. "That's Winston!"

He'd made it to his camp and signaled his arrival to us by blowing a cow horn.

Sam pushed open the door, reached inside, and retrieved his own cow horn. He lifted it to his lips, tilted back his head, and blew into the horn.

Those two grown men—who when around one another acted more like young boys—spent several minutes echoing one another's horn blasts into the night sky.

I had to laugh. I leaned against the cabin, listened to the men-boy's horn blasts punctuating Skilak's crunch, crackle, and crash, and watched the Christmas show in the sky. I knew I was experiencing a Christmas I'd always remember.

CHAPTER TWELVE

Winter Song

One night in late January, a loud groaning startled me awake. I turned in the bed to face Sam. In the moonlight, he lay wide awake with his hand resting on his stomach as he stared at the ceiling.

"Sam!" I grabbed his arm. "Are you okay?" I blinked rapidly as my eyes adjusted to the too-bright moonlight.

He turned to me and smiled. "I'm just fine."

I rose on one elbow. "What was that?"

No sooner than the words were out of my mouth than the moan sounded again, followed by creaking and an odd screeching sound, something akin to nails on a blackboard. "Oh!" I said, as the source of the sound dawned on me.

"She's talking to us tonight, isn't she?"

I lay back down, adjusting myself on my side as Sam slid his arm beneath my head. "She sure is."

The *she* that Sam and I referred to was Skilak Lake. The wind had died down enough for her waves to still, and Ol' Man Winter sank his claws deep into her, freezing her surface solid. Another loud creak sounded, like a nail being pulled from a dry board, and I sprang to my feet and padded to the picture window looking over the lake.

Sam chuckled. "You can't see her freezing, silly," he said.

Ignoring him, I pressed my face closer to the glass. "Anything that sounds like that has to be seen." I stood for some minutes, listening to the creaking and pinging, and then a loud eerie moan that sounded like a distressed whale deep beneath the surface ice, but I saw nothing. Skilak's surface shone like white satin in the light of an almost-full moon, but other than an occasional ruffling of needles on the pines, nothing moved.

"Come back to bed, Bonnie. Get some rest."

I turned, and Sam patted the bed beside him. I climbed into bed and pulled up the covers. "Sam, isn't it nice that we can see the lake from our window? Not just hear it, but *see it*?" At the upper cabin we could only hear the lake—the roaring of waves during a williwaw, or the crunching and grinding of ice during breakup, and now the creaking, groaning and pinging during freeze up.

Sam pulled me close. "Yes, it is!" He tapped my forehead with a fingertip. "Now let's be still and listen to her winter song." He kissed me where his finger had touched me, and I snuggled closely against him. *Winter song!* When I next opened my eyes, it was morning.

Once Skilak Lake had frozen several inches deeper, we settled into the still silence that was winter on Caribou Island. We could now go trapping, usually on the south shore of the mainland or our side closest to the island, as we could travel on foot on the ice. Sam had already gone out to check the depth of the ice, this time using his chainsaw to cut through it instead of chopping into it with an axe, as he did our first winter on the island. We could walk across the lake now, but she still wasn't solid enough for us to drive the Jeep across her, though we knew that day was only weeks away.

Sam and I trapped at least three, sometimes four or five, days a week. We'd catch mink, martin, muskrat, and an occasional beaver. Days that I didn't go with Sam, Winston would join him. Winston spent most of his time at his tent encampment, as he was still steadily working to build a cabin of his own. Without a woman to care for, he was under no pressure to build, because—as a man used to sleeping under the stars—he was quite comfortable living in his wall tent. He always said he enjoyed "roughing it," so he took his time peeling the many logs needed to build his one-room cabin. After all, he said, "I'm living in the wilderness for the *experience* of living in the wilderness."

Sam and I understood that perfectly.

Now that we were the only three on the island, I felt more at ease when the men were out trapping and hunting, and I truly enjoyed having days to myself. I still had plenty of chores to do—remember, I washed our clothes by hand in my washtub, a.k.a bathtub—and I spent many happy days puttering in the kitchen, baking bread or creating my own recipes made up of the meat Sam brought home. I'd season with spices and add flavor with the garden vegetables I'd canned over the summer and fall.

One of my favorite things to do when I knew the men would be away for the whole day was to take a long soak in my bathtub. (Yes, I also mean my washtub.) It probably sounds silly to anyone who is used to walking into their nice, warm bathroom, turning on the faucet, and adding a dollop of bubble bath or a scoop of soothing bath salts to frothing hot water. However, my bath ritual took a little longer.

First, I'd haul water from the hole Sam had cut in the ice up to the cabin. I put every large kettle I had onto the cookstove, and I heated the water to nearly boiling. I dragged my round, galvanized washtub to the living area, and I placed it on a rug in front of the fireplace. Then I put on my thickest potholder mitts, and I carefully carried each pot of water to the tub and poured it in, taking care not to splash myself or the floor. Once I filled the tub, I retrieved my towel and soap, and sometimes I'd grab a book and place a cup of hot tea within reach. I tested the water temperature, always erring on the side of too warm, as one handful of snow or chipped ice would quickly cool it down. Then I undressed and climbed in, sinking down as far as I could go, submerging as much of myself as was possible in the little round washtub. Over time, I'd gotten pretty good at it, and I found I could cover most of my body in water, if I curled up tightly.

Then I sat and soaked. And soaked. And soaked. It wasn't until the water cooled enough that I felt chilly when I moved that I finally gave up and climbed out. I wrapped myself in a towel and then donned my robe, and sat in front of the fire and carefully combed my freshly-washed hair until it was nearly dry.

As thankful as I was for time alone to soak in my tub, I couldn't help but dream as I puttered around my kitchen making fresh tortillas. I rolled balls of dough, then flattened them, thinking of the future day when I'd sit in my new sauna. Yes, we had one small sauna high up on the hill near our old cabin, but by the time we walked up there, heated it, sat in it, and came back down, we were as chilly as before we started. I decided to ask Sam to build us a new one much closer to our new cabin in the spring. I dreamed of how it would look, with benches long enough to stretch out upon, and rocks that would sizzle and steam when doused with a ladle of frigid lake water.

I shared my dreams with Sam and Winston over a dinner of fried moose burritos.

"Yeah, I can do that," Sam said. "Easy enough."

I clasped my hands together. "Oh, thank you, Sam!" I knew it wouldn't be "easy enough," as he'd said, because it would mean cutting more trees, peeling their bark, turning them into lumber, and then making a roof. All that, of course, would come before finding and hauling the rock we'd need for creating fire and steam.

In the spring, I'd get my new sauna much closer to our cabin, where we could enjoy it during the many long winters to come!

Later that night, hours after Winston had headed back to his place, Sam and I took one of our late-night walks along the beach. We were dressed heavily in our winter gear, so we lay down in the snow to watch the stars overhead. Many nights we'd do this, and we'd gotten really good at spotting satellites as they moved overhead. We'd find one, and we'd watch it until it moved out of range of our vision, and then we'd spot another one and follow it. Sometimes we'd see a shooting star, and we'd always make a wish.

That particular night, I heard Sam gasp. "Did you see that?" he said, pointing overhead.

I tried to follow the direction of his finger. "What?"

"It was a meteorite!"

"A meteorite? How do you know? Where is it? I don't see it!"

He huffed. "It's gone now."

"Well . . . what did it look like? How do you know it wasn't a shooting star?"

"No. Definitely not a shooting star. First, it was really low on the horizon. And I'm sure it hit the earth somewhere way over there." He pointed toward the mountain. "I sure wish you'd have seen it. We may never see that again in our lifetime." Disappointment colored his voice.

I felt like I'd let him down. It was silly and petty of me, I know, but he'd just experienced something amazing—a once-in-a-lifetime event—and he wanted to share it with me, but I'd missed it.

I reached out for my husband's gloved hand, and I squeezed. "There will be another one. And next time, I'll see it with you."

In the semi-darkness, the corners of Sam's eyes crinkled. With his other hand, he scooped up snow and flung it in my direction, dusting me with white powder.

"No, you didn't!" I squealed. I jumped up, scooped up as much snow as I could gather in my thickly covered hands, and threw it at Sam.

He grabbed me and rolled me over in the snow, both of us laughing and giggling and playing on the snow-covered beach under the star-spangled Alaskan sky.

Sam building a dock. Notice our "ice road" behind him.

Trapper Sam with a coyote!

CHAPTER THIRTEEN

Plane Wreck

A late afternoon in February found me mending a pair of Sam's jeans at the kitchen table. Sam had just finished reloading bullets in his gun room and had returned to the living room to stoke up the fire.

I bit off the thread, put away the needle, and held up the jeans. "Good as new, Sam!" I examined my handiwork, pleased with the small, even stitches. "You can't even tell you had a crotch blowout." I winked at my husband. With our vigorous lifestyle, Sam and I were hard on our clothes, and there was always mending to do.

"Thanks, Bonnie!" Sam placed another birch log into the wood stove when we both heard it.

He turned to look at me. "Who could that be?"

The droning of a small plane flew over our cabin. We both grabbed our coats and headed out the door to see who it could be. Down on the beach, we scanned the sky as the plane circled back toward the lake.

"That's Harry!" I said, as the little blue-and-white Cessna 175 neared us. Right on cue, the little plane tilted, its wing waving in greeting. He revved his engine and flew right by.

"He's heading back to Anchorage," Sam said. "Just flying by to check on us. He's a good friend."

Just as Sam uttered those words, the Cessna banked into a turn and made a couple of circles over the lake in front of us.

"Noooo!" Sam said. "I think he's going to land!"

Neither of us could believe it. An experienced pilot, Harry knew better than to land on Skilak with this much deep snow covering the ice without skis on his plane. He only had his wheels on.

Sam and I immediately began waving our arms, frantic to stop Harry as he flew lower and lower, coming in for a landing that would surely end in disaster.

The pitch of the engine changed as Harry throttled down. We waved more furiously, both of us shouting. "Stop! Pull up! Don't land!"

The plane dropped lower, only a few yards over the lake. I stopped waving and covered my mouth with my hands. Sam and I watched in horror of what we both knew would happen.

The small Cessna dropped onto the lake's surface, and instantly the deep snow anchored the plane's wheels into a deadlock. The nose of the plane tipped, its speed pitching it forward into the deep snow.

I screeched into my gloved hands. I knew the plane would flip and possibly roll across the surface of the lake.

Miraculously, the plane righted itself back onto its wheels, and Harry shut off the engine. The propeller was obviously damaged by harsh contact with the rock-like solid ice.

Sam and I ran headlong toward the plane, terrified that Harry was hurt—or worse. Before we reached it, the door flung open. Out stepped—who? This man wasn't Harry!

A stranger we'd never met, looking roughed up and shook up, extended his hand. "Martin," he said, his voice cracking a bit. "Harry's mechanic."

After we ensured Martin was okay, though a little shaken from the jolt of the hard landing, the three of us walked around Harry's Cessna. The propeller was damaged to the point the plane couldn't be flown without repair.

"I was making a test flight, for a prospective buyer." Martin said. "I've heard so much about Skilak Lake from Harry, I decided to fly over and check it out for myself. Thought I'd make a landing and takeoff," Martin sheepishly glanced at Sam. "Didn't take into account that deep snow."

Sam clapped the man on the back and let him off the hook. "Probably can't gauge it from the air, anyway." He offered a tight smile. "Let's go up to the house and get a cup of hot coffee, warm up a spell. Then we'll check out that propeller."

And just like that, we'd made a new friend on Skilak Lake.

Martin made a quick call from the plane's radio before we headed to the cabin. He made arrangements to spend the night with a friend in Soldotna, though Sam had kindly offered to allow him to stay in our guest cabin. We were at the time of year when night came early and daybreak came late, and our daylight hours were few. There was no way we'd be able to repair the plane before nightfall. The ice was finally thick enough to drive over in the jeep, so after dinner, Sam and Winston drove Martin across the lake and into town, where Martin would meet his friends.

Late the next morning, just at daybreak, Martin returned with his friend on the man's snowmobile, following our ice road across the lake. It was a gorgeous, sunny day (though quite cold), and the sunlight sparkled on the snow covering the lake.

On Sam's advice, the men had hauled a trailer behind the snowmobile with two power snow blowers they'd rented. Martin's friend worked to clear a runway for the plane, while Martin, Sam, and Winston took the propeller off the Cessna. Winston soon joined in with the second snow blower, and Martin held the propeller steady while Sam used his sledgehammer to pound out the propeller tips, one at a time, carefully straightening them.

Sam placed each propeller tip onto the flat surface of his splitting log, then placed the flat-cut end of another block of wood atop the bent propeller. That way, he didn't directly hit the metal tip of the propeller with his sledgehammer, reducing the risk of damage to the tip.

Once he'd finished, Martin appraised the work with a mechanic's eye. "Sam Ward, aside from the chipped paint, you can't tell this propeller was ever damaged! That's amazing!" He and Sam worked for about half an hour, reinstalling the propeller onto the Cessna.

The four men took turns working the snow blowers, as it proved to be exhausting work. Then they shoveled out snow from around the wheels, and Sam placed a piece of plywood in front of the wheels to bridge the snowy gap between the tires and the snow-cleared, icy runway. Early afternoon arrived, and though I offered to make a hot and hearty lunch for the men, Martin was anxious to get back into the air. His big concern was that the crankshaft had cracked as the propellers hit the ice.

Finally, he was ready to give it a whirl, and we all stood back as he fired up the Cessna. Its deafening roar sounded much louder than before, and after Martin shut the engine, Sam voiced his concern about taking her airborne.

"I think she's running smoothly enough to get her back to Anchorage," Martin said. "Besides, there are a whole lot of little lakes between here and there, so if I need to, I can land her again."

I didn't say what was on my mind—that his last lake landing didn't go so well—and instead, I wished him a safe journey. The three men also wished him well, and we stood back as Martin pointed the nose of the plane in the direction of the newly-made airstrip and throttled up.

I held my breath and prayed as the plane shot forward and its wheels lifted off well in advance of the end of the ice runway the men had cleared. Once in the air, Martin made one turn around the lake, and as he flew overhead, he tilted the Cessna, waving goodbye with its wing.

Sam and Winston helped load the awkward, heavy snow blowers back onto the trailer, and Martin's friend left, following the ice road back across the lake. As he pulled away, the man raised his arm, fingers extended, palm down, and he made an up-and-down motion, waving goodbye with his own "wing."

The three of us laughed, and Sam wrapped his arm around my shoulder. "How about that hot lunch you mentioned a bit earlier? With those guys gone, should be more for me and Winston, right?"

I playfully punched him in the ribs, and we headed back to the cabin, our day's adventure behind us.

*The propeller is back on the plane and the runway plowed.
Ready for takeoff!*

CHAPTER FOURTEEN

New Friends

"I have to leave."

Sam's face registered concern, but then immediately went crestfallen. "Why? You haven't finished your cabin."

Winston shook his head. "My mother isn't well. Not well at all." He went on to explain that he'd return in late summer or early fall, depending on his mother's recovery and health.

I knew we'd miss him terribly. Winston was more than a neighbor—albeit our only neighbor this time of year—he had also become a part of our family.

Sam spent a good portion of that following day in early May with Winston, helping his friend pack up his wall tent and belongings, and they loaded everything onto the boat, and—as the ice on Skilak had only broken up a few days before—they made the treacherous journey to take Winston across the lake and drive him to the airport.

I felt somewhat forlorn and melancholy, even after Sam's return, as we were still some weeks away from Anna and Nels's return to Caribou. There was no time to mope about it for too long, though, as Sam and I started to work on building our new sauna—one of the two building projects we'd slated for spring and summer.

A few days into our prep-work for the sauna, a new friend sauntered into our lives, quite literally. He strolled up to us from the beach late one morning, smoking a cigarette, and introduced himself as "Ol' Donal," and at first, I thought he'd meant *O'Donnell,* but when a few minutes later he said his last name, McCrae, I thought then he'd meant *Old Donald McCrae.* Nope. Turns out, he hadn't dropped the *D* on his name after all. It was Donal McCrae, and his friend back in Minnesota had tacked the *Ol'* onto it.

Ol' Donal shared with us that he'd been an industrial photographer, but retired a few years back. He'd never married nor had children. He'd owned a hundred-and-fifty acres of land close to Shakopee, Minnesota, right along the Minnesota River, and just before he left for Alaska, he gave it all to the state.

"Sold, you mean," Sam said.

The seventy-something year-old man pulled out a pack of cigarettes, shook one out, and lit it from the one he was currently smoking. He took a long draw, finishing the last bit of his cigarette, then stubbed it out on a rock, and pocketed the butt. He took another long draw from his fresh cigarette, then squinted at Sam. "Nosir. *Gave* it. Told 'em they could have it. Build a park out of it, or something."

The way Ol' Donal raised his eyebrows when he looked at me, I suppose my mouth must have dropped open at his words, so I tried to appear nonchalant.

"I got my pleasure out of it." Ol' Donal shrugged. "Let someone else enjoy it, I say. Besides, who wants to deal with selling a big ol' chunk of land in Minnesota? I just wanted to get rid of it and get on with my life. I'm too old to mess with that stuff."

Sam glanced at me, then cleared his throat. "So, Mr. McCrae, where are you staying?"

"Don't know no Mr. McCrae," the man said, grinning. "Call me *Ol' Donal.*"

Sam returned the man's smile. "Okay, where are you staying, Ol' Donal?"

"You know Don?" He nodded. "Of course you do. Island this small, I reckon everybody knows everybody. Anyway, Don's lending me his cabin for the time being."

Don, whom Sam and I had met on our very first visit to Caribou Island, visited the island occasionally during the summer to fish, along with his son Adam. Don's cabin sat on the opposite side of the island from us.

"You walked here from Don's?" I asked.

Ol' Donal nodded. "Sure did. I walk everywhere. Haven't owned a car in can't say how long."

"Not even in Minnesota?" I bit my tongue immediately after asking. It was none of my business, and I'm sure I sounded like a nosey parker.

My question didn't phase Ol' Donal McCrae. "I've flown into towns all over Alaska, and I walk after I land. Walked from Fairbanks to Anchorage a while back. That's where I met Don."

Sam let out a low whistle. "That's quite a long walk!"

"See more when you walk," Ol' Donal said. "I walked all the beaches in Nome, Alaska. Did you know there are still gold miners out there today, panning and sluicing for gold? Sure enough." He took another long drag, twisted his head to the side, and blew out a plume of smoke. "Intrigued me," he said. "Fascinating, the way those men put everything into their search for a few tiny nuggets." He nodded toward our cabin. "That's a good-looking place you have here. Care to show me around?"

Now I'm sure that's an odd question to anyone who hasn't lived in the Alaskan wilderness, but it's quite common to give visitors a tour of everything you own or have built when you live off the grid.

"Sure," Sam said. "My pleasure."

And I knew it was. Sam had worked hard to build not only our cabins, but others on the island, and while he showed Ol' Donal around our property, I went in to make coffee and start lunch for three.

It turned out that Ol' Donal was quite a wonderful conversationalist. He loved to debate—not argue, but debate—almost any issue. He said playing devil's advocate and really trying to understand both sides of any issue made you a smarter person. I supposed he had a point.

After lunch, Ol' Donal left to hike the beach back to Don's cabin, and Sam and I picked up where we left off, clearing a spot for our new sauna. Sam, of course, did the majority of the work on our sauna, though I helped as much as I could. Not only were we building a sauna for ourselves, but Harry and Foster had hired Sam to build them a cabin on the island—on an interior lot they had recently purchased.

We purchased our wood from the local sawmill in Sterling, and they delivered it to the lower landing. A company from Anchorage likewise made a delivery to the landing with tin for the roofs and windows for Harry and Foster's new cabin. Sam made many, many journeys across Skilak that spring, hauling as much of the building materials as his boat could hold on each trip.

On one of his first trips, I spent the entire day scouring the beach for rocks for our sauna. Sam had instructed as well as shown me the types of rocks we needed. "They need to be dense and heavy—not too small." He had picked up a solid-looking rock. "Look for granite or greywacke—they won't explode when it gets hot—nothing too porous or with layers where water can get trapped inside." So I'd load a bucket with rocks, carry it to the site of our sauna, and go back for more. By the time Sam started building, I'd found all we needed.

Sam built our sauna with two benches; one for each of us. It was a fine sauna, much better than the one up on the hill. In the corner, we placed a wood stove on top of some of the gravel we'd carried, bucket by bucket, to the sauna site. The sauna floor was made of plywood, into which Sam had drilled holes for drainage. At the end of our benches stood five-gallon buckets, half filled with crystal-clear, icy water from Skilak. On top of the stove stood a huge pan, also filled with water, surrounded by the thickly piled rocks I'd collected.

Once the water on top of the stove was hot and wisps of steam curled from it, the sauna was ready. We'd splash a dipper of cold water from our buckets onto the rocks, and the sauna would fill with steam.

Sam and I stripped down and lay atop our benches, letting the steam soak into our pores, warming our bones and loosening our work-weary muscles. Now and then, Sam would rise and add another ladle of cold water to the rocks, and again we'd breathe deeply of the steamy air.

After a while, when we'd had enough steaming, we ladled hot water from the pan atop the stove into each of our buckets of cold water. Once we reached bath-water temperature, we'd pour ladles of water over ourselves, soap up until we were frothy, then rinse with more ladles of water. It wasn't uncommon to finish our sauna with a water battle, first flinging ladles full of water at each other, then dumping what was left in our buckets onto one another.

Once our sauna was built, we used it almost daily. A few times, my he-man macho Sam would run out of the sauna, buck naked, yelling like Tarzan, and dive headlong into frigid Skilak Lake.

"You oughtta try it, Bonnie," he said, red-faced and shivering after the first time he took the polar plunge. "It's exhilarating and invigorating! Really opens up the lungs and sinuses!"

"I can blow my nose and breathe just fine from the bank while fully clothed," I said. "No, thank you, Mr. Ward."

The sauna is taking shape, but sometimes a man needs a break!

Sauna's all finished!

A few days after we'd built the sauna, I decided to ride along with Sam as he headed across Skilak Lake for more building supplies for Harry and Foster's cabin. I'd been on the island a bit too long, and I needed some socializing. It felt good to climb back into our Jeep—we'd left it on the lower landing prior to the ice melt—and head into Sterling. We visited the hardware store, and then we picked up our mail before stopping at the diner for lunch.

At the diner, we chatted with people we'd known since we first moved to Caribou, catching up on all that had happened over the winter months. Sam asked everyone we knew (and a few we'd just met), if they knew of anyone selling chickens or other fowl. After several inquiries, he spoke to a man who'd recently purchased fowl from a couple who owned a farm a few miles outside Sterling.

Sam and I had talked about raising more fowl for their eggs and fresh meat, and now he had the name and address of the family who sold the birds, and we were on our way to find them.

Warner and Marion Murphy were a lovely couple. They and their four children, Josh, Sharon, Cheryl, and Jeremy, all came out to meet us as soon as we arrived, and the open, friendly faces of the entire family graced us with smiles. Marion immediately invited us in for coffee and led me toward their rustic home.

Over two cups of coffee, we learned the ages of their children—Josh, 13; Sharon, 12; Cheryl, 8; and little Jeremy, 4. We toured the Murphys' home, which had a gorgeous, curvy, wooden staircase leading onto their second story. It was, indeed, the loveliest feature in their otherwise rustic and functional home. I learned, too, that Marion was the sister of the kindly man Bob, who'd hauled a truckload of logs for our second cabin on his boom truck across Skilak Lake years earlier. We hadn't seen Bob in a long time, and it was nice to hear news of him and meet another kind member of his family.

After coffee, we all headed outside to their barnyard, which was filled from one end to the other with all manner of fowl—chickens of all kinds, quail, pheasants, and even showy peacocks. I wanted all of them!

Of course, that wasn't feasible, so instead, we let little Jeremy lead us around as he told us about each variety of bird. His knowledge was impressive, and he even taught me a few things. I hid my chuckle behind my hand a few times as the young, bibbed-overall-wearing boy watched his father and mimicked the man's every motion. If Warner put his hands in his pockets, Jeremy did the same. When Warner cleared his throat, so did Jeremy. As Warner side-stepped a small feed trough, Jeremy ran to catch up, then slowed and side-stepped the trough in the same manner. He was the most adorable thing I'd seen in ages!

After we toured the home and the barnyard, Sam and I made our selection of bobwhite quail, and we promised to return soon—not just for more birds, but to continue the instant friendship we'd formed with the Murphys. We loaded up our birds and headed toward the Jeep.

"Hey, Mister Sam!" young Jeremy called, a thumb hooked into his overall gallus, standing in a pose identical to his father's. "Did you pay my daddy?"

Sam knelt on one knee, taking care not to grin. "Yes, sir. I surely did." He extended his big hand toward the little boy, who gave Sam a serious stare, then pumped his hand twice. "Pleasure doing business with you," Sam said.

Marion covered her mouth to hide her laughter, and as soon as Jeremy was out of earshot, chasing after a rooster, we all hooted with laughter over the seriousness of the young businessman.

On the drive back to the lower landing, I stared out the window at the stunning landscape—greening mountains still tipped in white, craggy rock cliffs in shades of gray and black, brilliant blue sky reflecting in the mirror that was Skilak Lake— and I again gave thanks. I gave thanks not only for the spectacular and dangerous place in which we lived, but also for Sam, and for my friends, old and new, whom I'd met in Alaska.

CHAPTER FIFTEEN

Come Again, Gone Again

Sam and I woke early one morning—I'd tell you the time, but we rarely bothered with clocks, as we slept and woke according to the weather, the time of year (you'll remember that, in Alaska, daylight can last most of the day, as can nighttime, depending on the season), and how we felt. We weren't ones to lie in bed all day, however, as chores and activities were plenteous on Caribou Island. Soon, Sam was chopping wood and I carried buckets of water to our sauna for our steam bath later in the evening.

As I returned to the lake to fill a second bucket, I heard a boat's motor. Shielding my eyes from the glare of sunshine on the lake, I spotted the small craft heading our way. "Sam! We have company!"

Sam stood and stretched his back, then walked down to the beach to stand beside me. "Don't recognize the boat," he said, "but they picked a great day for a ride."

He was right. The lake was perfectly calm, like a sheet of turquoise glass. Overhead, only a few puffy clouds dotted the otherwise clear sky. A perfect vee spread from behind the boat, causing ripples to travel across the otherwise smooth lake.

I grabbed Sam's arm. "Look! There's a woman on board!"

Sam chuckled. He thought it funny how excited I became over seeing another woman on our little island, but I couldn't explain to him the importance of female companionship in our very masculine environment.

I threw up a hand and waved, and the woman waved back. *Another* female friend!

As the boat drew near and the man cut its motor, letting it drift, Sam stepped into the water to help pull it onto shore, then he offered a hand to the woman, whose male companion helped her step off the boat.

Safely on shore, she straightened and smoothed her hair, then offered her hand. "Hi, I'm Laurie."

Sam and I learned that Laurie and Ralph were recently engaged, and Ralph wanted to show Laurie the island in hopes she'd want a home there. My heart leapt with joy as he said that.

"How did you find Caribou?" Sam asked. "I mean, why here?"

Ralph squeezed Laurie's hand, then let it drop. "I've been here before. I spent a summer out here a number of years ago . . ." He lowered his voice. ". . . with my ex-wife."

Sam glanced at me. He and I immediately knew who Ralph was. Nels had shown us the remnants of the man's so-called "camp" our first summer on the island. He and his wife had shared the same dream as Sam and I, which was to live in the Alaskan wilderness on Skilak Lake. The big difference was that Ralph never built his wife a cabin like Sam built for us, and so—tired of living in a tent that summer—his wife left him.

Sensing Laurie's discomfort, I cleared my throat and smiled. "Coffee, anyone? I have a batch of sourdough cinnamon rolls ready to go in the oven."

"Yes, please!" Sam said. "Bonnie's the best cook on the island."

I nudged Laurie with an elbow. "That's because, most of the time, I'm the only one."

We laughed, and the four of us sauntered toward our cabin. Inside, I quickly hustled about the kitchen as Sam gave our guests the grand tour, pointing out some of the intricacies of his work. Ralph voiced his appreciation of Sam's handiwork, while Laurie oohed and ahhed over the views of Skilak Lake and the mountains from our strategically placed windows.

When Sam took our guests upstairs to see the grandest view of all from our bedroom's picture window, I pulled out my best plates and quickly whipped up a batch of icing with confectioner's sugar and a few drops of vanilla to top our hot cinnamon rolls. On these rare visits of a female guest, I did my best to roll out the red carpet, especially wanting people new to the island to see that "roughing it" could be an elegant event, too.

Over coffee and cinnamon rolls at our table overlooking the lake, Ralph shared that he hoped to entice Laurie to live on the island. I squeezed Sam's knee under the table, and he covertly patted my hand.

"Before you decide," Sam said to Laurie, "let's take a walk around the island—let you see what Caribou Island has to offer."

I cleared our plates and cups with Laurie's help, and the four of us headed outdoors to stroll the island. We spent a few minutes with the birds, while Sam showed our guests how to cover the chicken pen with fishnet to keep out the predator birds. Our next stop was the sauna, which definitely enticed Laurie.

"You take daily saunas? This is more like paradise than roughing it!"

I couldn't help but giggle.

Next, we walked through the garden, where Sam explained which vegetables should be planted at which time of year to get the best yields. "Bonnie's canning rather frequently, too— not just vegetables, but barbequed moose, wild salmon, creamed bear, cranberry and rosehip jam, and so on—because in the winter months, our survival depends on what we've laid in store."

When Laurie's eyes grew round, I quickly added, "It sounds difficult, I suppose, but really, it's something I enjoy. My husband is a great hunter and provider, and I've come up with some recipes for delicious meals, so we eat quite well year-round."

Her face softened, and when Sam patted his belly and nodded, we all laughed.

Ralph wanted to see our old cabin, so we walked up the hill and gave them a tour. We then showed them other cabins Sam had built and the roads he'd cut.

I thrilled inside when Ralph slid an arm around Laurie's waist and said, "We could live here, don't you think?" She nuzzled her mouth to his ear and whispered, and while I couldn't hear what she said, the immediate glow on Ralph's face told me her response had been positive.

I would soon have a new female neighbor!

When we returned to our beach, Sam pointed at Skilak Lake. "We've got ripples," he said.

Laurie gave him a quizzical glance and stared at the lake. "Ripples?"

Sam nodded. "Storms stir up quickly around here. Ripples likely mean a storm is brewing."

Ralph shielded his eyes against the brilliant sun and looked at the nearly cloudless sky. "I don't see a storm coming. It's a gorgeous day!" He waved toward the lake. "That water's sparkling."

"Don't let her deceive you. She can turn angry in a minute."

Ralph's stomach growled loudly then, and it was his turn to pat his belly. "I'm so sorry!" he said.

I took my cue and placed a hand on Laurie's forearm. "Want to help me with lunch?

Laurie's face lit. "Sure! That sounds like fun!"

Ralph clapped a hand on Sam's shoulder. "I like their idea of fun," he said and laughed.

Sam gave another long stare at Skilak Lake, looked overhead, then nodded at me. "Should be okay for another hour or so, but then these fine folks will need to head back across the lake before she kicks up." He turned to Ralph. "We've got just enough time to show you where I'll be building a new cabin for our friends Harry and Foster and their families this summer."

Inside the cabin, Laurie sliced the bread, while I prepared a salmon salad for our sandwiches. I wanted to pull out all the stops to entice her to the joys of living on Caribou, so as we worked, I chattered brightly about the salmon runs, the taste of freshly smoked meat, the Northern Lights, shooting stars, and anything else that might cause her to want to move here.

By the time the men returned to the cabin, I could tell that Laurie was convinced. She took Ralph's hand to pull him toward the table we'd set, complete with a vase of wildflowers in the center, and she brightly announced, "I really like it here, Ralph. This place is incredible! And wait until you taste the salmon salad!"

Sam winked at me and mouthed the words, *Nice job!* Then his face grew serious. "I don't want to rush you folks, but as soon as we eat, you'd best get across that lake. Her ripples are larger now, and you don't want to get caught in the middle if she decides to act up."

Ralph smiled. "We'll be fine. I've been boating for years. And besides, the sky is still as clear as a bell. Only clouds out there right now are cotton balls."

We enjoyed our lunch and pleasant conversation, but when I got up to serve more coffee, Sam shot me a concerned glance and tilted his head toward the window. "We might want to skip that, Bonnie."

I felt my shoulders sag, but I nodded.

"We'll be fine, Sam," Ralph said. "You worry too much. I'm not a rookie, my friend."

Sam's lips pressed into a thin line, but he nodded. "All right. If you say so." He nodded toward me, his signal to go ahead and refill our cups. "Besides," he said. "You two are welcome to stay the night. You can have the guest cabin. Give Laurie a taste of what it's like to stay on the island."

"Oh, yes!" I said. "That'll be perfect!" My mind raced ahead to the big breakfast I'd prepare in the morning. I'd have Laurie help me gather fresh eggs, and we could make sourdough pancakes, and I'd open a jar of my homemade blueberry syrup. My grin felt like it might split my face as I set the coffee pot back on the stove and rejoined Sam and our guests at the table.

"Thanks, Sam," Ralph said. "I appreciate your offer, but we can't stay. We have to get back to work in Anchorage tomorrow."

Again, I felt defeated. My face must have shown my disappointment, as Laurie reached across the table and touched her fingertips to my hand.

"Don't worry," she said. "We'll be back soon." She turned to Ralph and smiled. "I think we're going to move here."

I couldn't hold in a squeal. Another lady on Caribou Island!

The four of us laughed, and the two men immediately began talking about building a cabin. That alone thrilled me, as a small part of me worried that Ralph would make the same mistake again by expecting Laurie to live in a tent like he'd lived with his ex-wife.

Before I could offer another refill of coffee, Sam squeezed my knee under the table to get my attention. He tilted his head toward the window and the lake beyond. My mouth gaped open.

"Ralph," Sam said. "If you two really intend on getting to Anchorage, you have to leave now." There was no more time for politeness. The gentle lapping of ripples had now turned to occasional whitecaps on the water.

Ralph peered out at the lake, and this time, he agreed, although reluctantly. "Yeah, I guess we should head back."

The lack of urgency in his voice disturbed me, and when Laurie stood and reached for Ralph's plate to help me clear the table, I stayed her hand. "I don't think you understand," I said. "As much as I'd love to have you stick around this evening, you have to go." I nodded toward the window. "She's about to get ugly."

Laurie registered my concern, and some of the color drained from her face. "Ralph, we should listen to them. They live here, so I'm sure they know what they're talking about."

Ralph again looked out the window, and indeed, there were more whitecaps now than just a moment ago. He stood. "All right, then. I guess we'll head back." He offered his handshake to Sam.

"We'll walk with you," Sam said, and we left the table as it was, covered with plates and cups. I knew he wanted to get them across that lake as soon as possible.

On the way to their boat, Sam again tried to coax the couple to stay overnight. "I really don't think you should do this," he said to Ralph, his voice low, so as not to frighten Laurie. "She's starting to kick up, and once she starts, she'll get nasty in a matter of minutes. I don't think you'll reach the midpoint before it'll get treacherous."

Ralph seemed a bit annoyed. "We'll be fine, Sam. Remember, I lived here a little while, too. Besides, we have work tomorrow. Responsibilities. We can't stay, though I appreciate your hospitality."

As we reached the boat, Ralph climbed in and offered his hand to Laurie to help her board, but she quickly turned to me and gave me a big hug.

"This has been an amazing day!" she said. "I can't wait to come back and see you." She released me from her hug, but then grabbed my hand. "We're going to be great neighbors!"

Her words made me happy, but my concern caused my smile to feel tight. "Yes, we will, but right now, you two need to get moving. I don't mean to rush you off, but really . . . if you're going, you've got to go *now*."

Sam helped push the boat off, and he and I stood arm in arm, watching the two head out. By now, the whitecaps were already solid all the way across the lake without any smooth breaks between. This was bad.

We watched the boat pound the waves, both of us knowing it would only get worse once they cleared the island. I held a fist to my chest, as if it might slow my rapidly beating heart.

The boat cleared the island, and that's when they hit the first big wave. Their small craft went so high in the air as it rode the wave that we could see the boat's floorboards. I watched as Laurie gripped the stern, holding on for dear life, and the boat disappeared as it crested the wave and dropped down on the other side with a thud so loud we easily heard it on the shore. Laurie screamed.

The boat appeared again, almost vertical as it rode up another wave, and again Laurie screamed, her shrill voice followed by another loud BAM as their boat smacked hard against the water on the other side of the wave.

Sam and I watched, terrified for the couple as the screams and slams repeated. I tried to look away, but I couldn't tear my eyes from the horrifying scene in front of me. I'd been in Laurie's situation before—many times, actually, and I knew how white-knuckled her grip would be, how weightless she felt as her body went airborne each time the boat dropped, how her bones jarred as the boat slammed against the lake, how terrified of drowning she must be right now.

We scrutinized the lake as the boat soared upward and then disappeared again from sight, Laurie's screams and the slamming sound growing softer as they moved farther from the safety of our island.

Minutes later, the tiny dot that was their boat finally disappeared, and I wrapped both arms around Sam's middle and held him close, still unable to take my eyes from those now-raging whitecaps on Skilak.

"Lord, protect them," I prayed, and as frightened as I was for the couple, I was also just as angry with Ralph for being so cocky and staying too long, his self-assuredness causing the terror Laurie was surely feeling. I knew firsthand she'd be shaken for days, even after she was safely on dry land.

"They won't be back, will they?" I said. We continued to stare at the place where we last saw their boat.

"I highly doubt it."

Just then, the sky cracked open with a sudden deluge of rain. Sam and I jogged toward the safety of our cabin as thunder—a rare occurrence here—rumbled across the lake behind us.

As I cleared the dishes from the table, I thought of Laurie's words, "We'll be great neighbors!" and I blinked back tears of loss.

I'd never see her again.

CHAPTER SIXTEEN

Grand Central Island

One day shortly after we last saw Ralph and Laurie, Sam and I were working in the garden when a small boat pulled into our shore.

I set the basket of fresh-picked vegetables on the ground near my feet and stretched my back. "I wonder who that could be." I raised a hand to shield my eyes against the glare of the sun's reflection on the lake.

"I don't know." Sam shrugged. "Let's go find out." He propped the hoe he'd been weeding with against a nearby birch tree, and together, we walked down to the beach.

A young man was helping a woman step out of the boat, and I noticed she was holding a baby. *A baby!* As we neared, the man helped three more young children out of the boat. I headed toward the woman. She was about my size and height with black hair that hung in soft waves below her shoulders.

"Hello, I'm Bonnie." I steadied a toddler just as he was about to stumble.

"Hi! I'm Adelle—and this," she said and nodded toward the baby in her arms, "is Claire."

I tilted my head toward the little bundle. "May I?"

Adelle nodded, and her bright smile thrilled me. I pulled back the blanket and peeked at the sleeping infant tucked inside. Honey-colored hair, fine and soft as down, crowned an angelic face. I couldn't resist the urge to reach out and touch her tiny hand, so velvety soft, and which resulted—to my great pleasure—in one corner of her rosebud lips to turn up into a smile.

"Ohhh, Adelle, she's the prettiest baby I think I've ever seen." I adjusted the blanket back over Claire and raised a brow at Adelle. "But, how on earth can she still be sleeping after the long boat ride across the lake and all that noise?"

As if on cue, the sound of children's squeals and laughter interrupted our conversation. We turned to see the two smaller children chasing each other in a circle, while an older girl, who appeared to be keeping an eye on them, giggled at their antics.

Adelle waved her free hand toward the children. "Claire's used to all the racket—she can sleep through anything."

Beyond the children, I saw Sam helping the man, whom I assumed was Adelle's husband, unload their boat and carry bags and boxes higher up on the beach and place them in a pile.

I turned to Adelle. "What brings you folks to Caribou Island?"

"We purchased a lot here and plan to build a little cabin."

My mouth dropped. I couldn't believe what my ears were hearing. "You mean you're moving here?" I couldn't keep the excitement out of my voice.

Adelle laughed and shook her head. "Oh, no—not yet, anyway. We live in Kenai, and John works as a carpet layer. We plan to come out on weekends when we can and start working on a cabin."

I resisted the urge to jump up and down and clap like a school girl—*and it wasn't easy!* I smiled at Adelle. "That's the best news I've heard in a long time. It will be so nice to have another woman on the island." I gave her a hug, taking care not to squeeze Claire too hard. "Welcome to Caribou Island!" Before I could get any mushier about the prospect of having a female neighbor, Sam called to me.

"Bonnie, are we going to stand here all day, or are you going to invite our new friends in for some coffee?" He shot me his most disarming smile, and winked when I looked at him. Evidently, he and John were finished unloading the boat. Sam clapped John on the shoulder and pointed him in the direction of our cabin.

"Of course! C'mon, Adelle!"

"Oh, it's lovely!" Adelle gushed as she stepped into my cabin, her next-to-the-youngest hiding behind her leg.

John looked around, nodding, and then offered Sam an appreciative smile. "Fine craftsmanship, Sam. You've done an excellent job."

"Thank you, Bonnie," Adelle said, taking a sugar cookie from the platter I held out to her. "You're so generous! We couldn't have asked for a nicer reception."

After coffee, milk, and cookies, Sam and I showed the family around our homestead. They were exceedingly complimentary, and when Adelle looked at John and gushed about how she believed she really could get used to this lifestyle, my heart soared.

"Oh, you absolutely could! It's so peaceful here. There's nothing like it in the world," I said.

John asked Sam if he knew the approximate location of their lot, and Sam pulled down his plot map. Adelle and I watched as Sam drew with his finger, pointing out the roads he'd cut and the locations of the various cabins on the island, as well as places where some day he hoped to build. And, of course, he showed John where their lot was located.

Beaming a smile at Adelle, John clapped a hand on Sam's back. "Thank you so much, Sam. We don't mean to rush off, but my wife and I want to head there now and get our tent set up before nightfall."

"Oh, Sam!" I said, after the family left. "A woman! And four children!" I clapped my hands and did a little dance.

"And a man," Sam said, wagging a finger at me. "Don't forget the man." He laughed at my antics.

John, Adelle, and their four children set up and moved into a tent up on the hill about an eighth of a mile from ours, with the intention of visiting weekends throughout the summer. They began building a cabin that, for the life of me, looked like an upright shoebox.

Some weeks later, we had more visitors to the island. Clark and Mary Walker, who lived in Anchorage, purchased a lot on the island on which to build a small getaway cabin. Clark was an avid fisherman, and while I was happy to have them working on a cabin, I was happier when Clark went fishing, because Mary would visit me, and the two of us became fast and dear friends who looked forward to sharing coffee and conversation.

On one of their weekend visits, Clark surprised Sam and me with a big stack of large carpet squares that he'd removed from a bank he was remodeling in Anchorage. They were commercial grade, beige, and looked brand new. Sam and I easily installed them over our upstairs bedroom floor. It surely made it easier to hop out of bed on frigid mornings, since my bare feet no longer had to touch the cold wooden floor.

By mid-August, Sam and I had finished Foster and Harry's cabin—about the size of our first cabin on the hill. We sent word that it was ready, and on a sunny day shortly thereafter, Harry's newly purchased 1969 Cessna 185 soared from the sky, its amphibious floats settling on the lake with hardly a splash. Sam and I hurried to the beach to greet them, and it thrilled me to see not only Harry and Foster step out of the plane, but also Foster's wife, Jane; their two children, Ruger and Missy; and Harry's wife, Marie. Both families had joined the men!

"Sam!" Marie called, heading toward him with her arms wide open. "I need a hug! You know, one of your special hugs."

I laughed and watched as Sam wrapped his arms around Marie, lifted her off the ground, and squeezed. Even from where I stood a few feet away, I could hear Marie's spine cracking like walnuts.

"Ahhh," she said after Sam placed her feet back on the ground. "I've waited all winter to have my back cracked like that." She patted Sam's arm. "Best chiropractor on Caribou Island."

Everyone laughed.

Just as it had happened on their very first visit to our little Alaskan home several years ago, Jane and Marie made themselves immediately at home in our new cabin. Marie climbed the steps to the second floor on a self-guided tour, as Jane pulled mugs from the cabinet and poured cups of coffee for everyone. The men talked about the picture window Sam had installed, and about the new propane stove and cupboards in my kitchen, while young Ruger discovered Sam's binoculars and planted himself at the window, observing loons on the lake. Little Missy found my stack of books, and she browsed the pages carefully, as if she were actually reading.

Soon everyone gathered again downstairs, and Marie asked the all-important question. "When can we see our new cabin?"

Jane jumped right in. "I know! I don't even know where it's located! Harry and Foster chose the spot, and Marie and I don't have a clue of its whereabouts."

Harry chuckled. "Aww, Jane. I told you it's near the approximate center of the island."

Jane waved his comment away with a hand. "Needle in a haystack. I want a tour!"

Sam had cut a road inland from our beach cabin directly to their cabin site, following the designated roadway, according to his plot map. I touched Jane's arm. "You're going to love it. Honestly, I think Sam's cabin-building skills grow better with each one he builds."

Jane smiled. "I'm sure you're right. Let's go see it!"

We headed out the door, and Sam suggested we each grab an armload of supplies from Harry's Cessna to carry to the cabin. "No sense wasting a trip," he said, and the men agreed. I had to smile; our friends were only staying one night in their cabin before heading back to Anchorage the following day, but Marie and Jane always over-packed. The first night they stayed with me during our first year, right after Sam went to the slope, they packed enough stuff into our little cabin that I just assumed they planned to stay a week. Imagine my surprise when they gathered everything up the next day in preparation to leave. I chuckled now at the memory, because Jane had told me they hadn't packed enough to stay on the island longer.

Now Marie shouldered a large tote over her shoulder and carried another bag in her arm. "I guess this is how a pack mule feels," she joked.

"Hey," Harry said, "I'm not the one calling you a mule."

And the fun began. The men good-naturedly ribbed one another throughout the entire hike, and Jane, Marie, and I caught up on news from the island to the mainland, and beyond. It felt so good to be in the company of ladies again!

As happy as I was to see my dear friends Jane and Marie, I loved how Caribou became a different place with the children running around. The first time I'd seen the kids, Ruger was three and Missy was only three months old. Now Ruger was a bright six-year-old, and Missy was the most inquisitive three-year-old I'd ever seen. That little girl was into everything!

We'd been in the woods no time when she walked up to Sam, tears brimming in her eyes as she held out a hand to him.

Sam took one look at her and knelt in front of her. "What's wrong, Missy?"

She thrust her open hand toward him, and Sam gingerly took it in his own big hand and bent over it. "You've got splinters," he said matter-of-factly. "Will you let me take them out for you?"

Missy straightened her tiny little spine, and her tears disappeared as if by magic. She nodded, and she stood quietly, never sniveling or protesting as Sam gently and methodically removed the splinters one at a time.

Instead, it was me whose eyes now filled as I watched my big, masculine husband earn the unwavering trust of a little girl who had a handful of splinters. Sam's gentleness with all living things touched my heart to the point of making me tearful, but

I quickly sniffed and turned away, as I didn't want to frighten Missy.

In a matter of minutes, the splinters were out, and Missy and Ruger were romping among the trees again.

By the time we reached the site of the cabin, Missy's hands had become black and sticky from pine rosin, and pine needles clung to nearly every surface of her body. Pinecones protruded from the pockets on her jacket, and she had an adorable smear of rosin across her nose. Ruger was still several yards behind us. He stood spread-legged, the binoculars pressed to his face, his head tilted backward.

"What do you see, Ruger?" Foster called.

He dropped the binoculars onto his chest, and when he turned to his dad, his eyes bulged. "It's the biggest birdie you ever saw!" He pointed up into the tree.

We all peered upward.

"Ruger," Foster said, "that's our national bird. It's a bald eagle."

High in the top of the spruce, a nest the size of a johnboat wedged into the forks of several limbs. The eagle looked down at us, turning and tilting its head as it watched us, assessing us as prey or threat.

I thought of the freedom the giant bird represented, and a chill ran through me. How could anyone be freer than we were here, making a life of our own choosing in the Alaskan wilderness?

"Ruger!" Jane called. "Come see our new cabin!"

The little boy ran toward his mother, his arms flapping at his sides like the wings of the bird above me. I stared upward at the majestic eagle. I thanked God for the liberty He'd given us to choose how and where we live, for the independent spirit of Alaskan homesteaders, and for the spirit of helpful camaraderie we shared with our friends.

Sam finished building another cabin. This one for Harry & Foster.

Summer's air seemed filled with laughter as our seasonal island population grew by tiny increments. I enjoyed our frequent cookouts, fish-fries, and pot-luck dinners with Harry and Marie, Foster and Jane, John and Adelle, Clark and Mary, and Ol' Donal, plus a herd of children running and playing around us on the weekends.

One weekend afternoon, Adelle came to the door with the baby on her hip. "Bonnie, could I borrow your wash basin? The baby really needs a bath."

I happened to have a pot of water on to boil, and I took it off the heat and tested it with my wrist. "Of course! But I just started heating this water, and it's the perfect temp for the baby's bathwater. Why don't you just bathe her here?"

Adelle's pretty eyes grew wide. "Are you sure? I'd like that, yes!"

I nodded, and I pulled my wash basin from its wall hook, carefully poured the big pot of water into it, then retrieved a washcloth, towel and a bar of soap.

Soon the baby was splashing and cooing as her mother covered her in suds.

"You know, Bonnie," Adelle said, "we're seriously considering moving here full-time." She nibbled her lower lip and looked at me with an earnest face. "Do you think I can do it?"

"Move here from Kenai?" I asked. "I'm sure you can! Sam can help bring over your stuff on our boat. Make as many trips as you need."

"No, I don't mean the move itself. I mean . . . the wilderness lifestyle. We have four kids. Do you think it's crazy to try to make it work out here?" She glanced around the kitchen and living room. "I just don't know if I can do what you've done here. It's so beautiful, but it seems so . . . *hard*."

I put my hand over hers, which was slick with soapy water. "If I can do it, anyone can do it. Besides," I nodded toward the window overlooking the beach, where the kids were romping and squealing, "the kids already love it here. Caribou would be a great place to raise a family!"

Her face relaxed. "I could homeschool, I suppose."

I nodded eagerly. "And I could help you!"

Adelle nodded, but her smile was tentative. "That's a nice offer."

As Adelle dried the baby, I went on and on—perhaps going overboard—about the joys of gardening, fishing, hunting, canning, and cooking on Caribou Island. Though she tried to appear hopeful, I could sense Adelle's doubt about raising and homeschooling her children on Caribou.

"Winters are tough though, huh?" she asked.

I bit my lip. I had to be honest with her. "Sometimes, yes." I rushed onward. "But we all help each other, and as long as you've stocked up with meat and supplies and firewood, you'll do fine."

Adelle smiled weakly, and with a slight nod, she finished dressing the baby, not meeting my eyes.

Summer came to an end far too early for me, and with its exit, the occasional visits from all of our friends slowed to a trickle, only to be followed by the isolation of winter. I still held out hope that Adelle and John would move to the island and make it their permanent home. They had finished building their cabin, but still had much to do to finish the interior. Clark and Mary had spent most summer weekends building their cabin on the interior of the island, within view of Harry and Foster's cabin. As with my other lady friends, I had thoroughly enjoyed my visits with Mary throughout the summer—Mary often came for coffee and girl-talk, and I'd grown to think of her as my big sister. I would really miss her come winter.

The island seemed almost too quiet after a summer of activity. Ol' Donal had moved out of Don's cabin and into our guest cabin up on the hill, and he'd began taking all of his evening meals with Sam and me. We quickly came to look forward to his visits, and the three of us had great conversation and debates, and we loved listening to the North Wind Messages together. Still, it wasn't the same as having women and children around, and I was already looking forward to the next summer. But first, we had a winter to get through.

CHAPTER SEVENTEEN

Caribou Hunt

The first week of September brought with it caribou-hunting season, so the morning of the seventh found Sam and me at the kitchen table, sipping coffee as we watched the lake, waiting for Harry's plane to land.

Sam's excitement was palpable. Beneath the table, he tapped his foot impatiently.

I, on the other hand, grew anxious as the time drew near for Harry's arrival. "Have you packed everything you need?" I asked.

"And then some." He laughed. "I expect Harry might ask me to leave some stuff behind, just to lighten his load."

I knew better. Sam can pack lighter than anyone I know. "When was the last time Harry flew across the inlet?" I tried to keep the concern out of my voice, but Sam recognized it and reached across the table for my hand.

"We'll be fine, Bonnie. Harry has been flying longer than anyone we know, and those mountains are no match for him."

Before I could argue, the low droning of Harry's engine reached our ears, and Sam hopped up from the table. "Let's head to the beach. I know he's anxious to get on our way."

He's not the only one, I thought.

Sam was right, however. Harry's plane hadn't even taxied all the way to the shore when Dean, Harry's cousin, flung open the door. The men quickly loaded up Sam's gear, and after a handshake from Dean and quick hugs from Harry and Foster, the three men boarded the plane.

Sam gave me a tight squeeze, but it was much too short for my liking. He kissed me goodbye and climbed aboard the plane, and before I knew it, I was waving as they took to the air.

"Lord," I prayed, "please see them safely there and safely home again." While I agreed that Harry was the best pilot we knew, I knew my Heavenly Father was an even better one, and He's the one I really trusted to bring my husband home.

The men would fly across Cook Inlet, which stretches over 180 miles from the Gulf of Alaska to Anchorage. Cook Inlet holds what some say is the most treacherous ocean water in the world. It's known for its thirty-foot tides and dangerous waves, which meant, should Harry need to make an emergency landing on the water . . . well, it could be a life-or-death decision.

Even *when* (I couldn't and wouldn't consider *if*) the men flew safely across the inlet, the danger wasn't over. They'd then fly into the Chigmit Mountains, the northernmost extension of the Aleutian Mountain Range, and home to two active volcanos: Mt. Redoubt (which we can see from the island on a clear day even though it's eighty miles away) and Mt. Iliamna.

The Chigmit mountains' sharp and jagged peaks make up one of the most perilous and rugged terrains imaginable. It was this mountain range that held Lake Clark Pass, one of Alaska's most dangerous passes. Lake Clark Pass was the route to what was arguably the best caribou hunting in the country, and that's where Sam and the men were heading.

Once the Cessna was out of sight, I knew I'd have to find something to occupy every waking moment; otherwise, I'd be sick with worry until my Sam returned.

I scooped up some scratch from the grain barrel and headed to the chicken lot. I chattered to my little birds as I scattered feed about, stepping cautiously around them. Our little bobwhite quails acted as though I was their best friend, scooting close to me, following me like baby ducks would follow their mother.

I spent most of the day picking cranberries. Caribou Island was practically carpeted in lowbush cranberries, and I harvested them throughout the late summer and early fall, gathering as many as I could to turn into jams, jellies, and syrups.

Just before afternoon turned into evening, Ol' Donal arrived for dinner. I stewed some of the cranberries as a side dish to fried moose with gravy served over mashed potatoes, and we scooped the sweetened berries over biscuits as dessert.

I'd just rose to pour us more coffee when my chickens started squawking in alarm. I bolted to the front door, grabbed the twelve-gauge shotgun that stood beside it, and rushed out to the chicken house. I lifted the gun and slowed as I neared, not wanting to scare away what I suspected was a weasel trying to kill my birds.

Sure enough, a low-down, sneaky weasel was snaking through the chicken pens, causing my quail and chickens to flap and squawk and scatter as they ran for their lives. We'd lost chickens to weasels before, and the terrible thing about a weasel is that it won't kill just for food—they'll slaughter for sport. They won't stop after killing one chicken—more than enough to fill their small bellies—but they'll rip apart every bird in a coop, leaving a mess of dead birds and feathers in their wake.

I crept up on the weasel, and when I was within range, I lifted the twelve-gauge to my shoulder, took aim, and squeezed the trigger. The weasel lifted a few feet off the ground as my shot found its mark.

I ran to the pens and checked on all my birds, counting as I walked among them, talking and cooing softly to calm them. "You're okay. You're okay. Thanks for the warning cries, boys and girls. It saved your lives."

Every bird was accounted for.

I shifted my shotgun to my left hand and picked up the weasel by the tail in my right, and I headed out of the pen.

That's when I noticed Ol' Donal standing on the porch, his grin splitting his face wide open.

"Well, I'll be, girlie! You got 'im!"

If I didn't know better, I'd say Ol' Donal was prouder of my kill shot than I was, and he called me "Skilak's Annie Oakley" when he said goodbye before heading up the hill to our guest cabin.

Before it got too late in the day, I decided to treat myself to a long, hot sauna. I headed to the lake to fill up my bucket, and soon I was reclining on my bench, letting steam swirl around me.

Several ladles of water later, I felt more relaxed than I had in days. Yes, I still worried over Sam, but that worry no longer paralyzed me. I had prayed for him and the other men, and I knew God was in charge.

The next morning, I slept a little later than usual, perhaps because the great amount of work I'd accomplished the day before had exhausted me. I dressed and headed to the kitchen to can the cranberries I'd gathered the day before.

Later that afternoon, jars filled with cranberry jam were still cooling on my kitchen counter, and the aroma of freshly baked sourdough bread filled the little cabin. I was about to slice a piece of bread, eager to try it with the still-warm jam, when I heard the drone of an airplane.

Who on earth could that be?

I quickly wiped my hands and headed to the window, my chest growing tighter as I saw Harry's Cessna coming low for a landing on the lake. What had happened? Why had they returned so quickly?

I told myself that perhaps the weather had turned bad and the men had turned back. But that didn't quite make sense, as they'd have turned back earlier yesterday, not today. I couldn't imagine what might have gone wrong, and Harry's plane couldn't stop fast enough for me to get answers.

Relief washed from my body when Sam flung open the door of the airplane and stepped out.

"Oh, Sam!" I cried, rushing to the edge of the lake. He smiled and waved, and I knew my worries were for nothing.

When Harry also stepped out, I realized Dean and Foster must still be back at the hunting camp, so I knew all was okay. But I still puzzled over why the men had returned.

Harry walked around the plane's amphibious floats to where Sam stood, and the two of them dragged out a large caribou, which Harry draped over Sam's back and shoulders. Then, Harry reached inside the Cessna and grabbed Sam's backpack and rifle, and the two men headed toward the table Sam had built for cleaning meat.

"Wow!" I said. "You've already got one!"

Sam grinned, clearly pleased with himself. "Yep!"

"Goodness! You men did well quite quickly."

Harry nodded toward Sam. "You mean Sam did well. He's the only one that got a caribou. Got it this morning, so his hunting is done. Time to butcher and stock your smokehouse for winter."

My mouth dropped open. I knew the rolling tundra at the far side of Lake Clark Pass was known for its plenteous caribou and bear, but getting one so quickly? I could hardly believe Sam's great fortune.

"Harry," I said, "are you going back to the pass?"

"Oh, yeah. Dean and Foster are still there." He grinned and waved while Sam came toward us with the rest of his things from the Cessna. "Besides, we've got some catching up to do."

I hugged Harry goodbye, and Sam reminded Harry to stop in Kenai for fuel. The two of them clapped each other's backs, and soon Harry took to the air again. As I'd done before, I said a prayer for his safe journey there and back, and for safe and productive hunting for the three men.

Ol' Donal must have heard the Cessna coming or going, because before Sam had skinned the caribou, Ol' Donal came sauntering down the path from the guest cabin. He was quite happy to see the caribou Sam had brought home.

Deep within the crinkled skin, Ol' Donal's eyes twinkled. "I bet I know what we're having for supper."

"Sam, slice off about a pound-sized chunk of fresh meat for me, would you?" I said. "I can use it for our supper."

Now I don't know what the men expected our supper to be, but when they came into the house an hour later to discover I'd prepared chicken-fried caribou, their mouths gaped open. I'd taken the fresh caribou meat Sam had offered me, and I cut it into serving-sized pieces, pounded it flat, then dredged it in flour seasoned with salt, pepper, and garlic. Then I dipped it into a mixture of egg and milk, then back into the seasoned flour, before deep-frying it in bear fat in my cast-iron skillet.

I'd also whipped up a large bowl of creamy mashed potatoes, and with the skillet drippings, I'd made a pan of brown gravy to go with the meat and potatoes. Of course, I rounded out our meal with fresh bread and cranberry jam.

"Oh, boy!" Ol' Donal said. "It's been ages since I've had chicken-fried steak."

We ate like starving animals. I'd worried that I'd made too much chicken-fried caribou, as the platter I'd placed on the table was heaping with steaming portions, but the men finished off the last two pieces, each smothering their slices in warm gravy.

"Bonnie, I don't know how you do it," Sam said, leaning back in his chair. "You never fail to surprise me. Your cooking is better than any I've had in the finest of steakhouses."

Ol' Donal nodded. "Can't beat chicken-fried caribou steak."

I laughed. "Yeah, it would be hard to find that on a steakhouse menu."

"Sam," said Ol' Donal, "tell us about Lake Clark Pass and your hunting trip. I've never been that far out—can't exactly walk over there—and I probably won't get there in my lifetime. I'd like to hear about it."

Sam pushed back from the table and stood. "How about we save that conversation for later?" He looked out the window toward the sky, which was quickly losing the light of day. "I'd like to get that caribou quartered and hanging in the shed before dark."

I cleared the dishes away, and we headed back outside to finish skinning and cutting up the caribou.

Later, after the caribou had been taken care of and hung in the shed, the three of us sat with our coffee and oatmeal cookies in the living room.

"Sam," I said, "tell us about your hunting trip. What was it like?"

He set his coffee cup down on the end table. "Incredible!" He paused a minute, and I found it difficult not to prompt him to continue. Then he raised a hand in the air, palm down. "Harry flew the plane in between these wicked-looking, cragged mountains." He looked at Ol' Donal. "You know they're volcanic, right?"

Ol' Donal bobbed his head.

"Did you fly close to Redoubt Volcano?" I asked.

"We sure did! That's a big volcano—stands over ten-thousand feet."

No wonder we can see it from here!

"We must have flown about an hour through the pass." Sam took a bite out of his cookie and brushed the crumbs off his shirt. "After we cleared the mountains, it was just lakes and rolling hills and tundra." His eyebrows rose. "That is some prime bear and caribou terrain. The darndest thing, though—" Sam leaned forward. "Was the bears. They were everywhere! We saw at least a couple dozen. Black bears, brown bears . . . even a brown bear treeing a black bear."

Ol' Donal's eyes grew round, but since he worked a mouthful of cookie in his jaws, he didn't speak.

"I'm serious!" Sam said, as if Ol' Donal hadn't believed him. "The black bear looked to be a lot bigger, but it hugged the top of a big ol' spruce, and that brown bear paced around the trunk, like he was waiting on his dinner to come down." Sam shook his head and crammed the last bite of cookie in his mouth. After a swig of coffee to wash it down, he continued. "Saw some cubs from the air, too. Harry flew low enough to scare them, and it angered their momma, so she rose up on her hind legs and roared at the plane." He looked at me. "I wished you could have seen it."

"Me, too. To think of how you and I traipsed all over these mountains hunting bear last winter, and you found a whole community of them."

Ol' Donal chuckled. "You call that a *sloth* of bears."

I'm sure the look I gave him must have been incredulous, because he tried to hide his grin, but failed. "I thought a sloth was another creature altogether," I argued.

"It is. It's a slow-moving animal, and the way the bears lope around when they're grouped together is why they call them a sloth."

"Hmfph. Learn something new every day," I said.

"Now let's get to it," Ol' Donal said. "Sam, tell us how you got your caribou."

Now it was Sam's turn to chuckle. "Mostly luck, but there's a story to be told, for sure." He sipped from his coffee, and I began to think he was purposely tormenting us by waiting to tell us.

"See, Harry flew us all around the tundra on the other side of the pass, and that's where we saw all those bears. He finally found a small lake where we could land, so we found a level clearing and set up our campsite." He sipped the last from his cup and looked at me, my cue to fill it. I went for the fresh pot

I'd put on just after I'd poured the last, and before returning to the living room, I picked up a dish of blueberries, since the men had devoured the rest of the cookies. As Sam talked, we picked and nibbled at the blueberries as if they were peanuts.

"We bedded down and conked out right away," Sam said. "Dean and I woke up early, ready to hunt." He shook his head. "Harry and Foster wanted to sleep late. I asked Foster if we saw caribou, if he wanted us to go ahead and shoot, or if he wanted us to wait on them."

I didn't understand. "Why would you wait? Were you afraid of waking them?"

Ol' Donal answered for Sam. "If you shoot one, the rest'll scatter. The whole herd will run off, and then your hunting's over. Best to have everyone out there at the same time, so everybody can get one." He looked at Sam. "So, what did he say?"

"Foster said to go ahead and shoot. I reckon he figured we'd be out there for three or four days, like we'd planned, so he'd have other opportunities for a shot." Sam popped a couple blueberries into his mouth, chewed, then took a sip of coffee.

"Dean and I walked up a little hill, just a short way from our camp—you could actually see the camp well from where we stood, no trees in the way—and when I looked down the other side, there came a herd of caribou, walking single-file into the clearing just below us." Sam's eyes grew large and bright with recollection. "Dean and I lay down and watched them. They just kept coming, probably fifty or more of 'em, one right after the other.

"I asked Dean if he wanted to shoot one, and he said, 'No, you go ahead.'" Sam shook his head, as if he couldn't imagine turning down a shot like that. Then he jerked a thumb toward the front door, where his guns hung. "I had my Sako .375 H&H Mag Rifle, and just like that, I pulled the trigger. It was a one-shot kill."

"Did the rest of the herd scatter?" I asked, thinking of Ol' Donal's earlier explanation.

"They did run," Sam said. Then he started to laugh.

"What's funny about that?" Ol' Donal asked.

"That's not what was funny." Sam took another swig of coffee, and I had to resist the urge to swat him. He loved keeping me waiting for the punch line.

"My shot not only woke Harry and Foster, it made them think we were at war, I reckon." Sam laughed again at whatever memory he still had to tell us. "I heard Foster yelp, and when I looked behind me, both of them had run out of the tent half-dressed, waving their guns. Poor Harry didn't have shirt nor boots on." Sam waved his arms, mimicking the two men as he laughed, and Ol' Donal and I joined in the laughter.

"I suppose me shooting a caribou was the last thing those two expected. Dean and I cracked up, laughing at them. I hollered down that I'd made a kill shot, and Foster waved me away, like he didn't believe me. They thought we were playing a prank on them to wake them up, until Dean yelled down that we needed help to drag it up the hill and down to our camp."

Sam grinned. "Even then, I'm not sure they quite believed us. It wasn't until we were down with my caribou and looked up to see them standing at the top of the hill they realized I'd shot a caribou while they were still in bed."

"Like shooting fish in a barrel, huh?" Ol' Donal said, pointing a finger into his coffee as he mimed shooting a gun.

"Miz Bonnie," Ol' Donal said, "I'd best be heading back home. Would you care to fill an old feller's cup for the walk? I promise I'll bring it back tomorrow evening." He stood and stretched a bit as I carried his mug to the kitchen for a refill.

"Yeah," Sam said, "Bonnie and I should probably turn in early, too." He stood and stretched out his arms, carried his and Ol' Donal's plates to the kitchen, and winked at me. "Looks like we will be canning caribou tomorrow."

I traded the plates for Ol' Donal's mug of coffee and planted a kiss on Sam's cheek. My day tomorrow would be even better than today. Nothing could make me happier than spending a day canning meat with my handsome husband.

CHAPTER EIGHTEEN

Too Many Goodbyes

Winston returned to the island in late September. Now both he and Ol' Donal joined us nightly for dinner, so I had the pleasure of cooking twice as much to feed everyone. I say *pleasure,* because I truly enjoyed the creative part of planning a variety of meals to feed us, and many recipes lent themselves more easily to serving four than two.

Sam and I still enjoyed our quiet breakfasts together, and usually it was only the two of us for lunch, though I never minded it when Nels or Winston or Ol' Donal popped in around noon, and I'd try to keep a sweet treat on hand for those occasions.

John and Adelle and their children still visited some weekends, though not as often as throughout the summer. Before September ended, however, they made a visit that I remember fondly. The children were outside playing, and the

143

men—or so Adelle and I thought—were showing Red, a friend who'd come to see their cabin-in-progress, around the island. Adelle joined me in the kitchen where I prepared lunch, and we caught each other up on news from the island and the mainland.

Just then, we heard raucous laughter coming from the men just outside the front door.

"What are they up to?" Adelle asked.

I rolled my eyes and smirked. "Who knows, with those guys! We'd better go see."

I opened the door. Winston, surrounded by Sam, John, the children, and Red, held the end of a long-handled sledge hammer in one hand, his arm extended straight out in front of him. Oh-so-slowly, he let the hammer tilt back toward his head without bending his arm.

My hand flew to my mouth as I gasped. The ball of that hammer had to weigh at least fifteen pounds—maybe more—and it rested atop a thirty-five-inch long wooden handle. Winston let that hammer-head drop closer and closer to his face. At any minute, his grip could slip, his grasp could loosen, or his arm could weaken, and his face would be smashed.

The sledgehammer dropped closer toward Winston's face, but he kept on smiling.

The head came another three inches closer, then another inch, then another. Winston's arm muscles bulged, and his face grew red.

I grabbed Sam by the arm and whispered—so not to disturb Winston's concentration—"Sam, if he drops that on his nose, he's going to break it."

Sam only chuckled.

"You got this!" John called out, and Red hooted with laughter.

The sledgehammer slowly dropped toward Winston's face, and as I held my breath, he lowered to where it touched against his nose, then almost as slowly, he raised it to its former upright position.

The kids jumped up and down and squealed, as the men cheered and shouted.

"That was amazing!" Adelle said, bouncing the baby on her hip.

Winston dropped the sledgehammer onto the ground, then headed toward the barrel where we caught rainwater and sipped from a ladle of water. "Whoo weee!" he said, wiping sweat from his brow.

I released Sam's arm. "I'm going to finish lunch." I shot my husband a warning look. "Don't you dare try that."

Inside, while Adelle fed the baby, I made biscuits to go with the cranberry jam, then put the finishing touches on a rhubarb pie. Bear stew made with new potatoes and carrots fresh from the garden simmered on the stove, and soon the house smelled decadent.

As I put out plates, I heard more laughter from the men outside, so I pulled open the door to see Sam, his arm cocked back with a hatchet hanging from his hand. He flung that hatchet toward a big slice of wood the men had affixed to a stump, and the hatchet sank its blade deep into the dead center of the wood.

"Bullseye!" John shouted from where he stood not three feet away from the target.

"Boys!" I yelled. "Dinnertime!"

I shook my head and turned to find Adelle looking over my shoulder. "Bunch of show-offs," she said, grinning. "I'm just glad John has found some new playmates."

I relaxed enough to laugh. Adelle was right. The men were having their own brand of fun, and I needed to loosen up and stop worrying, especially if I wanted Adelle to think Caribou Island was a safe place to raise her children.

By weekend's end, Adelle and John left with their children. Over coffee, with tear-filled eyes, Adelle told me they'd decided against living on the island full time. She wasn't confident in her wilderness-living skills (not that anyone is— it's a learn-as-you-go lifestyle), and she felt it would be too difficult with four young children.

"We'll probably still use it as a getaway cabin," she said.

The word *probably* didn't feel very encouraging to me, but I told her I understood, and I told her I'd eagerly await their next visit.

September and October seemed to pass before Sam and I had an opportunity to blink. We'd been so busy over the spring and summer building our new sauna and Harry and Foster's cabin that we had to double-time it to lay our own stores for winter. We'd been fortunate with Sam's caribou kills, but we still needed to cut and cord a great amount of firewood to keep us warm through the winter.

And in between all this were the daily chores, most of which I enjoyed, particularly cooking for everyone. Ol' Donal, who—besides Sam—was the most vocal about my cooking abilities, sometimes even made special requests for something he'd enjoyed before. He loved my moose burritos and the creamed bear I'd serve over biscuits, but as November rolled around, it was his Thanksgiving request that threw me.

"Why don't you make us a goose for Thanksgiving dinner, Bonnie?" he asked, pushing his glasses back up on his beaklike nose.

My eyes immediately went to the lake. The williwaw had already kicked up, and I hadn't seen a goose on the lake since early September.

Ol' Donal laughed. "I didn't mean for you to shoot one. Too late in the season for that. Naw, I thought I'd pick one up at the store." He lit a cigarette and drew a puff. "That is, if you don't mind fixing it for us."

"Well . . . okay. I mean, if we can get across the lake another time between now and Thanksgiving."

"Sure, we'll make it," Ol' Donal said, blowing a billowing cloud overhead.

It turns out that Ol' Donal was right. The williwaw winds rage this time of year, but they finally quieted down long enough for us to boat across the lake and get to town. Ol' Donal bought a goose at the grocery store, and I picked up a few extra things to make and serve with our Thanksgiving dinner.

What I neglected to pick up, however, was a recipe for how to cook a goose. I decided it couldn't be much different than cooking a chicken, so I prepared it as I would a chicken. I made stuffing using old sourdough bread that I'd cubed and dried on top of the wood stove. I added in seasonings, then placed root vegetables around the bird in my roasting pan. Easy peasy.

Except it wasn't.

An hour into the baking process, smoke began to curl out of my oven. I ran to the kitchen and flung open the door to get a big faceful of oily smoke and heat. I waved it away, grabbed my potholders, and pulled out the heavy pan.

"Eeeek!" I said. "What in the world?"

Sam looked up from where he sat in front of the woodstove, whittling sticks for spearfishing. "What's wrong? Did you burn it?"

"No, I didn't burn it. It's not even close to being done, yet. But Sam . . . my goose is *swimming!*"

Now I had my husband's full attention, and he put his stick and pan of wood shavings aside. "What?" He headed to the kitchen.

"It's swimming! The pan is full of oil!"

"How much did you put in there?"

"None! Well, I used about a stick's worth of butter on the goose's skin, but . . . goodness gracious! There must be three or four cups of oil in this pan! My vegetables are sloshing around in it!"

Sam started laughing. "Bonnie, a goose is full of fat. You knew that, didn't you?"

I shot him a scathing look. "Obviously not." I pulled a large bowl out of the cabinet, then motioned to the roasting pan. "Here. I'll hold the bowl, and you pour the oil out of the pan, before we're smoked out of house and home."

Between the two of us, we managed to dump out most of the oil, then I ladled much of the rest into the bowl and returned the goose to the oven.

"Oh, Sam! I've cooked a lot of things, but never a goose." I removed my oven mitts and set them on the counter. "Ol' Donal had his heart set on goose for Thanksgiving dinner. What if he hates it?"

"Relax, Bonnie. I'm sure it will turn out scrumptious and he'll love it, and if he doesn't, he can hit a McDonald's drive-thru."

My mouth went slack for a moment, but then I grabbed an oven mitt and flung it toward him. "Rotten, Mr. Ward. You're simply rotten." I picked up the bowl of hot grease and headed toward the door.

"Where are you going with that?" Sam asked.

"I'm going to dump it out."

"Hold up! I can use that!"

"Sam, what in Sam hill will you do with a bowl of hot goose grease?"

He grinned and rescued the bowl from my arms. "I'll let it cool and put it in a jar. It'll be great for moisturizing my leathers."

I shrugged. We'd learned over the years to utilize or recycle many things we might have tossed out while living on the mainland. Sam had used bear grease for years on his leathers, but still . . . goose oil leathers?

As it turned out, the goose oil was quite wonderful at adding suppleness to Sam's holsters, his belts, and our jackets. He rubbed it into his gun stocks, too, plus anything else that needed a bit of conditioning and shine. One afternoon shortly after Thanksgiving, Sam sat out front—yes, in the cold—with the jar of oil at his feet and an oil-soaked cloth in his hand, boasting about what a great job the goose oil was doing to rejuvenate his leather chaps.

"Well, Sam," I said to him. "You know what they say. . . ."

He looked at me so expectantly that I'm surprised I was able to tease him with a straight face.

"What's good for the goose is good for the gander."

I successfully dodged his playful swat, and giggling, I ran inside to start dinner.

A few days later, just as the williwaw winds were beginning to die down, Sam made his final trip on the boat to take Ol' Donal back to the mainland.

"It's too brutal out here over the winter months for an ol' feller like me," he said.

I hugged him goodbye. "You'll be back in the spring, right?"

He shrugged. "Maybe not. I'm thinking Soldotna might be a good place for me to settle down. You'll visit me there, right?"

I promised him I would. As it sank in that we'd have no more nightly dinners with our friend Ol' Donal, I hugged him again, this time more fiercely, not even minding the strong smell of cigarettes that clung to him like a second set of clothes.

When I let him go, he took my hand, and he pressed a wadded handkerchief into it.

"What's this?" I asked.

"Just a little something to repay you for all those wonderful dinners, but mostly for your company."

I carefully unfolded the tiny package. "Oh! Oh, my! Ol' Donal, are you sure?" Nestled in the fabric lay a sparkling diamond.

"I'm sure, girlie. I've no use for it. It came out of my mother's engagement ring. She'd probably want you to have it for taking care of her little boy."

My jaw dropped when he said "little boy," and then I giggled thinking of him as a child, probably always pushing up his glasses on that beaked nose of his.

As if he'd read my mind, he said, "Yeah, hard to believe it, but I was a little boy once." He folded his hand over mine where I held the diamond. "You take this, and one day you can make a pretty ring out of it for yourself."

I sniffed and blinked back tears, knowing how much it meant for him to give me this token of affection.

Thankfully, before I could become too weepy, Sam cleared his throat. "Best head on across, before the wind picks up again."

Ol' Donal touched the brim of his cap and climbed onto Sam's boat.

It was the last time I'd see my dinner conversationalist, though Sam ran into him a few times in town, and sometime later Sam drove him to the Soldotna Senior Citizen Center, as he wanted to meet some people his own age. Ol' Donal ended up getting an apartment near the senior center, and later in the year when on a supply run, Sam stopped by to visit him. He said Ol' Donal had quit smoking and had taken up woodworking, and he made and sold small furniture to a store in town. Indeed, Ol' Donal was our diamond in the rough Alaskan wilderness.

Shortly after Ol' Donal left, I walked to Anna's for a last visit before she headed to the mainland until late spring. Anna was quieter than usual as we sat at her kitchen table, savoring a cup of hot tea, and I assumed it was because she was sad to leave Nels and Caribou Island for the winter.

"Why don't you just stay?" I asked.

Anna's lips parted, and she gave me a long, blank stare.

"Anna?" I finally prompted.

Oh, how I'd misinterpreted her hesitance.

"I'm leaving him. For good this time, Bonnie."

Surely I'd misunderstood her words.

"You—you two are—you mean, you're not coming back?"

Anna's shoulders sagged, and she stared into her cup of hot tea as if it held answers. "I'm divorcing him." She let out a jagged breath. "We don't get along anymore. And living separately most of the year? No. I'm tired of it." She turned away from me and stared out at the lake. "I've had enough."

My mouth worked for several seconds before words finally tumbled out. "But you love—I mean, he loves—you both love

. . . oh, Anna. Are you *sure?*" Tears stung my eyes, and I reached for her hand in a weak effort to comfort her.

But when she squeezed my hand firmly and stared into my eyes with a leveled gaze and clear eyes, I realized she was serious. And she wasn't one bit tearful.

Anna had had enough.

Before the sun set, she was gone.

CHAPTER NINETEEN

My Thirtieth Birthday

Early in December, Skilak Lake started to freeze all the way across. The ice was thickest around the shoreline where water was shallower, and it remained thin in the center—much too thin to drive or even walk across.

On the morning of December 2, the wind picked up and blew quite stiffly, breaking up the ice once again. Sam decided that he and I should use this fortuitous breakup to boat over to the south shore to trap mink.

It turned out to be an excellent idea, because within that week, we trapped over a dozen mink, which he'd skin and sell for their hides, providing us with cash for extra supplies and gas on our next visit into town.

When December 8 rolled around, I reneged on Sam's offer to go trapping. "Why don't you ask Winston to go? I'm taking the day off for my birthday."

Sam laughed. "That's an excellent idea! Both the day off, and taking Winston. I'm sure he could use the break." Winston was nearing the end of his cabin-building, and he was now working to install cabinets and finish the interior. "What will you do with the day to yourself?" Sam asked.

I hummed and tapped my chin. "I think I'll bake myself a birthday cake, and then maybe make myself a special treat for dinner."

Sam grinned. "Sounds like a birthday for me, too!"

I shooed him toward the door. "Go get your hunting buddy. And tell him to bring an appetite to dinner."

Once the men were gone and I had the house to myself, I sat by the stove with a cup of hot tea, and I thumbed through my cookbooks, deciding what I'd make for dinner. After browsing what I thought the men might like, I thought, hey! It's *my* birthday! I'm going to have what *I* want.

And I wanted my delicious moose burritos!

Decision made, I dressed warmly and went out to feed the chickens. Then I carried water to the sauna, filling Sam's and my bucket and the big pot on the sauna stove for later.

Back inside, I started rolling out tortillas. I don't mean to brag, but my homemade tortillas are amazing! Made with fresh dough, when fried they bubble up and turn golden brown, and as if by magic, they're somehow both tender and crunchy at the same time. They're so good, and perfect for a birthday treat!

As I worked, I stared out the window. The day remained gray, but it had started to snow, and the big, white flakes made a lovely contrast against the gray sky and the dark sheen of the lake. I knew the men would be quite hungry, so I made a huge—and I'm not kidding when I say *huge*—stack of tortillas. I spiced up the moose meat and bean mixture, and one at a time, I rolled up the moose burritos and placed them in the sizzling hot oil in my cast iron frying pan and fried them on both sides until golden brown, and continued until I had a platter piled dangerously high with my treat.

Soon enough, the tangy scent of moose burritos was replaced with the decadent aroma of chocolate, as my birthday cake neared completion. I melted a pan of chocolate to cover my cake in fresh ganache. Oh, my birthday was going to be grand!

As the men returned, a thick fog accompanied them, settling all around the cabin and onto the lake. The temperature in the cabin seemed to drop a good fifteen degrees—it was toasty from my baking and deep-frying—when the men opened the door, allowing the wintery wind to gust inside.

After they'd shed their heavy garments and washed up, we sat around the table, devouring every last one of the huge tray of burritos I'd prepared. Oh, my! We lost all self-control with moose burritos! Winston could eat a half-dozen or more all by himself, and Sam and I nearly kept up with him.

I cleared the table and brought out the cake, and the men shyly sang "Happy Birthday" to me. I even blew out the candle I'd added, wishing for my thirtieth year to be as wonderful as my twenty-ninth had been.

We took our time eating the cake, as we were stuffed with moose burritos, but also because the companionship and conversation flowed easily that evening.

"Look at that," Winston said, pointing out the window toward Little Caribou Island.

The island had been shrouded in fog, but as quickly as it came, the fog started dissipating, and in the distance, on top of the heavy copse of pines turned solid white with snow, twelve bald eagles stood proudly. It was as if they materialized out of the fog, their ebony bodies standing out against the snow-covered trees, their brilliant white heads crowning the scene. It was a scene fitting of a calendar shot; ethereal, breathtaking, and somehow even eerie in its perfection.

Perhaps it was that otherworldly scene, or perhaps it was the knowledge that I'd entered a new decade of life, but an odd sensation came over me just then. I looked over at my beloved Sam, appearing so physically fit and handsome, his charming smile and his sparkling eyes melting my heart. And then I looked at Winston, his western accent reverberating as he talked, he and my husband laughing in deep timbres, and joy bubbled inside of me.

I glanced around me at the cabin we'd turned into a cozy home; the propane light above the stove casting a warm, golden glow over the knotty pine walls. A sense of deep, inner peace settled around me like the lovely fog that had covered the lake only minutes ago.

Bonnie, I said to myself, *you are living the best part of your life right now. Right here. Right in this very minute. Enjoy it. Embrace it, because it will never get better than this!*

I said a prayer of thanks, and as I did so, a Bible verse I'd read just that morning as part of my daily devotionals came to me.

"And the peace of God, which passeth all understanding, shall keep your hearts and minds through Christ Jesus."
Philippians 4:7 *King James Version*

I realized in that moment that the heavenly sensation I was experiencing was, indeed, heaven-sent. It certainly passed all understanding, and even now, my words of description seem weak. I again gave thanks to God for speaking to me this way, through His still, small voice.

". . . she even listening? Bonnie?" Now Sam's voice reached me. I had no idea how long I'd been in that serene and blissful state in which the men's voices both were and were not heard.

"Yes! Sorry. What were you saying?"

Sam grinned, and under the table he squeezed my knee. "I was just saying that some homemade snow-cream would be really good with another slice of birthday cake later this evening. What do you say?"

"Oh, Sam! Yes, that'd be scrumptious!"

Winston laughed and nodded. "I second that emotion."

"Hey, Winston," I said. "While I heat the water and do the dishes, and Sam makes snow-cream, why don't you be the first one to take a sauna? I put the big pot on to heat earlier today, so it should be ready by now. Sam and I will take a sauna later."

His eyes lit up. There was nothing quite as relaxing at the end of a frigid Alaskan day than a steamy sauna. "You sure?" he said, already standing from the table.

I smiled, trying not to laugh at his eagerness. "Of course! Go ahead."

I didn't have to tell him again. As Winston bolted out the door, Sam hooted with laughter. "You want to bet that Winston spends next summer building his own sauna?"

"Yep! I'd bet you're right!"

While I cleared the table, Sam gathered one of my large stainless-steel bowls, a big spoon, vanilla, and a small container of sugar, and he headed outdoors to make my birthday snow-cream.

As night fell, the three of us—sweet-smelling and cozy from our saunas—gathered in the living room, each of us nestling a bowl of rich birthday cake with chocolate ganache icing and a large dollop of Sam's sweet snow-cream. We each *mmmed and ahhhhed* as we savored the decadent treat.

Only one thing could have made my birthday celebration any more special, and that would have been to share it with my family. As our mail was often delayed, I hadn't received even a birthday card from my family, so while my birthday was one of the most amazing days I've ever lived, I still felt that tug toward my family back home.

I was grateful when Sam turned on the seven o'clock news, as it pushed away what I felt were selfish thoughts. After all, only moments earlier I'd received an amazing spiritual blessing—a heavenly birthday gift.

After the news, we all perked up from our sleepy positions, as the North Wind Messages began. We each loved hearing news about and to folks in the Alaskan bush who lived completely off-grid.

"This first message tonight is for a lassie on Caribou Island, name of Bonnie Ward," the announcer read.

I hopped to the edge of the chair where I'd been curled up. "Oh!"

"Here we go," the announcer continued, and we heard him shuffling papers. "'To Bonnie on Caribou Island. We want to wish you a very happy birthday. Love and miss you so much! Mom and Dad.' Aww, well isn't that sweet? Happy Birthday, Miss Bonnie."

Tears sprang to my eyes, and Sam chuckled when I swatted them away. "Well, there you go," he said. "Now isn't that better than a card?"

Love for my husband poured out of me when I looked at him. Without me saying a word, he somehow knew I was thinking of my parents and wishing I'd heard from them.

With no phones or mail delivery—and in those days no cell phones or internet—messages from home were more precious than you might imagine. My parents' delivery of a North Wind Message was indeed the cherry on top of the icing.

Frost covered trees on Little Caribou Island. We can see the island from our kitchen window, and often watch eagles and coyotes eating on salmon carcasses on the shoreline.

The wind really picked up in the days immediately following my birthday. Outdoors, the roaring of the whitecaps pounding against the ice shelves that had broken up and piled near the shore filled the air. The sound was a pleasant one, but one that nevertheless reminded us of Skilak's ever-impending danger.

Our days on the now almost-vacant island stayed quite busy. Though we'd had to cease trapping due to the rough waves and ice break-ups on the lake, we stayed busy with our ever-present daily chores—feeding the chickens, hauling water from the lake, chopping wood, skinning the last of the minks, and—quite literally—keeping the home fires burning.

Occasionally Sam and I would bundle up well enough to make the long walk in the stiff wind to Winston's cabin. He'd finished the exterior just as winter arrived, and it pleased me to see the attention he was putting into making the inside look like a cozy home. Winston could finally break down his wall tent, and soon his encampment was no more.

Winston had a real home.

On Caribou Island, neighbors helped neighbors. Especially, if you only had one or two neighbors. It wasn't even a question—it was a requirement. In the Alaskan wilderness, the land, the water, and the weather can turn on you in a moment, and if we were to survive it, we all needed one another.

CHAPTER TWENTY

Homesick

Our Christmas, while pleasant, remained subdued. It didn't achieve the "Merry" status usually reserved for the holy holiday, but we managed to celebrate it with a comfortable—and comforting—evening in front of the sparkling tree, nonetheless.

Heavy winter snows and increasingly frigid temperatures caused Caribou to seem more isolated than usual. A cloud of loneliness settled around me like a dense fog, and I missed the summer months when our little island was populated with happy voices.

Sam and I celebrated his birthday on December 29, and though I baked him a German chocolate cake and sang to him, I struggled to remain upbeat once he'd blown out his one candle. The house seemed too empty, too quiet, too lonely. And I was so homesick for my family that even a quick memory of them—and I thought of them almost hourly—brought tears to my eyes.

Worse than feeling lonely was the guilt I felt for letting Sam see my loneliness. He missed his family, too. He rarely spoke of it, but I knew a vein of sadness ran through his body, too. Isolated winters on an island in the Alaskan bush can do that to you.

When the guilt and loneliness became too much, I began to pray for an opportunity to see my family again. Two years had passed since I'd seen them, and Christmas had passed without a card or gift from anyone back home. I figured there may be something for us at the post office in town, but with the biting wind creating way-below-zero wind-chill factors, a trip across Skilak Lake was out of the question.

And then, the morning of January 15, as I fried the fresh eggs I'd gathered the morning before, Sam came in the door with a big grin on his face.

"Wind's died down," he said. "Brutally cold out there, but there's no wind." He pulled off his gloves and rubbed his hands together near the stove. "Thought I'd see if Winston might head across the lake with me and into town. He said the other day that he was in desperate need of some supplies."

As quickly as I'd gotten excited, I calmed down again. While a big part of me would love nothing more than to take a trip into town and perhaps make a quick trip to see Marion and Warner, I knew I'd be miserable heading into the bitter-cold air with the icy spray of the lake blowing around me. I would wait until the lake froze solid—if the hateful thing would ever get around to freezing—to make a trip across the ice in our warm Jeep.

"Y'all be careful," I said, "and eat a good breakfast before you hike over to Winston's."

Sam shouldered out of his heavy coat, hung it by the door, and headed toward the table. "Don't have to tell me twice. I've been thinking about another cup of hot coffee since I walked out the front door."

Some twenty minutes later, I'd filled a Thermos with steaming coffee for the men to take on their trip across the icy lake, and Sam was on his way to get Winston and head toward town. Or so I thought.

As it turned out, Sam couldn't get the boat motor started. He came through the door, his lips pressed into a thin line. "Water pump is frozen. Motor won't even turn over."

It wasn't the first time the weather had been so frigid that we couldn't get a motor to start. Knowing the drill, I pulled out a large pot and filled it from the bucket of water I kept in the kitchen, then put it on the stove to heat.

Once curls of steam rose from the pot of water, Sam, his hands gloved, took it out to the boat. I followed him with a heavy towel, just in case. He slowly poured the heavy pot of water over the water pump and motor, thawing it out, while Winston occasionally tried to start the boat. After several minutes, the motor wrenched itself to life, and soon it was thrumming again.

I kissed Sam goodbye, waved at Winston, and I took my pot and headed toward the cabin, stopping just long enough to fill it with water to replenish my stores. I could hardly wait to get back inside where it was warm!

Alone in the cabin, I made a cup of coffee and tried to read a book, but again I felt too lonely to really concentrate. I desperately wanted to hear from my family.

To "hear" them speak to me, I pulled out my box of letters from home, and I read through each of them, placing special emphasis on the parts I needed to hear right now—especially letters from my mother. I pulled out each of Mom's letters, reading and re-reading snippets that somehow seemed most important to me right now:

> *Call me. Reverse the charges. I would love to hear your voice telling me you are coming home for a visit . .*
>
> .
>
> *I'm really praying for you to come home. I'm praying that Sam gets on the pipeline again. I know you two could use the money, and you could stay with us while he's away, like you did the last time . . .*
>
> *You and Sam give each other a hug from us. A big one! Keep writing, Bonnie. Maybe we'll even see you soon. I know Sam's hoping to get back up on the slope, and we're still praying that'll happen . . .*
>
> *We would love to see you again! Tell Sam we're glad he got that coyote. We miss you so much! . . .*

Each of my mother's letters ended the same way:

> *We love and miss you. Love, Mom and Dad.*

I dried my tears and blew my nose, grateful that Sam wasn't there to see what a sentimental, slobbering mess I'd become. I always felt exhausted after a good cry, but I resisted the urge to curl up into a nest with my blanket and sleep. I had chores to do, and then after that, I planned to finish sewing the leather shirt I was making for Sam.

Some hours later, the sound of Sam's boat startled me. *Oh, goodness! I haven't even started dinner!* I was surprised at how long I had spent punching holes in the leather with the awl and hand stitching Sam's shirt at the kitchen table. I used a saddle stitch with the stitching so close and even that it could almost pass for a machine stitch.

I quickly cleared the table and lit the propane light, as the gloaming already darkened the cabin. I placed my biggest skillet on the stove, thinking salmon patties would be the quickest dish I could throw together. The men would be starving after a day in the cold wind, and I was thankful that I'd already baked extra loaves of fresh bread the day before that I could serve with jam.

I scrubbed and cut potatoes for frying, not taking time to peel them, as "rustic style" was Sam's favorite, anyway. By the time Sam and Winston were stomping snow off their boots outside the front door, dinner preparations were well underway. I quickly dried my hands and flung open the door.

"What in the world!" I said.

Sam stood loaded down with three large boxes and a big stack of mail, and behind him, Winston carried another large box, plus bags of supplies.

"Boxes from your parents," Sam said, a grin splitting his face. He pushed past me, followed by Winston, and the two deposited the boxes between our chairs near the stove.

I took the bags of our supplies from Winston as Sam stacked the mail on my end table. I nearly salivated over that pile of envelopes, and I picked them up, hefting them in my hands. *No, wait until after dinner. Sam will want to read them, too.*

The men headed out to secure the boat, and Sam said he'd bring in another load of wood, as the thermometer was sure to bottom out by nightfall.

"Wind is worse than the temperature," Winston said, his mustache and beard white with ice. He nodded toward the kitchen. "If it wouldn't put you out too much, I could sure use a cup of hot coffee as soon as I come back in."

"You got it!" I put down the letters where Sam had laid them, and hurried back to the kitchen to start coffee and set the table. As I worked, my eyes kept drifting toward the stack of mail.

By the time the coffee was ready, Sam and Winston were back inside, shedding their boots and layers. Sam stoked the fire with wood he'd brought in, and Winston headed straight for a coffee mug, wrapping both hands around it as I poured. I took Sam's cup to him, and on my way back to the table, I picked up a letter.

I couldn't wait any longer!

I quickly put the food on the table, and then I ripped open the envelope postmarked January 8, nine days earlier. As I refilled the men's coffee cups with one hand, I held the letter with the other.

"Read it to us," Sam said, grinning. "Go ahead. I know you can't stand it any longer."

I giggled and happily started reading my mother's letter aloud.

> "... *Did you receive all your boxes, yet? I think all together, we sent four of them. Again, I'm sorry we didn't get them out in time for Christmas.*
>
> "*Say, Bon, did you get a message over north wind messages on your birthday? We had a great Christmas with the family. Your niece and nephew were so excited! Laura got her Cabbage Patch Doll, and we got Daniel a Knight Rider and his car Kit. We also got each of them a pair of roller skates. Now they are saying they can't wait until Aunt Bonnie comes home to take them roller skating again. I think that's a good idea, too!*

*"We sure miss both of you. We hardly have any
snow, but, of course, winter is just starting. How is your
weather? How about the lake? I wonder if you are
waiting for it to freeze over."*

Sam chuckled at this, but I kept reading.

*"Would love to hear your voice. I wish you'd call
me and say, Hi, Mom! It's me, Bonnie, and I'm flying
home for a visit!"*

My voice cracked as I read this part, and I folded the letter
up and set it aside. I didn't want to get too tearful in front of
Winston, though I felt on the verge of sobbing.

As fate would have it, a few days later, my mother's
prayers—and my own—were answered. Harry's airplane
buzzed our house, and then he landed on the lake and taxied
toward the beach.

"Sam!" he said, calling his news before he even reached us.
"Foster's got a job for you up on the slope! Better getcher
affairs in order." He nodded toward me and grinned. "You,
too, Bonnie. I expect you'll want to spend a couple of months
with your family. Am I right?"

Winston must have heard the plane—or my squeal all the
way back at his cabin, because as Harry secured his plane,
Winston turned up, and Harry kindly invited him to tag along,
telling him Foster could likely find work for him, too.

"I 'preciate it, but I reckon I'll stick around here," he said,
scuffing his boot in the snow. "Just moved into my new cabin,
and I don't want to leave her just yet." He cocked his head
toward our place. "Besides, I can look after the trap lines and
the chickens while Sam and Bonnie are away."

"Oh, Winston!" I gushed. "Thank you!" I clutched my hands together to keep from clapping, and then I turned and ran toward the cabin.

"Bonnie?" Sam asked. "Where you going?"

I looked over my shoulder, but kept moving forward. "I'm going to fix dinner for y'all. And then I'm going to start packing!"

The three men chuckled behind me, but I didn't care. I was going to see my family!

CHAPTER TWENTY-ONE

A Visit Home

Hugs, squeals, and kisses announced my arrival at the airport in Minnesota as my dad and my sister Dawn greeted me. When I'd been turned loose of hugs for a moment, I peered over Dawn's shoulder. "Where's Mom?"

A cloud of concern briefly flitted across her face and she masked it with a smile, but not before I saw it. "She's at home. She didn't feel up to the trip."

My face must have registered equal concern, as Dawn put her hand on my forearm and spoke brightly. "Don't worry. Mom's fine, Bonnie. It's her emphysema—she has her good days and bad days, and today the weather is taking a toll on her."

My own lungs opened then, and my dad took my carry-on as Dawn tugged on my backpack. "Let me carry something!" she demanded.

I laughed, and soon we were loaded into dad's car and heading toward my parents' house.

Once we arrived, I nearly tumbled out of the car into my parents' driveway, as I couldn't wait to see my mother. My dad held open the door for me, and I rushed in, planning to find and surprise her. But it was she who surprised me.

"Bonnie!" my mother said, stretching out her arms from the hospital bed in the middle of my parents' living room. "You're home!"

My mouth went dry and I dropped my bag and rushed toward those outstretched arms. "Oh, Mom!" I practically fell on top of her, and without meaning to, I found myself weeping on her shoulder.

"Shhh," my mother said. "It's okay. You're home now. Everything is okay."

Afraid she'd misunderstood, I straightened from where I sat on the edge of the hospital bed, and I dried my face with my hands. "I'm okay, Mom," I said, "but are *you* okay?"

She clasped my hands in hers, and her grip was strong. "I'm fine. Just a little breathless. That's all." She spoke between sips of air, her sentences short and crisp.

I studied my mother's face. Her eyes were as bright as I remembered, and her smile still seemed to light up the room. At fifty years old, she didn't have a gray hair on her head. Her cheeks appeared a little too pale, and there were red pressure marks from the tubing of her nasal cannula on the sides of her face. Otherwise, if it wasn't for the fact that she lay upon a hospital bed and had an oxygen tank perched near her head, one might never know she was ill.

I hugged my mother again, and then my niece Laura tugged at my arm. "Aunt Bonnie! Let's play Monopoly!"

My mother pushed me away. "Go play with the kids. They've been about to burst to see you."

And play Monopoly we did! I bet I played fifty or sixty games with Laura and my nephew Daniel and my sisters Dawn and Connie during my two-month visit. Occasionally Dad would play with us, and he'd intentionally pass by properties without purchasing them so the kids could beat him.

"What!" he'd say. "You won again? How did you get so smart?"

The kids would giggle and run off, and we'd put the game back in the box, only to drag it out again a short time later.

We were playing Monopoly at the kitchen table one evening when I felt a hand on my hair.

"Bon-Bon," my mother said, "your hair is so beautiful and shiny. That crystal-pure lake water must be good for it."

I turned to see my precious mother standing behind me, oxygen tube attached to her nose as she held onto the back of my chair for support. "Thanks, Mom!" I said, and I almost immediately returned to the game in which I was engrossed.

It didn't dawn on me then, but it had taken quite a bit of effort for my mother to make the extra distance from the hospital bed to the kitchen, when it was all she could do to make the few steps from the bed to the bathroom. Her tender, loving gesture should have meant as much to me then as it does now . . . now that she has passed from my life.

My mother always had strong intuition where her children were concerned, and she missed nothing. She'd notice if I appeared sad as I sat quietly thinking of my husband, and to this day I have no idea how she'd figure out I was missing Sam. Outside, I made sure I kept a smile on my face, because—truly—I was thrilled to spend time with my family. But inside . . . inside, I felt broken without my husband. My mother always seemed to know what was happening on my inside. She could see everything; even what others never saw.

Once Mom noticed that I was squinting while watching television and recommended I get my eyes checked before going back to Alaska. I thought she was being overly concerned for nothing. I mean, for starters, I didn't watch television in Alaska—I didn't even own a television! When Mom and I would watch a show together thereafter, I'd feel her watching me, and I'd take great care not to squint. How silly of me!

Finally, my mother insisted that I see an ophthalmologist, and yes, I needed eyeglasses. Always, my mother spent more time caring about me than she did about herself. As did my sweet father.

One afternoon early into my visit, my dad pulled me aside. "You got a minute, Bon? I got something I want to show you." I followed him out to his workshop, where he pulled an old sheet off an antique Singer sewing machine. "What do you think?"

"Oh, Dad! Where did you find this?" I ran my hand over the faded and worn wooden cabinet, and then my father lifted the lid and pulled up the sewing machine.

"It's a treadle," he said, and his eyes sparkled when they met mine. "No electricity required."

It dawned on me then that it was a gift for me. "Really? You bought me a sewing machine?"

"She'll need a little work, but I figure we can have her ready before time for you to leave."

That same afternoon, my dad and I started breaking down the sewing machine. Over several days, we took it completely apart, cleaning and oiling the ornately designed head and all its components. We painted all the metal parts glossy black with touches of metallic gold. Once we'd put it back together, we started on the cabinet. We each worked to sand the antique oak cabinet using fine-grade steel wool. When the wood reached an almost velvety softness, we then oiled it down with a light coat of Tung tree oil, then sanded it again. We repeated this process several times. Days—and many hours of work later—the cabinet seemed to glow from within.

Soon we completed the refinishing process, and I began to sew. Little Laura took advantage of my sewing skills, as I made a whole wardrobe of clothes for her new Cabbage Patch Doll, even making her and the doll matching Easter dresses so she could play Mommy-Baby-Dress-Up when the holiday arrived. I also sewed dresses for my sister Connie, and she bragged to all her friends that I'd created them on a treadle sewing machine.

"On an antique sewing machine!" Connie said. "She made this with no electricity!"

I thought of the many days I'd spent with needle and thread in hand, stitching curtains, clothing, even a beaver-fur hat, and I laughed. I'd lived years with no electricity!

Before I left Minnesota, I'd become quite proficient on my "new" treadle Singer. I handled the sewing machine delicately as Dad and I took it apart once again and carefully packed it into boxes to ship to the little log cabin post office in Sterling, Alaska.

On the plane ride back to Alaska, I thought of my sewing machine, and how Dad and I had taken it apart, cleaned and polished its many parts, then put it back together to make it better than before. I thought of how precious was the time I spent with my family, with my generous-hearted father and my loving mother who appeared so much more fragile than when I last saw her. I thought of Sam, and how I'd moped and pouted around him the last months we were together. I considered how hard he'd been working on the North Slope to make a great amount of money to see us through the upcoming year. I knew he loved that job, and I knew he enjoyed the camaraderie of his friends and their antics as they worked the pipeline.

I hated being away from my husband, away from the cabin we'd built together, away from the stunningly gorgeous and dangerous wilderness we called home.

Yes, for a short while before leaving Caribou Island, I'd been broken by loneliness and homesickness, and maybe in that brokenness I hadn't realized that Sam was feeling broken, too. We are one, after all. But just like the old treadle Singer, we'd been taken apart—he'd gone in one direction, and I'd gone in another. While we were apart, we'd been cleaned and polished by those we'd greatly missed seeing.

When Samuel Ward walked toward me at the airport in Kenai, his smile broad and his eyes sparkling with happiness, I felt as if my life was put back together, and I knew we were somehow stronger and better than we ever were before.

CHAPTER TWENTY-TWO

Spring Is Here

On our trip back to the lower landing, Sam shared with me news from a letter he'd received from Winston. "Winston left a couple weeks ago. He sold his cabin," Sam said. "Sold it to one of Clark's friends. I'm guessing we won't meet the new owner until spring thaw."

The news saddened me, but I couldn't imagine Winston not coming back to Caribou, and I wondered if perhaps he'd do like Sam and I did, building another cabin for himself, using money from the sale of his first.

When Sam and I arrived at the lower landing, I was surprised to see a small three-wheeler with a trailer attached sitting beside our Jeep. "Wonder whose that is?" I asked Sam.

He winked. "For the time being, it's ours."

"What?"

"I borrowed it. Until we can test the ice for ourselves, I don't want to put the weight of the Jeep—plus us and our luggage—on top of it."

A shiver ran through me that had nothing to do with the temperature. I recalled the time I watched from the island as Sam walked across the lake toward the mainland, and how he disappeared from sight, then later reappeared, as the ice on the center of the lake sagged with his weight. "Are you sure we'll be okay?"

Sam put his hand on my shoulder. "As sure as I can be." He grabbed the largest of the boxes in which my Singer was packed and dropped it onto the trailer. "Let's get loaded up and get home."

To say that our ride across the lake was brisk would be an understatement. The icy wind added to the speed we were making across the ice, and it felt as if it cut into my cheeks, even through the scarf I'd wrapped around my face. Minnesota had spoiled me.

Soon we were back on Caribou Island, and Sam pulled the little three-wheeler right up to our front door. He stepped off and offered me his hand. "Madam," he said, and as I took it and stepped off, he bowed deeply.

I laughed. "You're a nutcase, Mr. Ward." Then I hugged him. "I'm so happy to be home!"

He quickly turned his face from me, and he scanned the satiny surface of Skilak Lake. "It is home, isn't it?" He wrapped an arm around my waist, and the two of us stood there a moment, appraising the gorgeous scenery.

I gave silent thanks to God for allowing me a trip to see my family, for bringing Sam and me safely back to Caribou Island, and for letting us live our Alaskan dream in a place that felt like home to both of us.

We shouldered our luggage, but at the front door, Sam stopped me. "Wait here."

"Why? What's wrong?"

He pointed toward the window beside our front door. There were deep gouges around it, as if someone had pried it open. Sam had put in our windows solidly, and they were made of Thermopane glass—they didn't open or shut. The molding was missing from around the window. "Someone's broken in." He gave me a warning glance. "Let me make sure they're not still here."

Minutes later, Sam came out holding a folded piece of paper in his hand. "Derik's been here. Left a note. Said he came down over the winter and couldn't get his cabin warm. Couldn't get a fire built." Sam shrugged. "He broke in and built a fire. Spent a couple nights, until he could get back to the mainland." Sam waved toward the window. "He put the window back in before he left."

"Oh."

It was as simple as that. It was perfectly okay with us that Derik had broken into our home, torn out a window to do so, and replaced it before he left. Derik's cabin sat on the northern side, the windiest side, of Caribou Island. It was a small, one-room, shack-like cabin, and when you stood inside it, you could see the light from outside through the cracks between the boards.

Sam and I had no problem with Derik sleeping in our home, eating our food, and burning our firewood while we were away. It was the wilderness way. He did what he had to do to survive.

After we carried in our luggage, the boxes I'd shipped from Minnesota, and the supplies we'd picked up in Sterling, Sam and I headed toward the chicken coops to check on our birds.

He threw out large handfuls of scratch, and though our birds were free-range fowl and could go anywhere they wanted to rummage for food, they came flocking toward us, some running up from behind the cabin, others flying in from the large pines overhead.

I laughed, and though I wanted to pick each one up and hug it, I let them be, knowing I could get pecked by a sharp beak if I interfered with dinner. "Looks like they're all here!" I said.

Sam surveyed the flock. "Almost all of them. We might be missing a couple."

Northern goshawks, owls, and other predatory birds were always a threat to our flock, and without us here to protect them, they were easy pickings. Winston had done a good job of feeding our birds—they were nice and plump—though I didn't see any sign of our bobwhite quail. I suspected they were scouring the forest, and I figured they'd be back soon enough.

Sam and I spent our first night back home stoking the fire to warm our large space, unpacking, and cleaning (the cabin had gotten a bit dusty while we were away). The next morning, as we made a quick walk around the rest of our property to make sure everything was okay—and it was—we realized the temperature had warmed.

"Forty degrees," Sam said, eyeing our thermometer. "Spring is here. Looks like we made it across the ice just in time. We need to get that three-wheeler back across the ice before the winds break up and wash out the ice."

"Will it be safe to bring the Jeep back, do you think?" I asked.

Sam stroked his chin. "Let's buy a four-wheeler."

"Seriously?"

"Sure. Why not? It'll be a lot lighter than the Jeep, even with a loaded trailer attached." He waved a hand toward the forest behind us. "It'll be small enough that we can navigate through the rough terrain and woods, and I can use it to pull logs out of the forest."

The next morning, we headed to the mainland, where we purchased "Mojo," the name Sam gave our new Honda four-wheeler. Back on the island, we took turns riding and driving through the woods, and I used it that evening to haul water from the lake to the cabin. What a brilliant idea!

The next day, Sam and I sat at the table, sipping fresh coffee as we made plans for investing our now-sizeable savings account. We wanted to buy more land on Skilak to build more getaway cabins to sell. Sam tapped a finger on the map spread before us, and, almost like an echo, we heard thumping on our porch outside the front door.

"What was that?" I asked.

Sam shrugged and got up, and as he crossed the floor, the thumping sounded again.

I followed him, and when he opened the door, we saw Rooster Cogburn, one of our Rhode Island Red roosters. (Yes, Sam had named him.)

Sam scooped up the bird and held him in his arms. "He's got a frozen leg."

I peered closer. Sure enough, the poor rooster's leg was frozen solid, and what was once golden yellow was now whitish gray. "Oh, Sam! What do we do?"

Sam's mouth pulled to one side as he palpated the chicken's leg and thigh. "It's hard. He's suffering, Bonnie." He put the bird down, where it thumped its poor little leg against the porch again. "He's suffering. Let me get my axe. I need to put him out of his misery."

I hated the thoughts of losing Rooster Cogburn, as he was one of our first purchases from Marion and Warner, and I'd come to think of him as a pet. But that was my own foolishness, as the reason we had chickens in the first place was for meat and eggs. And tonight, we'd be having fried chicken.

Some minutes later, when Sam opened the door with the plucked bird in hand, a whistling sounded behind him. "Oh, Sam!" I hopped up from the table. "Our bobwhites are back!" I stepped out on the porch, and sure enough, here they came, whistling *Bob-white, bob-white, bob-white!* After losing Rooster Cogburn, it was a definite pick-me-up to know our other birds had returned home.

At least twenty of the bobwhite quail settled around and inside the chicken coop, and Sam and I rushed to grab a bucket and throw out feed to celebrate their homecoming. We knew if we fed them regularly, they'd stick around.

Later in the day, Sam checked our other birds one at a time, and he discovered that several of our chickens had frozen feet. I spent the afternoon and evening cleaning, gutting, plucking and cooking chicken. What we didn't cook and eat, we hung from the porch eave where they would stay chilled enough while waiting their turn for the frying pan or stew pot.

In the weeks to come, the ice indeed became honeycombed, making the lake unsafe for travel. While we were homebound, Sam decided we'd build a better chicken coup to protect our birds in winters to come. He built this one with plywood, making it a double-walled, double-roofed structure. In the space between the walls, we dumped in buckets full of sawdust collected from our log-and-firewood-cutting area.

Once the void was filled between those walls, we could indeed feel a temperature change in the new coop. Sam then installed a propane light overhead in the center of the coop, enclosing it in tight wire mesh, to prevent the chickens from flying into it. Not only did it provide light during the long nights, it offered an additional measure of warmth for the birds. Instead of small poles for roosts, Sam used two-by-fours. This way, the birds could actually sit on their feet while roosting, keeping their spindly feet warm.

Lastly, to make the plywood coop more aesthetically appealing, Sam attached first-cut slabs from logs (the outside of the logs, with the bark still attached to the rounded side), to the outside of the coop. When it snowed, the snow collected on the bark, and the little chicken coop looked like a homey little cabin for the birds. "Sam, we have the most spoiled chickens in Alaska," I said when he'd finished.

Sam chuckled. "Possibly. At least now maybe their feet won't freeze!" He waved a hand toward the wooded yard next to the chicken coop. "Later, I'll build huge outdoor pens and cover them with fishnet." He turned to me and winked. "We need to expand to make room for more fowl."

I giggled. "The birds will have their own little fowl city."

For the next five weeks, we waited for the ice to break up. It seemed an interminably long time, but we stayed busy traipsing the island, trying to find the best lots to purchase for building getaway cabins. Our post-winter chores also kept us hopping, and I started clearing my garden spot again to be ready for planting season, right around the corner. Daily busyness, like stoking fires, baking, cooking, sewing, and tending to the birds, filled the long days. Buttons, our little Black Cochin bantam hen, hatched out ten little biddies, and I looked forward to telling Marion about how our flock had grown the next time I saw her.

Right after the ice break-up, on our first trip back to the mainland, we received a letter from Winston. He'd mailed it over a month earlier. In it, he told us about Rooster Cogburn's frozen foot, and he told us he'd enjoyed taking care of our birds.

And then he told us something that shocked us and left us saddened.

"As you know, I've sold my cabin to Clark's friend—his name is Kenny," he wrote. "My Alaskan adventure has come to an end, and I'm going to spend my days back in Wyoming. Clark's friend plans to use my place as a get-away cabin, and I plan to use the money from the sale as a down payment on a little ranch. I reckon this cowboy has finally roamed back home.

". . . Sam, I hope to see you and Bonnie again one day. Maybe you'll visit me in Wyoming, and I promise to visit you sometime. You've been the best friends a man could hope to have. I will miss you.

"Love, Winston."

Sam folded the letter and stuffed it back into the envelope. I held out my hand, thinking he'd hand it to me to add to the other mail I held. Instead, he tucked it inside his jacket, slipping into the inner breast pocket, right over his heart.

The chickens love their new chicken coop, and the Mojo simplifies the chore of hauling water to my thirsty birds!

CHAPTER TWENTY-THREE

Stinky Feet

Sam and I went to work right away, putting our investment plan into action. We'd researched county records and located the owners of the beach lot next to us. Over a lengthy phone call from a phone booth in Soldotna, with the older couple, Bernard and Louise Hudson, we learned they'd acquired that lot and a few others on the island many years earlier in trade for doing some advertising over the radio station in Anchorage they'd once owned. "I've never even been on the island," Bernard admitted.

The Hudsons agreed to sell us their lots—seemed happy to do it, in fact—and we offered to host them on the island, if they'd like to visit. They promised to come in early summer, so we scheduled a visit in late June, when Sam would pick them up on the landing, and they'd spend the day touring the island, then Sam would take them back to the mainland that evening.

Once we owned the property, we immediately started building. On each trip to the mainland, we purchased lumber from the sawmill in Sterling, and Sam hauled load after load back to the island. In addition to breaking ground for the getaway cabins, Sam continued to work on our pens for the fowl.

Warner offered to come to the island with us to show us how he built pens made of PVC pipe and netting, so that we could keep pheasants and peacocks on the island. Of course, we accepted.

Sam picked Warner up at the lower landing on a clear day, and the two boated over to the island. Sam had already picked up all the materials to build the pens, and Warner brought wire crates from Sterling that held a pair of stunning Impeyan pheasants and two gorgeous peacocks.

While the two built the long, arch-shaped, pen—which to me looked a bit like a greenhouse—I worked in the kitchen, baking bread and a cake and preparing a hot dinner for their hungry after-work appetites.

I'll admit, though . . . I stopped often to spy out the window or walk outdoors to observe their progress.

Once they'd framed the structure, the men covered the pen in strong, black plastic netting that would survive both the predator birds and the harsh weather. Sam planned to add an internal structure the next day; a small building inside the pen where the birds could get out of the weather.

After dinner and dessert, Sam ferried Warner back across the lake to the landing, where he'd left his truck, and our friend returned home to his family, promising us he'd bring them all over in a few days to visit.

Three days later, Sam picked up Warner, Marion, and their kids, and the whole troop came to Caribou Island to spend the day. A wilderness family, of sorts, they were used to a simple lifestyle and were very down-to-earth, much like Sam and me. We had an easy camaraderie, and it lifted my spirits to have the island alive with the laughter and horseplay of the children.

The youngest child, Jeremy, checked out Sam's beaver hat that hung near the door. Tentatively, he reached out a hand to pet the fur. Then he turned to me. "Sure smells good in here."

I loved that child. "Are you hungry?" I had removed a carrot cake from the oven only minutes before their arrival.

His head bounced in an eager nod.

"Jeremy," his mother scolded.

Marion brought with her a huge chicken pot-pie, which I popped into the oven along with homemade biscuits. When our lunch feast was served, we ate until we could hardly move.

Cheryl, their youngest daughter, who was now ten years old, instantly became my shadow. She helped in the kitchen, and later she checked out the sauna, the garden, and the birds. As she examined my Singer treadle sewing machine, she turned to me. "I'd like to camp over here. It sure seems like a fun place."

I glanced at Marion, then back at Cheryl. "Well, why don't you? You're welcome to stay a couple of days here on the island. That is, if it's okay with your mother." I turned to Marion with raised eyebrows, to make sure I wasn't overstepping my bounds.

Marion took in her daughter's expectant smile. "Sounds like an adventure, Cheryl. Why not?"

Cheryl let out a squeal. "Oh, boy! Thank you, Mom! Thank you, Miss Bonnie!" She ran toward the door. "I'm going to go tell Dad and Sam!"

When Sam took the rest of the family back to the landing, Cheryl stayed behind with me. The two of us decided to take a hike around the island. We strolled the shoreline, Cheryl's eyes lighting at each new discovery.

"Look at those pretty flowers," I said as I pointed. We scurried toward them. "These look like the ones you showed me at your mom's house. The chocolate lilies," I said.

"Yes!" Cheryl nodded and bent toward them. "The stinky ones." She picked a couple of them and handed me the small bundle.

I held them to my nose and sniffed. "Whew! They're stinky, all right."

Cheryl's eyes danced as she giggled, and I laughed along with her. What a delight to have a child on the island again!

"You know . . ." I said conspiratorially, "we should surprise Sam with a big vase of these, don't you think?"

Cheryl hooted. "Oh, yes! He'll think they're pretty, and then *wham-O!* The stink will get him!"

Cheryl and I headed back to the cabin, stinky lilies in hand. We decided we'd make cookies "to surprise Sam." Between the cookies and the lilies, the poor man wouldn't know what was happening, we figured.

Cheryl was narrating her fascination with my hand-crank mixer as she used it to make the cookie dough when Sam came in the door. I nudged her, and we shared a secret grin.

"What are you two up to?" Sam asked, and I quickly turned to Cheryl and put a finger to my lips to shush her.

"Just making cookies," I said.

"Yeah, we wanted to *surprise* you," Cheryl added.

"Well, how sweet! Thank you, Cheryl. I love cookies."

Cheryl and I bumped shoulders and giggled.

We watched Sam as he looked around and sniffed the air. His nose wrinkled, and I had to turn away so as not to laugh. Cheryl and I continued to drop spoonfuls of cookie dough onto a cookie sheet, and when she nudged me again, I glanced at my husband. He'd taken off his boots and put them aside, as if they were the cause of the offensive odor. He sat back down in his rocking chair, and in a minute, he took off his socks, and carried them to stuff inside his boots.

Cheryl and I did well to maintain our composure.

Sam returned to his chair, then another minute later, he stood, retrieved his boots from where he'd placed them near the door, and set them outside.

To keep from laughing, I chattered about how long we'd need to bake the cookies. Cheryl again nudged me as Sam opened the door a second time. We watched, laughing, from the picture window as Sam walked barefoot down to the lake, cuffed his trousers, and waded in the water to wash his "stinky feet."

Momentarily, Sam came back in and relaxed in his rocking chair. He again sniffed the air, and this time his whole face scrunched up.

Cheryl and I couldn't keep it together, and we both burst into gales of laughter. Sam looked at us, his face red with embarrassment, and I could fool him no longer.

I stepped across the room and picked up the vase of chocolate lilies, and held it toward Sam. "Smell our pretty flowers."

With a quizzical look, he took the vase, and as he drew it closer to his face, his expression morphed into disgust. He thrust it away. "Aw, that's awful!" He looked at Cheryl, then at me, and gave us a stern look. "Shame on you girls. I thought it was my feet!"

We again broke into laughter, and this time, Sam joined us, and soon the three of us were wiping our eyes.

He carried the vase outside, and when he returned, it was empty.

"Better leave that oven door open after the cookies come out," he said. "Might even want to bake up a second batch, because a house that smells like cookies has to be better than a house that smells like rotten flowers!"

"Yeah," Cheryl chimed in as Sam deposited the vase on the kitchen counter. "Better than stinky feet, too!"

CHAPTER TWENTY-FOUR

A Wild Beast

Our summer filled with hard work and passed quickly as Sam and I worked on the getaway cabins. By now, we had a system in place, and we maneuvered concisely and with good speed.

In early August, we received a North Wind Message to pick up Warner and Marion at the landing, so the next morning, after we'd stoked our fire—yes, even in August, the mornings on Skilak Lake arrived with a chill—and I'd collected eggs and started breakfast, Sam made ready to head across the water to pick up our friends.

Before I could even set the table, we heard a boat motor drawing near, and we peered out the window to see a watercraft headed our way. The boat drifted onto our beach, and out stepped our friend Dave, who I'll always think of as "Bear-hunter," because he killed a black bear and brought it to the landing while we were camped there our first summer on Skilak Lake.

In the wilderness, you open your door and serve anyone who chances by your home, so of course, we invited Dave to breakfast, and he was happy to join us. After four years, Sam and I had become known as "the couple who live on the lake," so I always kept coffee on the stove, something sweet on hand, and we entertained hunters, fishermen, adventurers, fish-and-game officers, and anyone else who happened to land on Caribou Island.

Dave eagerly dug into a big bowl of scrambled eggs, hot biscuits, gravy, and cranberry jam as he told us of his plans. "I'm heading to the upper end of the lake to do some Dall sheep hunting." He eyed Sam over his cup of coffee. "Thought you might like to come along."

I knew Sam would be eager to go, but I also knew he'd have to decline.

"Aw, I'm sorry, bud. You know I'd love to go with you, but I'm picking up some friends from Sterling who are coming for a visit this afternoon."

As I poured our third cups of coffee, something caught my eye out the window. "Look!"

The men followed my stare, seeing the waves that, seemingly out of nowhere, were lapping at the shoreline. Only minutes ago, the lake was a satiny sheen of smoothness without a wave to be found.

"That could be trouble," Sam said.

Dave nodded and shoveled the last bites of his breakfast into his mouth, and held up a hand to decline my pour. "I need to head out of here. I don't trust that lake as far as I could throw her."

191

Sam and I chuckled at his words, but he agreed that Dave needed to run before the weather got worse. The sky remained a brilliant blue, but we knew that with the wind picking up enough to cause waves, it wouldn't last long.

True to our worries, by the time Dave had pulled on his coat and waders and made it to his boat, the lapping waves began to show an occasional whitecap. We waved Dave off and stood watching him disappear into the distance. Seemingly out of nowhere, the sky turned dark and it began to rain. Before we even made it back to the house, the wind began to howl, and the few whitecaps turned to many.

As Sam and I entered the cabin, the wind roared at our backs. "Oh, Sam! Surely he'll turn around, don't you think?"

Sam stood at the picture window a moment. "I pray he does. Those waves are spiking high now, with nothing but whitecaps."

I recalled the many beatings I'd taken in the past by the waves pounding our boat when Skilak turned ugly in a split-second, and I shivered.

Sam grabbed another armload of wood and brought it inside, and I was grateful for his foresight in building a fire that morning, as he added logs and stoked the stove to a warm blaze. With the overcast sky, monsoon-like rain, and raging wind, the temperature plummeted, as well.

Right about the time the roar of waves and wind became deafening, Sam spoke again from where he stood at the window. "Here he comes!"

I rushed to Sam's side, and we watched Dave's boat as it crested and fell, sometimes remaining completely airborne as the water disappeared from beneath it, only to see the craft slam down again to fight another big wave. My breath came in short gasps until he made it safely to the shore and dropped anchor.

The winds were so stiff that Dave walked bent forward toward our cabin. Once safely inside, he peeled off his coat and over-shirt, and he was soaked to the skin. I ran up the stairs to our bedroom and retrieved one of Sam's clean flannel shirts and a towel, and soon Dave was drying himself and re-dressing in front of our now-roaring fire.

"It was all I could do to turn my boat around," Dave said. "In all my life, I've never seen a lake turn nasty as fast as Skilak does. She can be downright wicked, can't she?" It wasn't a question, though Sam and I agreed, anyway.

The wind continued to howl into the evening, and we turned on the radio to hear weather reports and listen to North Wind Messages. We knew that Warner and Marion would have already headed back to their home—if they'd even left it—as soon as they saw the angry lake.

"Gale-force winds with gusts up to sixty miles-per-hour," the announcer said. We had no trouble believing him, though I might have guessed even stronger gusts here on Skilak.

Soon the rain stopped, but the wind continued to roar. Sam and Dave decided to walk around to the north side of Caribou Island, where the wind came in, to watch the wave action. Even though it was after 9:00 pm, it was still daylight out, as we were in the "land of the midnight sun" time of year.

Shortly after the men left, a knock at the door startled me. Sam wouldn't knock, and I couldn't imagine who'd be out in this kind of weather. I thought the island was deserted, except for Dave, Sam, and me.

I opened the door, holding it against the wind, and was shocked to see Foster, soaked to the skin in some kind of odd neoprene body suit, shivering and worried.

"Is Sam here? We need help." His teeth chattered.

"Come in," I said, but he shook his head and pointed toward the beach.

"The boat flipped and threw my friend into the lake."

"Is he—did he—" I couldn't voice the words.

Foster shook his head. "No, we were in chest-deep water when we flipped. He's out there with the boat, but he's standing up. Threw him about ten feet, though."

I grabbed my coat and quickly yanked on my waders. "I'll help you first, and then we'll go get Sam."

Foster practically had to yell over the wind as we hustled down to the lake. "The boat almost flipped over a wave at first. Richard was steering, and it threw him into the air like a ragdoll."

"Oh, no!"

"He panicked at first, beating at the water and the waves. Guess he thought he would drown. Then he realized he could stand, so he calmed down a bit. He's shaken, though."

As we reached the beach, Richard loped toward us, soaking wet and shivering. Together, the three of us pulled the boat to the shore and secured it. Then I ushered the men to the cabin, where they, too, stripped in front of the stove's fire while I brought down more towels and dry clothes. Once I'd offered them big mugs of hot coffee, I ordered them to stay by the stove while I ran to the other side of the island to get Sam and Dave.

By the time I reached my husband, I was out of breath, but even if I'd meandered over there, I'd have been breathless at the sight of those enormous waves. It looked like it churned from within, and as far as one could see, mountains of water rose and fell, pounding against one another.

"Hey, Bonnie," Sam said, not realizing I'd come with a purpose other than wave-watching. "We saw three waterspouts out there. Water tornadoes. She's wild tonight!"

I interrupted his weather report to tell him about Foster and Richard.

"They crossed *this?*" Sam's eyes bulged.

Dave shook his head. "You've got to be kidding me. It's a wonder they're alive."

The three of us hustled back to the cabin to find Foster and Richard almost shoulder-to-shoulder in front of the fire, both shivering even though they were now warmly dressed.

I tossed the lap-quilts Sam and I used toward the men, and Foster offered me his empty mug in return. "A refill, please?"

Of course, I obliged.

Another two pots of coffee later, Dave, Foster, and Richard spread out sleeping bags on the living room floor. Though you'd think the men would be on a caffeinated high, all three of them had fallen asleep before I could even mount the stairs to our bedroom.

Upstairs, Sam slipped an arm around me as we stood before our big picture window and stared out at Skilak Lake's latest temper tantrum. "She's a beast, all right," he said.

"A wild beast," I agreed.

We pulled down the covers and crawled into bed. "Looks like we'll have company for a couple of days, Bonnie."

"Suits me fine." I snuggled against Sam's warm chest. "I'm just glad everyone got out of that lake alive."

CHAPTER TWENTY-FIVE

Bear Terror

The mountains' mid-September colors of yellow, gold, and amber-orange reflected brilliantly on Skilak Lake, and the late-afternoon purple sky framed the scene I gawked at from my picture window. I'd had a busy day, feeding the birds, carrying water, baking bread, preparing meals, and general cleaning. I relaxed now at my kitchen table, enjoying the serene and inspiring view as I sipped hot chocolate from my favorite mug—a rare moment of respite following the busy harvest season.

Sam had taken a stroll to the center of the island to visit the man we called Arkansas Ed. Arkansas Ed was a friend of Don's, and Don had lent him the use of his cabin through summer and fall in exchange for Ed doing some odd jobs on the place for him. We rarely saw him, but when we did, it was always a nice time, and Sam enjoyed exchanging stories with him.

As dusk settled, the cabin grew darker, but the dim light inside suited my peaceful mood, and I didn't light the propane lamps as I'd normally have done before this hour. Sam's footsteps sounded on the porch, and I let out a soft sigh of relief and contentment.

"Hey, honey," Sam said, stepping inside the door. He held something large and flat in his splayed hand. Whatever it was hung off both sides of his palm and fingers. "Arkansas Ed sent you a surprise." He grinned. "I'm afraid I've eaten half of it, though."

"What is it?" As Sam drew near, a smoky scent reached my nose.

"Smoked salmon," he said. "It's pretty good! Almost as good as ours. I've been munching on it the whole way home." He held it out to me, and I took it from his hand and placed it on a platter that I set on the table. Sam pinched off another piece and stuffed it into his mouth as I turned to light the propane lantern.

Warm light suffused the room and cast a honeyed glow over the kitchen table. I inhaled the smoky aroma of the salmon, which Arkansas Ed had smoked with the skin still on, unlike the bare way Sam and I prepared it. I reached out and flaked off a bite-sized piece of the fish. I had it almost to my mouth, when I thought I saw movement. I leaned and held the piece of fish to the lantern. Instinctively, I dropped it, as if it were alive and dangerous.

And in a way, it was! The fish literally crawled with maggots!

"Ewww!" I squealed. "Sam! There's maggots on it!"

Sam's eyes widened, and he leaned over the fish, the surface of which in the lamplight seemed to wiggle. He coughed and gagged, then covered his mouth with his hand and bolted toward the door.

Sam flung open the door, ran down off the porch, and I heard him gagging and retching in the darkness.

I shuddered as I picked up the platter and followed Sam out the door, though I walked past him, holding the platter at arm's length, as if it could bite me, and I headed straight toward the beach, where I flung the infested fish toward the shoreline.

"Seagull food," I said as I passed Sam, who stood hunched over, his hands on his knees as he tried to purge the contents of his stomach. I stopped and turned back to look at Sam. "Almost as good as ours, huh?" I mocked. "Ha! Some surprise! Tell Arkansas Ed, when you see him again, that we'll pass on his smoked salmon next time."

Sam and I were pleased to have another late-season visitor in September, after our weekend warriors had left for their lives on the mainland. Loni, an acquaintance from Kenai, came to do some fall hunting. Like many men who came to Caribou Island to hunt, Loni asked Sam to please accompany him, knowing Sam knew Skilak Lake and the surrounding area better than most. While Sam never claimed to be a hunting guide, he was happy to show a fellow hunter the best spots for wild game.

"I'd feel safer if you came with me, anyway," Loni explained.

Sam, of course, readily agreed to go along. "What are we hunting?" he asked, not knowing if Loni wanted Dall sheep, bear, or moose.

Loni offered a small grin, and his face reddened. "I'd like to get a brown bear."

Sam let out a low whistle. "All right, then, start at the top! Brown bear, it is."

The men headed out the next morning, and they were gone all day. When they returned, Loni didn't come inside, which I found strange. When I stared out the window and watched Loni climb back into his boat—without a bear—I figured either he was disappointed at not bagging a bear or he wanted to get home before dark.

When Sam walked in, however, I realized the reason was more ominous.

Dried, rust-colored blood was smeared across Sam's cheek, and the collar of his coat was stained red with blood.

"Sam! What happened?" I touched my husband's chin to turn his head. Fresh red drops of blood oozed from his ear. "My Lord, Sam! What in the world?"

I quickly ran for my first aid kit and grabbed a bowl of water, then motioned for Sam to have a seat.

"Loni," Sam said. "Loni happened."

I gave him a mock-glare as I dabbed at the drops of blood still oozing from his ear. Sam winced.

"I'm sorry. Does it hurt?"

"It throbs. The whole side of my head aches, and my ear is roaring. I can't hear anything out of this ear," he said, lifting his hand toward it.

"Tell me what happened."

Sam's jaw muscle twitched, and he rolled his eyes to meet mine. "Bear terror."

"What? Oh!" Sam and I used the term "bear terror" as a pun on "buck fever." Men were said to get buck fever when they were so anxious when spotting their first deer with a gun in their hands, they'd tremble and shake and couldn't hit the deer even at close range. Only "bear terror" was more ominous. Sam had hunted with men who freaked out when face to face with a brown bear. One fellow had actually run and hid behind a boulder, and when he joined Sam later—after Sam dispatched the charging bear—his face was pale and he looked sick.

It's one thing to spot a black bear in the wild, but it's something entirely different—and more terrifying—to see a brown bear. Brown bear are notoriously more aggressive and won't hesitate to charge and attack, whereas a black bear will more likely spook and run or amble away.

"I let Loni use my Ruger .458 Win Mag for our bear hunt," Sam continued. "You know he wanted a brown bear, so I took him to the upper end of the lake. I knew we'd have a good chance of getting one up there on the glacier flats.

"We climbed up on that huge, rocky mound that protrudes up from the flats. I told Loni that we could sit up on those rocks and just wait for a bear. We'd have a good line of sight, and could get a good bead on it."

I rinsed the washcloth in the bowl of cool water, and then began to clean Sam's bloody cheek and neck.

"We'd been there about an hour," Sam continued, "when I spotted a huge brown bear chasing salmon in the creek. He was moving along at a fast clip, heading right toward us.

"Loni jumped up and aimed, but I tugged at him, told him to sit back down and wait for the bear to get closer. That bear was some good five-hundred yards or more away, and that's too far to shoot from that distance.

"Of course, Loni didn't listen. He was shaking in his boots, and he stepped sideways toward me, and he fired off his first shot while the barrel of my Ruger was only a few inches from my ear!"

"Oh, Sam. I'm so sorry! No wonder your ear's bleeding. I'll bet your eardrum has ruptured."

Sam's lips were twisted to one side when he looked at me, and he nodded. "No doubt. I grabbed my ear and started rocking, it hurt so bad, Bonnie. I couldn't hear a thing. Still can't, on that side.

"Then, without even pausing, Loni ejected three rounds right onto the ground. That man was shaking and trembling, and meanwhile, the bear had turned and bolted to the edge of the glacier flats, and it ran right into the woods."

"What a shame," I said.

"What's crazy is that Loni looks at me, and I'm having to read his lips as much as hear him, and he says, 'I had that hide on the wall.' Made me so mad, I could have punched him! I said, 'Bullshit, Loni! You just ejected three rounds into the ground! I told you to wait until he got closer, and sit down and get a good bead on him.'"

"What did Loni say?"

"He said, 'I shot four times at that bear!' Then I told him, 'No, you didn't. You shot once prematurely, and then you ejected three bullets. Look!' And I pointed to the ground."

"That's when I saw the blood on my hand, and I knew my ear must really be messed up."

"It's messed up, all right," I said.

"It's ringing and roaring," Sam said. "And that Loni, he just stood there shaking his head. Said, 'I can't believe it, Sam. I was sure I shot that bear four times. I was sure of it. I can't believe it.'"

"Bear terror," Sam and I both said in unison, and for the first time since he'd walked in, Sam smiled.

I bent and kissed my husband's forehead. "It's not bleeding anymore, but I have no doubt you'll have hearing damage for some time to come. Maybe permanently," I said, tugging Sam's collar out so that he could see it. "You really should see a doctor."

Sure enough, to this day, my poor Sam can't hear well in that ear, and I have no doubt it's from the Ruger's blast so close to his head.

CHAPTER TWENTY-SIX

More Fish!

Early one September morning after the bear incident, Sam and I strolled the beach, coffee cups in hand, admiring the autumn foliage. Skilak Lake mirrored the yellows and oranges of the aspen, birch, and cottonwood trees, which stood out against the deep greens of the spruce and hemlock.

"Moose-hunting season is still in and we need a moose," Sam said. "Want to go with me?"

"Absolutely! When do you want to go?"

Sam stroked his chin. "I need to finish that cabin before the weather turns. Need to put the ridgepole on it . . . need another set of hands for that." He let out a hum. "I would like to take a day off work to hunt though. Maybe we can just head over to the south shore and take a look. Might spot a moose over there."

As if our talk of moose-hunting conjured him up, a boat motored across the water toward us. Captaining the craft was our French-voyager friend, Lucas, Sam's co-worker on the pipeline.

"Should have expected him," Sam said, grinning. "He hasn't missed a moose season yet."

"And there's your second set of hands for that ridgepole." I knew that, despite my construction skills and abilities, I wasn't strong enough or tall enough to help Sam maneuver a heavy, awkward ridgepole into place.

Lucas only spent two days with us, and during that time, he didn't get a moose, but he was happy to help Sam with the ridgepole. He went on about the great use of space Sam had made in the small cabin. Later, Sam would build cupboards and a double-wide bunk bed, and add a small wood stove. I added curtains and matching bedspread and tablecloth, and the cabin was complete—sturdy enough for a hunter, but adorable enough for his wife.

Our new guest cabin

After Lucas left, Sam decided to take a day off from construction, and he and I went hunting. We arrived on the south shore and had barely trudged inland a short way when we saw what appeared to be a decent-sized bull moose browsing on willows in the distance. Sam made a clean shot, and the moose dropped with one bullet.

"Good job, Sam!"

He grinned, then looked back through the woods in the direction where our boat was anchored, out of sight. "At least we won't have to drag him too far."

It wasn't until we closed the distance between us and the moose that we realized his enormous size. He'd looked average from where we stood, but up close, he was a monster! His antlers alone measured fifty-four inches.

Sam and I worked *hard* getting that moose prepped! We spent the day gutting, skinning, and quartering the beast that would sustain us through the long winter ahead.

"Bonnie, move the leg this way," Sam would say, then, "Now pull that leg the other way."

I put my full weight into tugging those massive, long legs this way or that as Sam worked to skin and butcher the moose. After we finished, we packed it one load at a time, trip by trip, to the boat. Hours after we started, we arrived home and hung the meat in our shed.

For a solid week, I canned moose while Sam went back to work on the cabin we were building. Using a hand-grinder that my parents sent me a few years earlier, I ground moose into burger and made moose meatballs, moose burgers, and moose meatloaves. Then I cooked and canned moose stew, moose Swiss steak, moose pepper steak, and moose barbeque. I filled my pressure canner with jars of moose meals, then pressure cooked them and set them out to cool so the lids would seal. That pinging sound as the lids sealed was music to my ears!

Just as I lifted the last jar of moose meat from the canner, movement out the window caught my eye. The surface of Skilak Lake churned, but not as if a storm approached.

The source of the churning dawned on me right away—the salmon were in! Just as the thought entered my mind, a huge fish jumped high into the air and landed in the lake with a big splash. "Sam!" I ran to the door, shouting. When Sam wasn't near our cabin, I kept running and kept shouting his name.

Now when I think of it, I realize I may have frightened him, but I hope my yells and yelps related my happiness and excitement.

Of course, we went fishing. We hadn't caught many fish in the prior runs, and since the fish were literally jumping out of the water just off our own boat dock, it only made sense to get on it right away.

And catch fish we did! For the next several days, I canned (and also ate) plenty of salmon. My pantry shelves quickly filled with colorful jars filled with the land's bounty. I often worked myself into a sweat over the stove, but appraising a pantry stocked with jars of moose, salmon, cranberries, and a variety of other jams and sauces . . . well, it filled me with a deep sense of pride. We would eat well through the harsh winter ahead.

It seemed that no sooner than I'd finished canning and put away my pressure cooker, Foster and Jane arrived for a visit, along with their two children. We were so excited to see everyone! I tried not to let my disappointment that they were only staying one day show, and I dove in to have fun with them.

And they wanted to go fishing.

Again, we caught an amazing amount of the silver Coho salmon, as well as a fair catch of trout. We filled Foster's coolers until they would barely close, and we still had a lot of fish left over.

"We can bag them up for you, or put them in buckets to take back home," I offered.

"No, thank you," Jane said. "Our freezer is still full of fish from last year. You two keep this. You'll need it to survive the winter."

Sam clapped her on the back before I could protest. "Thanks, Jane. That's generous of you."

I held back a sigh and smiled. It was a generous offer. But it meant more canning.

After the family left, I surveyed the fish. "Sam, there's more here than I can process in a day. Get a bucket."

Sam carried a five-gallon bucket of water from the lake, into which I dumped about a cup of salt. The salt solution would help preserve some of the fish, while I canned the rest.

And, of course, we had fish for dinner.

And breakfast.

And lunch and dinner the next day.

As I canned the last of the fish from the bucket on the second day, I looked longingly at the jars of moose meatballs. "Tonight," I whispered to them, "you will be on my dinner plate!"

"Hey, Bonnie," Sam called from the front door.

I hustled out of the pantry, glad he hadn't heard me talking to the food. "Yes?"

He had his shotgun in his hand. "I'm taking the boat up the lake. Going to bear hunt for a few hours."

Bear! Bear roast! Creamed bear! My mouth actually watered.

Of course, I'd have to can it, but maybe the smell of fish would finally dissipate from my kitchen.

Later that afternoon, Sam's boat motored toward the dock, and I walked down to meet him, visions of fresh bear meat dancing in my head. (No sugarplums on Skilak, I'm afraid.)

Sam arched his back and stretched, and a big grin spread across his face. "You won't believe it!"

"What?" I felt the stretch in my cheeks as I smiled. Oh, boy, a *big* bear!

Sam reached down into the boat, and he held up a big stringer of—you guessed it—fish.

The breath hissed out of me.

"I found the *best* fishing hole!" Sam said, holding the stringer up high over his head. "Dolly Varden trout!"

Back to my pressure cooker. By the time I'd processed all that fish, I didn't want to can, fry, eat, look at, or even smell another fish—ever!

The next morning, Sam loped across the living room, again his gun in hand. "Going to go get a black bear today."

Oh, boy. I'd heard that one, before. "Sam Ward, don't you dare come back here with a stringer of fish. You hear me?"

He laughed and held up a hand in surrender. "I won't!"

"I'm serious, Sam. If you come home with a stringer of fish, I'm walking out on the pressure cooker and the fry pan both. You got it?"

"I won't even get my line wet." He reached the door and then turned to me. "You okay canning bear meat, though?"

It was my turn to laugh. "I'm tired of canning, yes, but I'll be happy to can some fresh bear meat. Anything but fish."

It was true. I wanted variety over our winter meals, and having another bounty of meat in the house would be a wonderful thing, even though it meant more canning.

When Sam returned home, I again went down to the dock, but this time I didn't run. Though I hoped he'd gotten a black bear, yesterday's letdown kept me calm. "Did you get one?" My voice came out more tentative than hopeful.

"Nah." Sam stepped around his meat pack, which bulged with something.

"Well . . . what's in the pack?"

"Oh, that." He casually waved it away.

"Sam?"

He looked at me, his grin weak and sheepish. "I got a little sidetracked."

"Meaning?"

He shrugged. "Found myself back at that amazing fishing hole."

Yes.

More fish.

More. Fish.

I let my husband live.

Sam the great hunter, fisherman, and provider.
All of our meat came from the land.

Bonnie canning salmon!

CHAPTER TWENTY-SEVEN

Rosie the Riveter

Winston returned to the island for a visit in late September—said he couldn't stay away—and Sam and I couldn't have been happier! He really had become a member of our little island family, and we'd both missed him greatly.

We offered to let him stay in the guest cabin, but he kindly refused, saying he would be more comfortable in his wall tent. *No surprise there!* He set up his tent—complete with little wood stove—in his old campsite near the cabin he'd built and later sold to Kenny. In celebration of Winston's return, I made a heaping platter of moose burritos for dinner. I knew it was one of his favorite dishes—not to mention, Sam and I liked them too!

A few days later, Winston, Sam, and I went camping at the upper end of Skilak Lake. After weeks of canning moose and fish—and more fish—I was ready for a break. The spectacular views of the still-golden foliage proved to be just the vacation I needed. Snowcapped mountains framed the brilliant-yellow leaves that still furiously clung to the trees, and the deep-blue sky reflected onto the turquoise lake water. To say it was stunning would be an understatement.

We set up our pup tents in a cove near the glacier flat, Winston's right beside the one Sam and I shared. We placed a powerful scope on a tripod, and the three of us took turns with our eye pressed to the lens much of the day, birdwatching. We found it fascinating. There were perhaps a few thousand birds on and around the lake—flying in, landing, sometimes squabbling and taking off again—and there were so many different kinds! Geese, ducks, even trumpeter swans were gathering to prepare for their flight south ahead of the coming winter. We watched massive eagles on the opposite shore ripping apart salmon carcasses. Their raucous noise remained constant all day and evening.

When it became too dark to birdwatch, the men built a fire, and I pulled out a tin of homemade tortillas and jars of moose barbeque, along with a container of moose jerky. As I put together our dinner, Sam placed a pot of coffee over the fire, and soon we feasted. The birds settled down at about the same time Winston, Sam, and I started yawning, and soon we called it a night.

I curled up next to Sam, and within minutes—maybe even seconds—of my head hitting the pillow, I slept.

Sometime close to dawn, a loud snap outside the tent jolted me awake. It was too loud for a twig—something large had broken a small branch. Sam and I simultaneously sat upright. Even in the dark silence, I couldn't hear him breathing, and I held my breath, as well. I felt his hand move over to his rifle.

Then I heard the click of Winston's gun as he cocked it in the tent next to ours.

In the next instant, all those birds that had quieted to near-silence during the night raised an unbelievable noise—such loud squawking and flapping and screeching that I held my hands to my ears. Those thousands of birds all took to the air at the same time, and the sound was deafening. The noise lasted at least a full ten minutes, possibly more.

Sam and I remained upright as the sound disappeared, and I knew Winston was equally alert next to us. After the birds left, the night fell silent. *Completely* silent. No twigs snapping, no birds, no morning animals rustling. It was eerie.

"Sam," I whispered as quietly as I could, "was that a bear?"

"Yeah, probably was. Birds must have scared him off."

We lay back down, but it was some time before I again drifted off. I continued to listen for any sound that a bear might make. There's an abundance of brown bears around Skilak Lake, and huge ones, at that.

The next morning, the three of us crawled out of our tents at about the same time, and I put on coffee while the men traipsed our camp, seeking the source of the night's visitor. I checked the scope, but other than a few eagles still pecking on salmon bones on the opposite shore, the lake was void of birds. Not one of the thousands had remained behind.

"Over here, Winston," Sam said as he pointed to the ground a few yards from our tents. "Brown bear, all right. And he's a big one."

Sure enough, the tracks the brown bear left behind were larger than the length of Sam's foot. He was a monster, indeed. If those birds hadn't taken flight when they had, scaring away the bear, we would've been attacked.

After our vacation, I spent the last of autumn helping Sam clear a spot for a new cabin next to ours on the beach. Sam and Winston made trips to town between storms for more lumber, and on one of those trips, Sam surprised me with a new boat. He'd bought the Bayrunner, a bigger and more seaworthy boat than our last. In addition to lumber, he carried on it large sheets of sheet metal and boxes of rivets.

"What's that for?" I asked. It wasn't the usual roofing materials we used, so I couldn't imagine what Sam planned to do with it.

"Gonna turn the Bayrunner into a bow picker. We'll build us a little cabin on the boat, so we can stay warm crossing the lake."

I hugged my husband. "Brilliant!"

The two of us worked hard, and in a couple days' time, Sam had cut the sheet metal, clamped it in place, and drilled holes where the rivets would join the cabin walls to the metal framework. I helped by holding a heavy metal bucking bar against the tail of the rivet inside the boat's cabin, while Sam riveted it in place from the other side.

"Rosie the Riveter," Sam said, laughing. "That's my gal!"

Sam has the framework done.

Bonnie posing for the camera.

Our hand-riveted cabin is finished. Sam added a little woodstove to keep us warm during those cold weather lake crossings. What luxury!

Rosie the Riveter

We'd hoped to make it back across the lake for more lumber the following day—and truth be told, I wanted to try out the new boat and sit in the cabin we'd built—but Skilak kicked up her waves against another windy storm, so we stayed put.

We didn't know until four days later when we finally made it to town, but on those days while we were snug and warm against the storm inside our cabin, six strong men from Elmendorf Air Base fought for their lives at the east end of Skilak Lake. Only four survived.

The six men had boated over from the mainland to camp and bear hunt, staying in a forest service cabin in Doroshin Bay near the glacier flats. Two men stayed behind in the cabin, while the other four returned to the boat to ferry their gear to the upper campground. Before they reached the campground, the weather turned bad, and the boat, which only bore a small outboard motor, capsized against the stormy waves.

The men clung to the capsized boat for hours as the waves beat against them. When they drifted closer to the mainland, all four swam toward the shore. Fighting the waves quickly sapped their strength, so they turned and headed back to the boat. Only three of them made it.

Sometime later, when the boat drifted close to shore a second time, the three surviving men swam toward the shore, but again, exhausted, they turned back to the boat. Only two made it back. The lake claimed its second victim.

Finally, late that Saturday evening, the boat drifted close enough to the shore that the two chanced it again, and this time, they made it to the shore. The men shot their rifles, and fortunately, a Kenai fish and game officer who'd been fishing on the lake heard their shots, and he summoned a float plane to rescue the two men.

The two airmen who'd been left behind at the cabin without supplies had meantime decided to hike out, fearing they'd be stranded by bad weather and would starve. The two weren't located until late Monday afternoon, and both suffered hypothermia.

When Sam and I learned of this tragedy, we were deeply saddened. "If only I'd have known," Sam said, "I could have saved them all."

Despite the wicked storm, Sam was confident enough in his boating to insist that he could have rescued those men. He'd never choose to go out in that kind of weather, but would not hesitate to brave Skilak's nasty moods to save a life. Those losses weighed heavily upon us for some time to come.

October seemed to fly past as Sam and I stayed busy with winter chores. Not only did we work hard, day and night, on the cabin we were building on the beachfront property next to us, but we also had to cut and haul enough firewood to last us through the coming winter. The long days that lasted closer and closer to twenty-four hours during the summer morphed too quickly into night, and we often slept deeply to wake the next morning to start a new day of work.

Sam and I were thankful for Winston's help, as he often pitched in to help with the cabin, or to help Sam with other heavy-lifting-type chores. I would try to repay him—not that repayment was required, for helping and teamwork are a necessary part of the wilderness lifestyle—with hearty meals and special desserts. Sam and I appreciated my extra efforts in the kitchen, as well, and the three of us looked forward to dinners in front of the picture window, looking out at the land we loved.

Early in November, Sam and I decided the new cabin we were building would be ours. We would move yet again. We sat at the table drawing out plans as a large chicken potpie baked in the oven. Winston returned to his camp with supplies he'd purchased while he and Sam were in town earlier in the day to get lumber. He would join us later for dinner.

"Panoramic views," Sam said, waving toward the paper. "That's what I want." He drew full-length windows along the entire front of the cabin sketch. "We can see the lake from every room, this way."

"Ohhh, that sounds amazing! I love watching the lake while I'm working," I said. "Or resting."

Sam laughed. "Any other time?"

I gave him a playful push, and hopped up as the timer went off, telling me it was time to rescue dinner from the oven.

Winston arrived just after Sam had cleared away the cabin plans, and I set the table. We huddled around the steaming chicken potpie and dove in, as Sam paused between bites to tell Winston of our plans to move.

"Could use your help again tomorrow," Sam said to Winston. "I have the sawyer working on another load of lumber; he said it'll be ready by late morning."

"Not a problem." Winston tilted a head toward the window and the lake beyond. "Long as she obliges."

"Right." Sam hopped up to turn on the radio so we could catch the weather report.

We grew quiet as we listened to the news and focused on filling our hungry bellies, and then I retrieved the large slices of spice cake I'd made just before baking the chicken potpie. As I was drizzling vanilla glaze over the slices, mention of my name on the radio caught my attention.

"We'll start tonight's North Wind Messages with a note to Sam and Bonnie on Caribou Island," the announcer said. "Dear Sam and Bonnie, Nathan Donald Buchholz was born at 4:25 this afternoon. He's eight pounds and two ounces. Both mom and baby are doing fine. Love, Mom and Dad."

"Woo hoo!" I jumped up and down in my kitchen. "My baby sister had a baby!"

Winston chuckled. "Didn't know babies could have babies, but okay."

The three of us broke into happy laughter.

"Auntie Bonnie," Sam said.

"And Uncle Sam," I said. The image of Sam in a red, white, and blue suit popped into my head, and I laughed even harder.

"Gonna have to retire your beaver fur hat," Winston said, scrubbing Sam's head with his knuckles. "Bonnie's gonna have to make you a new one out of an American flag."

Sam pulled a stern face, and he pointed a finger at me, mimicking the old Uncle Sam recruitment posters. "I want *you!*"

The three of us roared with gales of laughter.

But even as we laughed, a tinge of pain stabbed my heart. How old would my nephew be before I could hold him in my arms?

CHAPTER TWENTY-EIGHT

Those Turkeys!

January 1986 came in with a clear but frigid day. We celebrated New Year's Day by—you guessed it—working on our new cabin and doing our daily chores. Such is the sustainable life.

Sam and Winston went to Anchorage the next day for windows and building supplies, and while they were gone, the wind began to howl. I kept one eye on the lake, which began to churn, slowly at first, but then with an increasing presence of small whitecaps. The drive to Anchorage from the landing on the other side of the lake was just over 150 miles. The men would be gone all day, giving the storm time to pass, I hoped.

My hopes didn't materialize.

I brought in water from the lake, fed the animals, carried in wood to stoke the fire, and finally decided to make our upcoming week's worth of fresh bread. Though I tried to stay busy to keep my mind off the lake and the wind, my line of sight never failed to venture toward those ever-increasing whitecaps. Outside the window, the tall spruce leaned and twisted and groaned in the stiff winds.

Soup. I'd put on a big pot of bean soup; something warm and filling to welcome the men home. I got to work sorting and cleaning the beans, and I put them on to boil, adding plenty of salt and spices, and a nice chunk of canned bear to add flavor and seasoning.

As I worked, darkness crept in, and in the gloaming, Skilak grew angrier. The waves were now too rough to risk crossing the lake. I tried to send mental messages through the atmosphere to my husband. *Sam, please don't try to cross that lake. Sam, stay on the mainland. You can come home after the storm passes.*

I knew Sam was wise to the dangers of Skilak Lake, but I also knew he correctly considered himself an above-average, skilled boater. And the pull to come home is always stronger than the pull to leave. He might try it. He might fail.

I turned to prayer. That's all I could do to assuage my fears. Though I often prayed as I worked, this time, my worry brought me to my knees, and I knelt in front of the fire to talk to my Heavenly Father.

When I finally rose, night had fallen. I felt more at peace, confident that Sam had not ventured across the water.

I settled into my rocking chair before the fire, a quilt on my lap and a book in my hand. And then I heard it: scraping along the outside of the cabin, right behind where I sat. I put my feet on the floor to still the rocker, and I froze, listening.

The scraping sounded again, louder this time.

My mind raced to find the source. Trees? No, there were no trees with branches long enough to reach the cabin, even in the stiff wind. Tools? No, we'd put all the tools away, and there were no pegs on that side of the cabin where anything would be hanging. A person? I thought I was alone on the island. Nels had left a few weeks ago and it was hard to say when he'd return. Maybe a bear?

Go see what it is. You can do this, Bonnie.

I scrabbled together what little courage I had and pulled on my coat and hat, and then I picked up the 12-guage shotgun. I checked to make sure it was loaded, released the safety, and opened the door.

Icy rain and a blast of fierce wind pushed me backward a step, but I quickly regained my balance and stepped out onto the deck. I treaded carefully to the end of the deck, as if someone might hear me, even though I'm sure my steps couldn't be heard over the screaming wind.

Go ahead. Step around the corner. You can do it.

I lifted the shotgun to my shoulder, preparing to take aim at whatever might be scraping the side of my home.

I heard it again.

Terrified of what I might find, I sucked in a steadying breath, and I leapt around the corner.

I'd imagined anything *except* what I actually saw.

There stood three of our full-grown turkeys! They'd squeezed together as tightly as they could, huddled up against the side of the cabin.

I let out my breath in a relieved *whoosh,* my muscles weak with relief. I ran back into the cabin to put up the gun, then I returned to scoop up one big turkey at a time, carrying each one to the safety and warm protection of the chicken coop.

By the time I was done, some ten or fifteen minutes later, I was soaked to the skin and freezing. Back indoors, I stripped and dried off, then put on my old fuzzy blue robe, and I again curled up to the fire with a blanket to listen to North Wind Messages. Between messages, I chuckled as I thought of the turkeys and how terrified I'd been of them. I knew Sam and Winston would get a big laugh out of my adventure.

Early the next morning, I woke to find a much-calmer Skilak Lake. Before I'd even put on coffee, the purr of Sam's boat drawing near reached my ears. "Thank You, God!" I bustled about the kitchen, quickly making biscuits and gravy for my hungry husband and our friend.

The two looked haggard when they came through the door, and both were eager for coffee, breakfast, and a warm fire.

"Rough night?" I asked.

Sam grimaced. "Slept in the Jeep on the landing."

"If you can call that *sleep*," Winston added. "Cramped quarters, for sure."

"Skilak was much too rough to cross in the dark," Sam said. "Didn't want to risk it."

"I'm so glad you didn't," I said. "I was worried."

Sam pulled me close and hugged me, then kissed me on the forehead. "I knew you would be." His next kiss found my lips. "I knew you were praying for us, so I knew we'd be all right."

As we three devoured breakfast the men shared news of the mainland. I was thrilled to learn that our friend Clark Walker had given us three large windows that he'd removed from a bank in Anchorage during a remodeling job. The windows were made of heavy, double-paned glass, and were exactly what we needed for the front of our new cabin.

"Sturdy stuff," Winston said. "It'll make a strong barrier between you two and the weather."

Sam's tired eyes twinkled mischievously over his coffee mug. "Make a strong barrier between Bonnie and her turkeys."

I mocked throwing a biscuit at him, and we all laughed, relieved to be together again and safe in our warm home.

CHAPTER TWENTY-NINE

Saving Willy

A few weeks later, Winston returned to Wyoming, and almost immediately, the lake froze over. Unfortunately, it wasn't frozen deep enough to travel across, not even riding on Mojo.

We weren't short on supplies, however, as Sam stocked us well when he'd taken Winston to the mainland, and a week later, Harry flew over and dropped packages from his airplane, as the lake was not frozen deeply enough for him to land. Among those packages were boxes including candy bars, cigarettes for Sam, coffee, and lots of other treats. Jane had sent several books and magazines to help me pass the time over the long winter. You couldn't ask for better friends than that!

That same night, as Sam and I sat listening to North Wind Messages, we received a surprising note from Clark Walker.

"To Sam and Bonnie on Caribou," the announcer read. "We hope you are the ones who removed the wheels and tires from your Jeep."

Sam's mouth dropped open, and I imagine mine did, as well.

"You've got to be kidding me," he said.

"Somebody stole the wheels and tires right off our Jeep!" I couldn't believe it. "What are we going to do?"

Sam shook his head and shrugged. "Nothing we can do. Not a thing." He sighed. "We'll get new tires and wheels when the weather breaks."

"Poor Nelly Bell," I said.

"Nelly Bell, nothing!" Sam said. "Poor us!"

"Yeah, that too."

Early in February, we had about six inches of ice on the lake in front of the house. Sam decided to chance it to check on the Jeep, though we knew the ice would be much thinner in the middle of the lake. He took the snowmobile, the lightest form of transportation we had, and headed out.

My breath felt shallow the entire time he was gone, but when he returned, he had good news—well, as good as it can get when you've had your vehicle stripped.

Our friend Ernie from Sterling Auto had heard of our bad luck, and he'd put on some temporary wheels and tires, and left a note that those should work until Sam had a chance to get some new ones.

"What a good man!" I said when Sam relayed the news.

"You haven't heard the bad news yet," Sam said.

"Oh, no! What's the bad news?"

"The ice was only a couple inches thick in the middle of the lake. We won't be traveling across it for a while."

It was no surprise! We were having an uncommonly warm winter so far, with daytime highs often reaching into the low forties. On the good side though, it made for great working conditions, and Sam and I took advantage by working on the new cabin, of which the walls were slowly but steadily climbing, one row of timbers at a time.

For the next four weeks we worked every day on the cabin, and periodically, Sam would knock off long enough to check the thickness of the lake ice. Finally, on March 3, the lake was frozen deep enough to safely travel across and into town, and even that time, Sam and I had to bundle up as round as Michelin men and ride the snowmobile across the lake. What a frigid ride!

When we went into town, Sam immediately drove us to Sterling Auto and ordered new tires and wheels for the Jeep. We profusely thanked Ernie for his help and kindness, which he waved away, saying, "Aw, you'd have done the same." And it was true.

A couple days later, I cheered as I watched Sam—straddled over the wall high above me—pound the last spike into the last timber. "Sam, you d-d-did it!" Even though I stood next to the woodstove that we had purchased for the new cabin (and which we kept a fire in so we could warm up while working on the cabin), I was so cold my teeth chattered. When I last looked at the thermometer it was only four degrees, but you'd never know it to look at Sam with his coat half unzipped. The cold never fazed him the way it did me.

"Yep!" Sam nodded his approval as he looked at the walls. "We sure did!" He climbed down the ladder and turned to face me. I noticed the tension in his face and thought he must be tired—and rightfully so. "Now all we have to do is roof it and put the windows and doors in."

"It looks great, Sam!" I put my arms around him and squeezed. "I'm so proud of you!" I looked up into his face and smiled. "How about some hot coffee?" I picked up the thermos that we always brought to our work site filled with hot brew. "And I don't mean this coffee, unless you like it *iced*. Let's go home, I'm freezing."

Sam wrapped his arm around my shoulder, and we turned toward home. By the time we entered our cabin, I knew something was wrong. Sam didn't seem his normal jolly self. After a productive day like today, he should have been thrilled with his accomplishment in finishing the cabin walls. Instead, he looked worried.

"Sam, what's wrong? Are you okay?"

Sam let out a pent up breath. "I'm okay, but I've got this nagging feeling about Willy, and I can't shake it. I think something is wrong, Bonnie. I'm going to pass on that coffee and go check on him."

Willy was a thirty-something man who'd been staying the winter in an old trapper's cabin built in the early 1900s. We hadn't seen him since late fall, and though that wasn't odd— the man was a complete recluse who abhorred human interaction—it still made us uneasy. Sam dressed warmly and took the snowmobile up the lake to Cotton Wood Creek, some five miles or so away. Sam's instinct—like always—was spot-on. He found the cabin with the door flung open and snow blowing inside. Willy was passed out drunk on his bed, nearly frozen in the four-degree temperature. The temperature inside the cabin was barely warmer than outside. Sam tried to rouse Willy, but the man was out cold, and several empty liquor bottles surrounded the scrawny man.

Immediately, my Sam went to work. He chopped wood, built a fire, and opened a can of beans from the man's cupboard and put the can atop the woodstove. As he warmed, Willy began to stir, and soon Sam was able to rouse him.

"I gave him a good talking-to," Sam told me when he returned home that evening. "Don't know if it helped, but I think it might have shook him a little to realize he probably would have frozen to death if I hadn't checked on him."

The fact that Sam—a man as rugged as they come—listened to his intuition made me love him all the more.

CHAPTER THIRTY

Wilderness Realtor

The second week of March came in with a wintery blast, and that blast blew in Nels. Sam helped the man ferry his supplies across the ice in the Jeep, and after a short visit of a few days on the island, Nels decided he wanted to return home to the mainland until after ice break-up, which would probably occur in May.

While Sam was gone with Nels, I went out to gather in wood, and I was surprised to hear a plane approaching. I stood in the edge of the woods out of sight, as I didn't recognize the plane. Being completely alone on the island could be a frightful thing at times, as not everyone who came to our island was kind—though certainly most were. I never worried when Sam was at home, but when he was away . . . yes, I'll admit it, I was sometimes afraid.

The plane landed on the ice in front of our cabin, and two men stepped out. I didn't recognize either, and I began to worry. Then a woman stepped out. I relaxed a bit, and perhaps I even felt hopeful.

I stepped out from the trees, firewood in my arms. "Hello!" I called.

One of the men, perhaps in his forties, had short brown hair that was graying at the temples, threw up a hand and offered a genuinely kind smile. "Hello! Are you Bonnie?"

I answered that I was, and he introduced himself as Gene, then introduced his wife Laura and their son, Carl.

"John and Adelle sent us to see you," Gene said. "We're here to look at their cabin."

My look must have been one of puzzlement, as Laura glanced at her husband, then stepped toward me. "You didn't know? John and Adelle are selling their cabin."

"Oh." I couldn't think of anything else to say.

Gene cleared his throat, obviously uncomfortable with my disappointment.

I put aside my load of wood, and I led the trio up the hill to John and Adelle's cabin. I could tell that Laura wasn't impressed, and I couldn't quite blame her. The plywood cabin was small—12' x 12' and two stories high.

Laura peeked through the window and shook her head.

Gene spoke for her. "This isn't what we're looking for."

Another woman neighbor turning away from my little island. I tried not to let my new disappointment show.

"Do you know of anything else for sale on the island—preferably something on the beach?"

I perked up. Boy, did I! "Yes, I do. My husband and I are building a new cabin down the beach from ours, and we plan to sell our cabin."

"The cute one where we anchored the plane?" Laura asked. My spirits lifted. "You bet!"

"Can we see it?"

The three followed me down the hill again, and along the way, I learned that Gene was an engineer on the North Slope, and he knew Harry and Foster. The couple lived in Anchorage, and they wanted a getaway cabin for vacations and hunting trips.

I invited the three inside our cabin, and then I stayed outside to allow them time to browse. When they stepped outside, all three were smiling.

"This is exactly what we're looking for," Gene said.

Laura and Carl nodded.

"If you sell this one, where will you live?" Laura asked.

I pointed to the lot next door to ours and the almost finished cabin.

"Mind if I take a look?" Gene asked.

Laura tapped her watch. "It's getting late, Gene. It'll be dark soon." We were in the season where night took up the majority of our twenty-four-hour day.

"Right," he said. "Carl, go ahead and start the plane." He touched his wife's arm. "I'll be quick."

Gene and I hustled to the building site. I gave what was probably the quickest real-estate tour in history, talking faster as I heard the propellers fire up in the background.

"This is a bedroom, and this is another bedroom," I said, flinging my arms as I spoke. "Here's the living room and kitchen, and it'll have a cathedral ceiling with blue knotty pine." I showed him the openings Sam had cut for the floor-to-ceiling windows in the front of the cabin, pointing out the panoramic view of the lake.

"I want this one," Gene said. "Sell us this one."

My mouth dropped. "But—but it's not even finished yet." It didn't even have a roof on it.

He shrugged. "I don't care. I can help your husband finish it. Besides, you won't have to move out of your cozy home."

My head spun. I truly loved the cabin Sam and I lived in, and the second story made it more special—to me—than this one with its single story. "Um—"

Gene pressed his business card into my hand. "Here. Tell your husband I want to buy this cabin. What will you sell it for?"

"I—I don't know. We'll have to talk about it."

Gene shrugged. "Doesn't matter. I'll pay it, whatever you ask. This is the one we want." He turned and hopped down from the deck to the ground. "Gotta run. Family is waiting."

And with that, he was gone.

I could hardly wait to tell Sam when he returned. We rarely ever had visitors to the island in the dead of winter, and not only had I had a visitor in my husband's absence, I'd sold him a cabin!

It was almost full dark when Sam returned, even though it was still early afternoon.

"How was your day, sweetie?" he asked as he kissed me hello.

"Oh, fine. I sold a cabin." I nonchalantly turned and walked toward the kitchen.

Sam laughed. "Yeah, right."

I turned back to him, now ecstatic. "I did, Sam! I really did!" I pointed in the direction of the new cabin we were building. "I sold that cabin today!" I thrust the man's business card toward Sam. "He wants you to call him as soon as you can."

"But it's not finished," Sam said.

"He doesn't care. He wants it."

Sam looked around us. "I thought you wanted to move into it, Bonnie."

"I love this home, honey. Besides, it's a little bigger, and I love having the second story view." I shrugged. "We wouldn't have to move everything again."

Sam's eyes lit. "Okay, then. Let's go."

"What? You mean . . . *now?*"

"Sure. It's still early. Bundle up, and let's roll."

We called Gene from town, and he immediately accepted Sam's price, even though Sam priced it higher than we'd initially thought we'd sell it for, as he'd allowed for some negotiation.

"As soon as the ice goes out, Carl and I will come help you put on the roof. I'd like to have a hand in seeing it finished. You know . . . pride of craftsmanship," Gene said.

Back on the island, Sam and I celebrated our good fortune with hot chocolate in front of the fire. "Not only did we get the price we wanted, I'll have help finishing it!" Sam toasted me with his mug. "Bonnie, you make a fine real-estate agent. You're hired."

Two days later, it was Al's plane that flew in and landed on the lake near our cabin. Sam and I welcomed Al in for a chat. We hadn't seen him for quite some time. He had taken me on my first bush plane ride during our first year on the island. We considered him a great friend.

"How many cabins have you built out here now?" Al asked, after Sam told him about the new one we'd just sold next door.

Sam reflected for a moment. "Seven."

"Seven cabins," I said, "but he's also built all kinds of outbuildings—sheds, chicken coops, saunas, outhouses—and he built some awesome pens for the pheasants and poultry out back of our cabin."

Al offered me his mug for a refill. "You're sitting on a goldmine here, Sam. But I guess you've already figured that out."

He nodded as I handed him his filled mug. "Bonnie, as cozy as you've made this place, you ought to start a bed-and-breakfast."

I laughed. "We have no problem entertaining guests, both here and in our guest cabin, but there's no way we could charge for simple hospitality. It's just not us."

Al smiled. "That's just like you two."

"Well . . . we're all friends out here," I explained. "Our door is always open to friends."

Al lifted his mug in salute. "And better still, your coffee pot is always on."

*The panoramic view of the lake from inside the cabin
is nothing short of spectacular! Bravo, Sam! Job well done!*

A girl's gotta stay warm!

Cabin is a little more than half-way up!

My hard working Sam just got the ridgepole up! Good job, Sam!

Almost ready to put the roof on.

The cabin is finished and looking great!

*Tongue and groove blue mountain pine
makes a beautiful cathedral ceiling!*

*Floors turned out gorgeous too! And the view of the lake from those
windows; priceless!*

CHAPTER THIRTY-ONE

Good News from Home

One night in early May, Sam and I awoke to the creak, shatter, crunch, and roar of Skilak Lake. "The ice is breaking up," Sam whispered.

I snuggled close to him and smiled. When I'd heard that noise during our first year out here, it terrified me. This time, I found it comforting. Soon, we'd be able to freely travel to the mainland.

The next morning, on May 7, Sam tried to take the boat across the lake, but there was still too much ice and he had to turn back.

That same day, Buttons, our little Black Cochin Bantam hen—and one of our best brooders—hatched out eight biddies. Tucked safe and warm under their mother's outstretched wings, the downy soft chicks intermittently poked their little heads out between her feathers and looked up at the two legged creatures with inquisitive bright eyes.

"Ahhh! Sam, they're so cute!" I squatted nearby to get a closer look, but the little heads quickly disappeared behind their feathered cover—only a beak or two still sticking out—which made me giggle.

"Yeah, they are!" Sam smiled as he carefully approached and placed two shallow pans on the floor nearby. One held water and the other grain.

That got Buttons' attention, and she stood and *clucked*, and for a few brief seconds I saw too many to count spindly little legs and feet sticking out from under her.

I say a few brief seconds, because just then, the ground started to rumble and shake. The water inside the pan that Sam had just placed in front of Buttons started sloshing. The chickens squawked in alarm, wings flapping—some flying up into the trees and others running to the chicken coop. Buttons crouched protectively over her chicks.

I gripped Sam by his pant legs, and he helped me to my feet. I'm sure the surprised look on his face mirrored my own. We held onto each other for balance as everything under and above our feet continued to rattle and shake. It seemed that everything was moving—even the trees swayed, and I worried about the chickens who sought safety in the branches overhead.

And then it stopped. Just like that, everything went still—everything, that is, but the pounding of my heart beating against my chest.

"Wow!" I gushed. "That was scary!" I looked at Sam and realized I still had a white-knuckled death grip on his arm.

"That was a big one, Bonnie!"

"I'll say. It was a doozy!"

Sam squeezed my shoulder. "Are you okay?"

I took a deep breath and nodded vigorously. "I'm okay. And you?"

Sam scanned the yard and the bird pens, and then turned to face me. "I'm fine, and everything looks okay out here. C'mon, we better check to see if anything is broken in the house."

Other than a few things knocked off shelves and one broken dish, nothing else suffered any damage—save a few shattered nerves. *Mine!*

That evening we listened to the radio news broadcast and learned the earthquake epicenter was located approximately ninety miles southeast of Adak, Alaska, and was 7.7 on the Richter scale. It was the largest earthquake to occur in Alaska in the last twenty years.

A few days later, the ice broke up enough and washed down river for Sam's boat to make it all the way across. We headed straight to the Sterling Post Office. Nancy, the postmistress, gave me a warm hug, and she handed me a box in which to gather all the mail that had accumulated over the seven weeks we'd been stranded on Caribou Island.

That evening in front of the fire, Sam and I poured over letters and packages, taking turns reading our mail aloud.

"Sam!" I squealed as I thumbed through a letter. "Dad and Uncle Bob are coming to visit us!"

Sam's face brightened. "When is that?"

"July!"

I grew tearful as I read a letter of concern from my sister Dawn.

"Please write soon! It's been an awfully long time, and we're terribly worried now. Are you stuck because of the volcano? Did the Chernobyl fallout harm you? Are you safe? Please, please, write to us."

The Augustine Volcano, the youngest volcano in the Cook Inlet, had erupted in March, bringing with it clouds of ash that stopped all air traffic in and out of Anchorage, and also left our seemingly airtight home covered inside and out with a fine layer of ash. Following that, on April 26, the Chernobyl nuclear explosion occurred in nearby Russia. No wonder my family was worried about us!

"Oh, Sam," I said, sniveling.

"Don't worry." He reached over and patted my hand. "We'll go back to town tomorrow, and you can call your family."

I leapt up, scattered the envelopes and pages of the letter I'd held, and wrapped my arms around Sam.

The next morning, I was up early to make breakfast so we could make a trip into town as soon as possible. I couldn't wait to get to a payphone and call my family. As Sam came to the table, he pointed out the window. "Wonder who that is?"

I peered out the window, spotting a small craft that looked like a canoe. "I don't have a clue."

Sam pushed back his chair. "I'd better go see."

Curious, I followed him out the door, and we walked to the beach to await the canoe's arrival. A few minutes later when it came near the shore, Sam pulled the canoe's nose up onto shore. "Good morning." He smiled at the woman, who I'd guess to be in her mid-to-late fifties, and a man who appeared to be in his thirties.

The man introduced himself as Roy, then pointed to the older woman. "This is my Aunt Barbara." Roy wore a burgundy beret and an army jacket over a thick-looking plaid wool shirt and jeans. Aunt Barbara's jet-black hair was medium length, and had grown out enough to reveal white roots. She'd wrapped a scarf around her face, but now pulled it down enough to uncover her smile.

Roy stared intently at Sam. "You must be Sam Ward."

"That I am," Sam said. "What brings you two to Caribou Island?"

"Just bought us a cabin. We're here to check it out."

It turned out that Roy had purchased John and Adelle's cabin.

Though we were in a hurry to get to town, at my invitation, Roy and Barbara joined us at the table for a quick cup of coffee. They were anxious to see their property, so insisted they couldn't stay but a moment, and we didn't disagree. Barbara kindly complimented my coffee, but Roy seemed unimpressed, although he guzzled two cups. He talked little, but his eyes searched every inch of our cabin. Of course, Sam and I were used to people—especially men—eyeballing Sam's handiwork, but where most would ask questions about how this or that was built, Roy only stared and examined.

And more than once, I caught him staring at me. Examining me. It was enough to make me uncomfortable, and I shifted in my seat or directed a question directly at Sam to get his attention.

Roy's aunt Barbara also noticed. Once, when Roy's upturned face appeared to be examining the ceiling, Barbara caught my eye. She tilted her head toward her nephew, and she raised an eyebrow. Then she winked and shrugged, and she let out a soft sigh.

I smiled, taking her signals to mean that Roy was a little "off," or perhaps just tired or not feeling well, so I tried to brush off his lack of friendliness.

Barbara accepted my offer to fill their Thermos with the last of the coffee, and she and her nephew headed out the door.

"Stop back in anytime," I said. "We'll be back from town late this evening." I motioned toward the Thermos she held. "But you're welcome to come back any time for a refill. As far as I know, your new cabin doesn't have a stove, so feel free to stop in for coffee."

Barbara thanked me as Roy stared hard at my long hair, and I self-consciously pushed it behind my back. He's an odd one, I thought, but then again, people who decide to live off the grid—including Sam and me—are often thought of as odd.

I had no clue at that moment, however, just how odd Roy would turn out to be.

CHAPTER THIRTY-TWO

Gertrude & Heathcliff

As spring led into summer, Sam received more and more messages to ferry the "weekend warriors" back and forth across Skilak Lake to Caribou Island. Two of the people he often ferried were Roy and Barbara. Roy's trips usually included a load of supplies, and Sam would always help him load those supplies onto our trailer attached to Mojo, and he'd haul the load up the hill to the cabin Roy had purchased from John and Adelle.

Roy's cabin didn't have a stove at the time, so Sam and I often invited him and his aunt for dinner, but they always declined, as they were working on the unfinished interior of their cabin. Aunt Barbara (as I'd come to know her), often walked down to refill her Thermos with hot coffee, and I always enjoyed her visits, brief though they were. She only stayed a few minutes, as she was anxious to get back to "check on Roy," or "see what Roy is up to now," or "finish helping Roy" with some project or another. I understood. Homesteading Alaska definitely kept one busy.

One day she brought me a gift—a set of kitchen towels. "Just a token of my appreciation for your kind hospitality. It isn't much, but—"

"Thank you! What a sweet gesture!" I gave her a hug, and her eyes sparkled. Though our visits were usually short and coffee-centered, she was always kind.

In short, I liked her.

I learned to overlook Roy's staring and occasional odd behavior, though it nevertheless unnerved me. He could instantly go from pleasant to dark, with even his eyes and facial features quickly morphing into a wicked-looking mask.

Even though Roy and Aunt Barbara stopped by our cabin for coffee and small chat every time they returned to the island, Sam and I still hadn't made it to theirs. We weren't being unneighborly—we were simply covered up with our own work, finishing Gene and Laura's cabin, the tending to our animals and home, hunting and fishing, and of course, Sam stayed busy ferrying folks across the lake. Also, we knew how much time it took to homestead a property on Caribou Island, so we gave the two of them enough space to work on their short weekend visits to their cabin.

We also had a very brief visit from Don, our first friend on Caribou Island. Don flew in to check on his cabin after the harsh winter. On the heels of his visit, Clark and Mary arrived, along with their friend Kenny, who'd bought Winston's cabin, and Kenny's wife Rachel. Kenny and Rachel came bearing an incredibly special and generous gift for us—a propane refrigerator!

I had no idea such an appliance existed, but you can bet I fell in love with it. Other than the great outdoors, I hadn't had refrigeration in the five years we'd been on the island. Kenny even had the propane refrigerator painted harvest gold to match my kitchen stove. However, due to space and because propane was precious to us, we kept the refrigerator outdoors. Sam built a little shelter against the side of the cabin especially for the appliance, and we only used it during the summer months. Winter, of course, brought its own chill, so the refrigerator wasn't needed then.

Early summer kept Sam and me busy. In addition to working the garden and doing our other chores, we made time for entertaining. We often had cookouts and nighttime fire pit chats with our steady stream of visitors—Foster, Jane and their kids; Harry and Marie; and our new neighbors, Gene, Laura, and Carl.

By the time July arrived, I was beside myself with excitement to see my father and my uncle Bob. Dad had written to Sam and me that Uncle Bob wanted to pan for gold. Dad said he'd be happy just to catch any fish that was larger than his usual catch, which was always under eight ounces. We laughed over that one, but I suspected it wasn't far from the truth.

I read my father's letter aloud to Sam, and as I folded it, we heard a knock at the door. We certainly weren't expecting anyone, and we hadn't heard or seen a plane or a boat head in our direction. Sam hustled to the door, and he opened it to find Willy, all the way from the Cotton Wood Cabin.

Thankfully, Willy was in much better shape than when Sam last saw him. Sam invited him in, and I quickly put on a fresh pot of coffee, and when I patted out biscuits for dinner, I made extra.

Willy joined us for dinner, and our visit was a pleasant one. I'm always happy when someone enjoys my cooking, and Willy helped himself to seconds, then shyly asked if I'd wrap one of the extra raisin bars I'd made for dessert into a package for breakfast for him. Of course, I was pleased to do it.

The purpose of Willy's visit was to ask Sam if he'd ferry him into town on his next trip across the lake. Willy needed supplies, and Sam was happy to have company on his trip across the lake. The two men planned for Sam to pick up Willy three days later at Willy's camp, and afterward, Sam and Willy would spend the day in Soldotna running errands.

While the two were away, I cleaned like a madwoman. I wanted my home spic-n-span clean for my father and uncle's visit, so I scrubbed floors on my hands and knees, hand-washed curtains, cleaned the windows, and worked until late in the night. I alternated between my Great-Grandmother Markeson's flat irons, heating them both on the stove, then using one to iron the curtains until it cooled, then trading it out for the other, until my curtains were crisp and fresh-looking.

Our new neighbors, Gene and Laura, who'd purchased the lakefront cabin Sam and I had built on the beach lot next to ours, kindly offered to let my father and my uncle stay in their cabin during their visit to the island. This thrilled us, as their cabin was much closer to ours than our guest cabin, and our own cabin only had one bedroom. I could hardly wait until July 26 arrived, when we'd pick up the men at the Kenai airport for their stay on Caribou Island. I knew my father would be astounded at the work Sam and I had put into the well-appointed cabin, and he and Uncle Bob would be blown away by the stunning panoramic view of Skilak Lake they'd see out the windows Sam had installed.

The day finally arrived when Sam and I went to the mainland to pick up Dad and Uncle Bob. The two couldn't wait to see our land and home, and neither could believe Sam's skill in cabin building.

"What a craftsman you are, Sam!" Uncle Bob said. "Who knew you had it in you!" He playfully ribbed my husband, and I knew he was just getting started. My father and uncle were jokesters, and it thrilled me to have the three men I loved and respected teasing one another.

Of course, we immediately went fishing. My father was shocked by the number and size of the sockeye salmon that filled the lake in front of the house, and after listening to him brag about what a great fishing place we had, Sam insisted on taking the two men up to his "special fishing hole" up the lake.

And fish we did. Dad wasn't used to the fight the salmon put up, and his muscles ached and fingers blistered from fighting to reel in his catch. Yet, he laughed and hooted the whole time. He and Uncle Bob had a blast! Dad caught a prize catch that was longer than his torso, and he beamed as I snapped a photo of him holding his trophy fish.

After a full day of fishing, we came back to the island that afternoon on a lake that was a bit too choppy. I wasn't worried, despite the occasional whitecaps I saw, as by now Sam had boat landing down to a science, and our sturdy bowpicker could handle chop better than any of our previous boats. Sam could easily beach the nose of the boat so that we didn't have to step out into water; instead, we could jump off the nose right onto the beach, without needing waders.

As we came inland, Sam slowed the boat. As always, he goosed the engine just a bit, giving a little forward thrust, while hydraulically raising the motor, so the bowpicker would rest upon the shore just to Sam's liking. He's expertly done this hundreds of times in all sorts of weather.

But not today.

Today, the boat's thrust was a bit too powerful, or possibly the wave on which we rode in was a little too high, so as we came in for our landing, the boat went airborne! Who knew the little bowpicker could fly?

Just about the time we went from sailing to flying, our neighbor Roy stood knee deep in water as he bent over, his dark hair falling over one eye as he worked on the outboard motor on his canoe. He straightened as Sam came in and offered a wave, but his arm froze and his mouth opened in a wide gape, and—realizing the boat's forward momentum was more than Sam had planned—Roy dove headlong into an old wooden dory that was dry-docked higher up on the beach.

Sam's calm-and-collected expression morphed into one of alarm as the bowpicker sailed into the air. I opened my mouth to scream, but only a little squeak eked out as the boat landed with a hard thud, completely dry-docked on the beach.

We sat in stunned silence for several seconds, and then Roy's head slowly appeared from behind the gunwale of the old dory, his eyes the size of saucers.

Sam looked at him and burst into a hearty guffaw. Dad and Uncle Bob laughed, and then I joined the three of them. Within a minute, the four of us were cackling so hard that tears rolled down our cheeks.

Roy stepped out of the dory, an odd look on his face, as if he couldn't understand why we found the whole thing so funny, but finally he smiled, and eventually he even let out a small laugh.

That evening, we again cleaned fish. And I cooked fish. Again. Even though I was getting tired of fish, my father and uncle were so happy with their catches that I caught their joyous spirit, and soon I found myself eating seconds.

And the men and I weren't the only ones stuffing ourselves with fish. Sam had tossed the scraps into the shallow water down the beach after filleting the fish. Two good-sized seagulls—Uncle Bob dubbed them *Gertrude* and *Heathcliff*—gorged themselves on the fish scraps.

"Look at ol' Heathcliff," Uncle Bob said. "He's going at it! He's trying to catch up with Gertrude, because she's putting that fish away."

We watched as the two even gobbled down entire sacks of salmon roe (eggs). Those two birds ate and ate and ate some more. When they'd had their fill, and then some, they tried to fly off, but were so engorged they couldn't get off the ground!

"Oh, poor Heathcliff," my dad said. "I know just how you feel!" Dad rubbed his belly, and we all chuckled. We spent a good half hour or more watching those two birds flapping their wings harder and faster, trying to get their bellies off the ground. It didn't work. Finally, they gave up and waddled out of site, as we again burst into laughter.

The four of us settled around the wood stove with cups of coffee, and before long, our laughter turned into yawning. When Dad's cup emptied, I stood to offer a refill.

He waved me away. "I believe I'm going to head on up the beach to that pretty cabin and get me some shut-eye. I'm about worn out." His deep yawn punctuated his words.

"I'll join you," Uncle Bob said. "Tomorrow's a new day."

My dad took his cup to the kitchen sink, and as he walked back toward the door, he stopped again in front of the picture window, pointing. "Did you see that! Bob, come look!"

Of course, Sam and I joined Dad and Uncle Bob at the window, just in time to see a huge sockeye leap out of the water.

"I'm going to get my fishing rod!" Dad said, heading—in a hurry—toward the door with infectious enthusiasm.

I couldn't believe it. Just moments ago, he'd claimed exhaustion. "Dad, it's eleven o'clock at *night*. I know it's still daylight, but you'll wear yourself out if you don't get a little bit of sleep."

Again, he waved me away. Minutes later, Dad, Uncle Bob, and Sam stood in the lake wearing hip waders, casting and, yes, *catching,* more fish.

My dad is beaming with his fresh-caught salmon!

Dad and Sam never tire of fishing.

Look at those smiles! Salmon is ready for the smoker!

Dad and me, watching Sam expertly filleting salmon.

Uncle Bob & Dad are intrigued with Sam's filleting skills.

Sam and Uncle Bob getting ready to fire up the smoker.

How wonderful to share our world with my dad and Uncle Bob!

Fortunately, Uncle Bob had different plans for the following day. He wanted to pan for gold. "Might as well seek my fortune while I'm here," he said. "It's eluded me everywhere else."

The morning was sunny and a balmy sixty-five degrees (yes, that's balmy on Caribou Island), so we went to a little creek that emptied into the upper end of the lake. The four of us shimmied and shook our pans in the water, seeking "color," as Uncle Bob called it. It didn't take long until we were successful, and Uncle Bob was the first to spot treasure.

"Go-go-go," he stuttered. He looked at me, his eyes wide. *"Gold!"* he finally managed.

I laughed and went over to examine his pan. Sure enough, "Color," I said.

Gold in that there pan!

*Uncle Bob is off and running with sluice box in hand,
leading the pack up the creek!*

That's all it took. Uncle Bob's energy for prospecting gold almost outweighed my dad's energy for fishing—and he wasn't the only one. Once I saw color, I had the fever! We spent a good part of their two-week stay turning over large rocks, shoving aside huge boulders, and possibly even re-routing the course of the creek in an effort to find "one big nugget" for the men to take home. On that last day of prospecting it wasn't Uncle Bob we had to drag away, it was me! The three men were ready to call it a day long before I was ready to put down my gold pan.

"Bonnie, let's go!" Sam picked up the sluice pan and slung it over his shoulder. "It's getting late and the three of us are tired."

"Just one more pan," I growled. Squatted on my haunches next to the creek, I tipped the edge of my dirt filled pan into the icy water and began swirling it from side to side. Surely I'd find a nugget *this time*. The three party-poopers had already started down the trail toward the boat and discovering that I wasn't following, had turned around and impatiently tried to coax me to *come on!*

"It's cold, and your lips are turning blue," Dad said, leaning on the shovel.

"We can hear your teeth chattering clear over here," Uncle Bob huffed.

I looked up from my pan. "Ahhh, you too, Uncle Bob? You're the one that got us into this *mining* operation."

"Yeah, but there's a sauna calling my name, and these old bones and aching muscles are ready!"

"Oh, okay," I grumbled, then stood and tossed the panful of dirt back into the creek. I stared at the men and pointed at the spot where I had tossed the dirt. "Are you satisfied now? There goes what might have possibly been the best pay dirt to date—but, since you guys insist we go—come on then!" They rolled their eyes and I could hear their snickers, as I stomped ahead of them and led the way to the boat.

We returned to the cabin hungry, tired, and happy. We each took saunas that night, and Dad teased Sam about his "red hot" sauna.

"You trying to boil me alive in there, son? It was so steamy, I couldn't see my hand in front of my face!"

Of course it wasn't that hot, but Dad couldn't miss an opportunity to poke at Sam, and Sam was always happy to give it back to him.

"You're going to turn me into Dad Soup!" my father complained.

"Well, we've gotta have something to live on out here. Those measly little guppies you've been catching won't get us through a midnight snack."

Dad was first to turn in that night, and as I headed out to the sauna with Sam, we passed Uncle Bob coming back, ready to head to Gene and Laura's cabin.

"Bonnie?" he said. "Can I have a word?"

I looked at Sam, and he nodded and headed on to the sauna. I turned to follow Uncle Bob back to our cabin.

"Is there something you need, Uncle Bob?"

His mouth drew to one side, and his eyes reminded me of a beagle puppy's—large, round and sad. "It's . . . it's your mother."

"What do you mean?"

He let out a long, hissing breath. "I don't know how to say this, so I'm just going to come out with it." He put a hand on my shoulder, and without meaning to, I trembled.

"Bonnie," he said, "your mother won't be around too much longer. Her health is failing her fast. You need to know that."

My eyes stung as if someone had splashed them with gasoline.

"Hey, Bonnie!" Sam called, walking toward us. "Grab us another bar of soap, will you?"

Uncle Bob squeezed my shoulder where his hand rested, and he nodded toward Sam, then he turned and headed on up the beach.

I stood fixed in my footsteps for a moment, and then I ran into the house for soap—and to dry my eyes. I didn't want Sam to see me crying. I didn't want to see myself crying, either. I didn't want to give credence to Uncle Bob's words.

That night—actually in the wee hours of morning—Sam and I were shaken awake. A low rumbling sounded throughout the house.

"Earthquake!" Sam and I said simultaneously.

For less than a minute, everything in the house shook, including us. Then, as suddenly as it came, it was gone.

"Do you think Dad and Uncle Bob are okay?" I asked.

Sam reached out and patted my leg. "Of course. We're okay, aren't we? Just a little shudder."

I lay awake for a bit, but drifted back to sleep soon enough.

At breakfast, Dad was quick to bring it up. "That was some earthquake!"

"You fare all right?" Sam asked.

Dad huffed and jerked a thumb toward his brother-in-law. "This one slept right through it! I woke him up, even gave him a good shaking, told him we were having an earthquake. By the time he opened his eyes, it was over. He thought I was lying to him. Told me I was dreaming! Said to go back to sleep! Can you believe it?"

I laughed. Uncle Bob was known almost as much for his hard sleeping as he was his loud snoring.

My uncle shrugged. "Wasn't no earthquake. Y'all are trying to out-prank the prankster."

Later, the news on the radio reported the earthquake measured a 4.1 on the Richter scale. Of course, Uncle Bob had just made a trip outdoors to relieve himself when that part of the news was announced, and though we all told him about the report, he still insisted we were in cahoots to pull one over on him.

Two days later, Dad hinted about the decline of my mother's health, but I immediately changed the subject. He caught me again alone in the kitchen, and—in his own kind and subtle way—he made me listen to what I was trying hard not to hear.

"I wish she was healthy enough to come out here and see you," Dad said. "I wish you could see her again . . . before . . . before she gets any worse. I'm afraid she won't be with us this time next year."

"Don't say that! She's going to be okay, Dad. Mom's a fighter!"

That night, after Sam had fallen asleep, I lay in bed and quietly wept. It hadn't been that long since I'd seen my mother, and while she was weaker, she wasn't *that* sick. Still, just the thought of her passing one day in the far-away future was enough to make me tearful. I blamed it on homesickness—Dad and Uncle Bob were here, but Mom wasn't—and a hefty dose of exhaustion, and I made myself think brighter thoughts until I finally fell asleep.

Too soon came the time to take Dad and Uncle Bob back to the airport. In addition to their luggage, we each lugged in a box filled with canned or smoked salmon. At the luggage check point, we looked around us and laughed. Nearly every person boarding the plane had a similar box, a case, or a cooler full of fish.

"That's gonna be a good-smelling flight," Sam said.

A man standing next to us held a big, red cooler. He turned to us and grinned. "I just don't know how we're all going to get off the ground with all this extra weight."

Uncle Bob's face lit. "Gertrude and Heathcliff!" he crowed. "We'll be like Gertrude and Heathcliff! That plane will have to flap its wings and get a running start, and we still might be grounded for a while."

After more laughter, some long, tight hugs, and a few tears, the boarding announcement was made.

Dad gripped my hand and leaned close to me. "Bonnie, please don't ignore what I said. Come home to see your mother as soon as you can." He kissed my cheek, and then he turned and walked away.

His words chilled me, but again I pushed them aside, and went to stand beside Sam at the window as we watched for the plane to take off. When it finally taxied down the runway, we held our collective breath.

"It's too heavy to get off the ground," said an older woman standing next to us. She wrung a damp handkerchief in her age-spotted hands. "Too much weight."

Sure enough, the plane seemed to struggle to get its wheels off the ground, and everyone watched with growing fear as the plane quickly neared the end of the long runway without taking flight.

At the last second, quite literally, with not more than a yard of tarmac left, the plane shuddered and lifted off the ground. Everyone standing at the boarding gate cheered, and Sam pulled me close and laughed.

"Gertrude and Heathcliff!" he said. "They made it!"

Dad told me later that everyone in the plane also clapped and cheered when the wheels finally lifted off the tarmac.

On the drive back to the lower landing, Dad's words circled again and again in my mind. I needed to go see Mom. "Sam, what do you think about us making a pre-Thanksgiving trip to see my parents?"

Sam briefly took his eyes from the road, and the look on his face told me that Dad and Uncle Bob had probably mentioned Mom's health to him, too. "I think that's a fine idea. It'll have to be short, weather pending and all, but we should be able to get away and back before things get too rough."

I squeezed Sam's hand, feeling much better. Once I saw my mother, I'd be able to assess her health for myself and allay Dad's fears. He was probably overly concerned, anyway.

Later, I'd realize both Uncle Bob and Dad were trying hard to prepare me for what lay ahead. I only wish I'd have listened and followed them home to Minnesota right then for another visit with my mother.

CHAPTER THIRTY-THREE

A Creepy Cabin

One day shortly after Dad and Uncle Bob had returned to Minnesota, as Sam and I walked along the beach, he turned to me.

"Say, Bonnie, want to walk up to Roy's place?"

The question caught me off guard. Roy and his aunt only came to the island for two or three days at a time, and though they almost always stopped by for coffee before heading up the hill to their place, we'd never been to see them. We knew Roy was working on his cabin, but Sam and I were also busy. Plus, we entertained quite a bit in the summer months. I suppose it had really never dawned on me to go up to Roy's cabin to visit Barbara and him.

"Um . . . okay." I felt a little hesitant, but I told myself there was no reason for that feeling. So Roy was a little odd. So what? Lots of people were odd. Hey, I might seem odd to some people. Maybe even a lot of people! And I liked Barbara. I enjoyed our coffee chats, even though we had them less often since Roy installed a stove in his cabin so they could make their own brew.

I walked alongside Sam past our cabin and chicken coops. We headed the short distance up the hill behind us, and when we topped the knoll, I stopped in my tracks. Sam did, too.

Roy had fenced his entire property with a tall, chain-link fence!

Sam and I stood there a full minute or more, without speaking. We were surprised, puzzled, and downright shocked. "Why on earth?" Sam finally managed. The fence had a gate bearing a huge, hand-sized padlock. "Who's he trying to keep out?"

"Everyone."

"Huh," Sam said. "We're his only neighbors."

We walked closer toward the locked gate. "Oh, Sam," I said softly, pointing toward the yard. Three small crosses stood in a cemetery plot he'd created in his front yard. A chill raced across the back of my neck and up my scalp, and I shivered. I touched Sam's elbow. "Let's go."

As I said those words, Roy stepped out onto the small, second-story deck and stared out at us. He didn't speak.

Sam, of course, did. He threw up a hand and gave a big smile. "Howdy, neighbor! Thought we'd pay you a visit . . . see what you've done to the place!"

Roy stood woodenly, not moving, still not speaking. After another minute passed, he gave a slight nod, then stepped backward, back into his house.

I squeezed Sam's hand. "Let's go," I whispered fiercely. I'd never felt so unwelcomed or unwanted in my life.

"Aw, it'll be fine."

Roy emerged from the front door on the lower level, and he pulled a fist-sized ring full of keys from his pocket. He fidgeted with them, picking through one after another, until he found the one that would unlock the massive padlock holding the property hostage.

I stared at him. Hard. I searched for any clue of the Roy I knew, of the man who had coffee in my kitchen, who—however odd—was polite and kind.

That Roy was gone. In his place was *this Roy*. This Roy's face held cold, dark eyes that were void of any semblance of emotion. It was as if he didn't even recognize me; it was as if I were a stranger, not him.

He deadpanned Sam, then me, then Sam again. "I don't much care for company." His voice had a hard edge to it. Unkind. "I'll let you in *this* time, though."

And Sam? He completely ignored the man's harsh tone and grinned. "Thanks!" Sam held onto my hand and pulled me through the gate, as if my feet hadn't grown roots deep into the soil on the *outside* of the fence, as if I were happy to come along with him into this bizarre man's yard.

Sam acted as if we'd just been gleefully welcomed into Roy's home. He continued to smile and strolled casually behind Roy as the man led us into the cramped little upright shoebox of a home.

And when we entered . . . oh! I blinked hard, thinking I must be in some kind of dream—nightmare, really. Roy's cabin didn't hold any of the usual trappings of a wilderness cabin—no tools, no survival gear, no equipment, no heavy clothing by the door.

No, the walls of Roy's cabin were decorated—*decorated!*—with scalps hanging from pegs. Some of those scalps were even pierced through the center by large nails, pinning them to the walls. Fake scalps, I hoped. Fake scalps, I prayed. *God, please let them be fake!* A rubbery-looking, fake, bloody hand hung in the window by a piece of rope tied to the wrist. He'd strung synthetic spider webs in clusters across shelves, in front of windows, and from candlesticks. Plastic or rubber tarantulas poised in odd places throughout the claustrophobic-feeling room.

I stiffened when Roy spoke.

"I like Halloween," he blurted.

Sam looked at me, then turned to Roy. "Yeah. Halloween's nice." Sam looked at me again, and his eyes seemed to say, *So what?* October was still two months away. "Not much trick-or-treating here on the island."

Roy scowled.

Barbara reached out and patted Roy's arm. "Halloween is Roy's favorite holiday."

"Better'n Christmas," Roy said, his voice hard and his face deadpan.

No one argued with him.

"Coffee?" Barbara asked, her voice artificially bright.

I shook my head, my mouth too dry to speak. I stared at Sam, willing him to decline her offer so we could get out of there. Though I didn't look at him, I felt Roy's eyes on me. He seemed fixated with my hair, but I told myself he probably hadn't seen many women with hair so long.

I was right.

"Your hair's long," he said, apropos of nothing.

I still stared at Sam, and he smiled.

"Yes," I finally managed. What more could I say?

"Halloween is good for scaring people," Roy said. "I got a Halloween tape of scary noises, wolves howling, women screaming. I scare people with it."

"Roy, how about another cup of coffee?" Barbara offered him the cup she held without waiting for his response.

Roy isn't right in the head, I thought.

I had no clue at that point how right I was.

He motioned toward a display of scalps nailed to a wall. "I scalp intruders," he said. He didn't smile.

"Oh, Roy!" Barbara said. She laughed, but her laugh eked out tightly; a nervous twitter unlike her usual, free-floating, easy chuckle. "Roy, let's offer our guests something to eat, shall we?" Barbara motioned toward the open pantry, lined with cans and boxes of food, and plastic containers filled with who-knew-what.

I shook my head without looking at her. I didn't want anything from this home, not even the coffee I'd supplied them. I was unable to speak. I couldn't turn my stare away from Roy. I'd never felt as unwelcome anywhere in my life as I did in that moment.

I wanted out of there! Roy's unwavering scowl made it clear that he didn't want us in his place. And those decorations . . . they didn't make sense to me. Halloween was still three months away. My eyes darted around the room as I tried to sort out all I saw and felt and heard. Could it be witchcraft?

Sam wiggled his fingers against me, and I looked down, realizing I gripped his hand so fiercely that my own knuckles were white. I loosened my grip, but I didn't let go. I had to hang onto the only thing I believed was normal in the whole place.

Barbara said something, but I was so wrapped up in what I was seeing that I couldn't catch her words. I looked at Sam, sending him a mental plea to get me out of there.

"Well," he said, looking first at Barbara, then at Roy. "I reckon we'll head back down the hill. We were out for a walk before doing our evening chores, and we thought we'd stop by."

Roy's face remained hard, though a muscle in his jaw twitched.

I didn't waste time in pulling Sam toward the door.

"Stop in and see us for coffee again," Sam said.

I glanced at Barbara, but I still couldn't speak.

We were almost in our own cabin before I again found my voice. "We are never, *ever*, going back to that cabin again! Do you hear me, Sam Ward? *Never!* There is something wrong with that man, and it's too dangerous to go in there."

"Uh-huh."

"I'm serious! That fence . . . those scalps . . . and the *crosses!* Who is buried there? Or, who does he plan on burying there? Who?"

"Awww, Bonnie. It's probably just for show. His own little haunted house." Sam rubbed the back of his neck. "He's odd, all right, but I don't think he's dangerous." Even as he said it, I could tell Sam wasn't convinced.

"Promise me, Sam. Promise me you'll never go in there again."

Sam turned to me and cupped my head in his hands. "Okay. I promise." He pulled me into his warm arms. "You're safe. I won't let anything happen to you." He kissed me. "You have my word."

CHAPTER THIRTY-FOUR

Island of Terror

As summer turned into early fall and the mountains donned their colorful skirts, Sam remained quite friendly around Roy. I, on the other hand, grew warier. Sometimes Roy would return a wave; other times, he'd act as if he looked right through us, unseeing. Though he sometimes chatted amicably enough with my husband, the man's comments to me were clipped, and he always seemed to be watching me from the corner of his eye, appraising me, spying on me. To say he made me uncomfortable would be an understatement.

I made sure I was never alone with him, not even for a second. I stayed close to Sam or to Roy's aunt Barbara whenever the man was around. Sam still ferried the couple back and forth across the lake as often as they needed, and one day when Sam mentioned in front of them that he and I were heading into town the next day, Roy spoke up.

"Can I go with you? Could use a few supplies before the holiday."

Holiday? Thanksgiving was two months away, and Christmas hadn't even blipped on my mental radar, yet. Then it dawned on me. *Halloween.* Roy's favorite holiday. I shuddered.

Before I could think up a reasonable protest, Sam spoke up.

"Sure. Be down about seven, if you don't mind. I want to get an early start, as we've got quite a few stops to make in town."

Our friends, Clark and Mary Walker, were at the lower landing when we arrived. They were heading across Skilak to the island for a weekend visit. We joked about being two ships passing in the broad daylight, and we shared some hugs and wishes for safe sailing, and then we were all on our way again.

One of our last stops in town was the gas station where Sam filled up several five-gallon gas jugs for the boat and for Mojo. While he went inside to pay for our gas, Roy, who sat directly behind me in the Jeep, leaned forward. I startled when he spoke near my ear.

"You know when we were on the dock the last time, back in the spring, and we ran into the Walkers then, too?"

I nodded and turned in my seat, as much to move away from his mouth that was too near to me as to watch his face.

"Remember when everybody started laughing? Like y'all were doing today?"

"Yes. What about it?"

Roy's dark eyes searched my face as a long pause settled between us. When he spoke again, his voice was low. "Were they laughing at me?"

His question stunned me. "Of course not, Roy! Did you—have you thought that this whole time?"

He nodded.

"I'm glad you asked me, but I'm so sorry you thought that this whole time. They're a really nice couple, and they'd never laugh at anyone's expense."

Sam opened the Jeep door just then, and Roy sank back into his seat, saying nothing.

I turned to face forward again, and as we drove back to the lower landing, I thought about Roy's question, and I searched my mind to recall everything that everyone had said each time we'd been around the Walkers. For the life of me, I couldn't think of anything at all that would make Roy think they were laughing at him.

What caused his mind to think such things? What would even put him in that frame of mind? What had happened to him to make him so paranoid?

I found no answers, and I didn't dare ask Roy, or even his aunt, those questions.

A few weeks later in mid-October, Sam got a call on the CB from our friend Warner—yes, we had finally after all these years installed a CB radio. The men made plans for Warner to pick Sam up at the landing and take him to Seward, to work on Warner's boat.

Other than Roy, I'd be alone on the island, as Barbara hadn't returned with him on this last trip to Caribou, and Nels had left the island a few weeks ago. Still, I wasn't worried, as having someone there was certainly better than having no one there.

Or so I thought.

My first night alone, a windstorm blew in. The trees tossed and creaked in the wind, and the wind blew harder as evening turned to night. I stoked the fire and lit an extra propane lantern against the chilly darkness.

In the kitchen, I put my teakettle on to boil water, and I was pulling down a box of tea sachets from the cabinet, when I heard voices. I stiffened and cocked my head, listening.

Nothing.

Bonnie, isolation is playing tricks on your mind.

I headed to the stairwell where Sam had built bookshelves and browsed the selection there, trying to decide which new book I'd start tonight. As I ran my fingers along their spines, I again thought I heard a voice.

It's just the wind.

Nevertheless, it unnerved me. I returned to the kitchen, removed the kettle from the heat, and turned off the overhead propane light. No sense feeding my imagination with caffeine. I was tired, and I was hearing things. I needed sleep.

Upstairs, I'd just curled up in bed when I heard a woman's scream. A *woman's* scream! My mind raced to keep up with my heartbeat. I was the only woman on the island.

I flung off the covers and ran to the window, searching the beach for the source of the sound. Sometimes a rabbit would squeal when cornered or caught by another animal, and while their screams could be likened to that of a woman, I was certain the shrill rise and fall of the shriek I'd heard could only come from a female human being.

As far out as I could see, there were only the rise and fall of the whitecaps glistening on the lake. In the distance, the sky began a lightshow as the *aurora borealis* illuminated the night.

"Breathe, Bonnie," I said aloud, as if the sound of my own voice in my ears could erase what I'd just heard. I peered out another minute, then turned to head back to bed. Just as I fluffed my pillow, another blood-chilling scream pierced the darkness. I nearly jumped from my skin!

I again ran to the window, fully expecting to see a woman being stabbed to death on the shore. (Oh, the awful things that go through your mind when you're terrified!)

Where is she? Who is she? What on earth is happening?

The scream came again, and I wrapped my arms around myself. How could those screams pierce the thick walls of our cabin? How could I hear them so clearly above the near-deafening fury of the storm outside?

I stepped away from the window and peered into the darkness of my room as my eyes tried to adjust from the moonlight and northern lights outdoors. Grotesque shapes seemed to morph from the dark shadows as the screams continued. I closed my eyes, afraid to move. *God, please help me! Tell me what is happening!*

Just then, the screaming stopped. I opened my eyes, now better able to see the room around me. No one was there.

Suddenly, maniacal laughter penetrated the air where the screaming left off. The sound of cackling, like that of a crazed witch, seemed to bounce off the walls of my cabin.

Roy!

He was playing the Halloween tape he'd once told Sam and me he owned. But why would he use it to scare me? And why tonight, when Sam was away?

That's it! He knew Sam was away. Roy monitored the same CB radio channel that Sam and I used, and he'd heard Sam making arrangements to meet Warner to work on Warner's boat. Tonight, Roy had watched me from outside, had seen me settling down for the evening, had waited until I turned out the downstairs lamp, had watched as my upstairs window illuminated, then went dark, signaling my bedtime.

Thankful for the moonlight pouring in through my bedroom windows, I quickly redressed in jeans and a sweater. As I pushed my arms through the sleeves, again the raucous, witchy laughter shattered the stillness. My heart thudded my chest.

"Why is he doing this to me?" My voice trembled as I spoke the words aloud, and the quavering angered me. I quickly grabbed my boots and flashlight, and, tucking my boots under my arm, I carefully made my way down the narrow steps in the darkness. When I reached the bottom, the laughter stopped.

I now had no doubt that I was being watched. I turned off the flashlight as another blast of wind howled against the sides of the cabin. Earlier, the weatherman forecasted up to sixty-miles-per-hour winds, and I now knew they were at least that strong. Using only the moonlight to see by, I picked my way across the room, trying my best to remain in the shadows. I reached my treadle sewing machine and opened its drawer, retrieving the Smith & Wesson .44 Magnum.

Carefully, I opened the cylinder to make sure the gun was loaded.

It was.

I moved over to the couch and lay the gun and flashlight by my side. My hands trembled as I tugged on my boots. I'd been frightened before when alone on the island, but never had I felt the terror that surged through me tonight. My legs felt like wet spaghetti when I stood. I realized I was breathing rapidly and shallowly, and I did my best to slow and steady my breath to keep from hyperventilating.

What now? I tried to figure out what to do next as another gale of witchy laughter, followed by a piercing scream, shot through the night.

My first impulse was to bolt out the door and run for my life. But where would I go? There was no escaping Caribou Island, not without a boat, and our boat was anchored on the other side of the now-raging Skilak Lake. In this weather, even if I had a boat, I'd capsize and drown before I could even make it to the halfway point.

The CB radio! I could call for help. They'd send a helicopter to come rescue me. It would take—what?—thirty or forty-five minutes? That is, if they could even fly out in this weather?

No, that wouldn't work. Besides, Roy monitored the radio. He would hear me, and then what would he do?

Fearing my trembling legs would give out from beneath me, I returned to the couch, where I sat on high alert, quaking with terror as the screams and laughter seemed to come from all corners of the house. I stared constantly at the big picture window, half-expecting to see Roy's face pressing against the glass, a machete in his hand. I moved the gun from beside me onto my lap as the northern lights danced against the wall and the front door. What I normally found beautiful now seemed eerie.

Several minutes passed without hearing screams or laughter. Still, I was afraid to move. What was he doing now? Where was he?

My body's constant trembling led me into an exhausted state as the steady surge of adrenaline burned off, yet I couldn't stop shaking. I dried my hands on my jeans and surprised myself with a deep yawn. I desperately needed sleep.

After a good thirty or forty minutes had passed in relative silence—the wind still roared—I figured Roy must have returned up the hill to his cabin. I chanced a walk to the window, peering first into the trees, and then letting out a pent-up breath when the dancing lights helped me relax. I scanned the beach, and that's when I saw the flash of light as the sound of gunshot reached my ears.

Roy stood at the edge of the surf, and he'd straightened just as he set off the firecracker. Roy was on my beach! *My beach!* This was my property, and there he stood beneath the Northern Lights, shrouded in moonlight, trying—and succeeding—in terrifying me. He had no business here, none whatsoever.

I felt so weak that I feared I might not make it back up the stairs. I quickly checked the front door again, my legs quaking as I crossed the floor, and then I made it back up the stairs. If Roy was foolish enough to break into my house, I would shoot him.

Never had I believed for even a second I could shoot another human being, but in that moment, I knew that if Roy came after me, I would shoot him, and I would kill him.

Fully dressed, I collapsed onto the bed, the flashlight in one hand, and my Smith & Wesson in the other. I don't think I lay there long before I fell into an exhausted sleep.

The next morning, I had chores to do. I needed water, the fowl needed to be fed, and I had to bring in more wood. The wind had died down, and I decided that, since I could likely hear him coming now, I'd be brave and face the day ahead of me.

As I went about my chores, I grew angrier. Caribou Island was my *home*. It was my safe place. Sam and I had settled not only our property, but had cleared lots and built cabins for others as well. Sam had cleared roadways. This was, in many ways, *our island.* And I refused to let a crazy man like Roy make me want to leave it.

The day before, I'd started building a walkway made of smooth rocks I'd collected on the beach. Now feeling courageous, I gathered another load of flat rocks into our wheelbarrow and pushed it up from the beach and continued my work. I wanted Sam to be surprised when he came home.

Regardless of my newfound bravery, I frequently looked around me, watching for Roy. Thankfully, he never appeared. *You have nothing to worry about, Bonnie. He was just playing a prank on you.* Wicked prank, though it was. I think he'd truly intended to terrify me, and he'd succeeded in that hateful mission.

Later that afternoon, my outdoor chores behind me, I came inside to make dinner for myself. I'd wanted a long, hot sauna, but I couldn't bring myself to get undressed in the sauna and relax in a steamy room, when that man might be *out there.*

As night crept in, it brought with it fresh fear. What if Roy returned tonight? I bustled about, checking and rechecking the front door to make sure it was locked. I loaded the shotgun and let off the safety latch. I again checked my handgun. I lit both gas lamps in the kitchen and living room. I loaded the stove with extra wood and adjusted the damper so I wouldn't have to mess with it later that night.

Though I'd consoled myself through the day that nothing bad had really *happened* last night, my mind again began to torment me with what *could* happen, with what Roy *might* do. His actions over the months I'd known him convinced me that he was paranoid and mentally unstable. With my own eyes, I'd watched him swing from an amiable mood to a dark one without provocation. I'd seen him grow unfriendlier to Sam and me as the weeks had passed since our only visit to his cabin.

As the sun began to dip into Skilak Lake, I sat at the window, scanning the beach and the woods for any sign of Roy. My chest tightened each time a bird flew past or a tree branch dipped. What was the man planning to do to me tonight?

I had two more nights before Sam would return, and I wasn't sure I could face them alone. *Father, please protect me from Roy. I'm afraid of him. I need your shield around me.*

I stared out over the water, feeling no less afraid after my prayer.

And then I heard the hum of a boat motor. Someone was coming!

I stared out the window, my foot jittering against the floor as the speck on the water grew closer. I couldn't imagine who it could be.

And then I realized whose boat it was.

It was ours! Sam was coming home!

I let out a yip and hopped up from the table, and I quickly gathered ingredients, along with a jar of moose Swiss steak from the pantry to make a hearty homecoming meal for my man. By the time Sam reached the shore, I'd run down to greet him, and before he could even tie up our craft, I leapt into his arms.

"Thank God, you're home!" I meant that quite literally. My prayer had been answered.

The biscuits were ready to come out of the oven when Sam and I reached the cabin, and the Swiss steak was bubbling on the stove. Everything was right in my world, again.

As we ate, I told Sam what had happened the night before. I tried to leave out any melodrama I might have been feeling, as I wanted Sam to be proud of me. I even tried to laugh, telling him I'd probably overreacted. Sam's face remained stoic the whole time I talked. When I finished, he changed the subject, telling me that Warner had to order parts for the boat repair, which is why he'd come home sooner. I didn't mind that Sam hadn't addressed my telling of the events of the prior night; I now felt perfectly safe with my husband back at home.

The next morning after breakfast, I was sweeping the cabin floor downstairs when I heard angry voices on the beach. I went to the door and opened it a bit, and I saw Sam and Roy standing no more than a foot apart, facing each other. I couldn't hear everything they said, but as their voices rose and fell, Sam's clearly became louder than Roy's, and I picked up bits and pieces of his sermon.

". . . and if you ever—*ever!*—scare my wife again, you'll wish you hadn't!" Sam said. "Nothing had better ever happen to her while I'm gone, do you hear me?" Sam shoved a finger at Roy's nose. "Not one hair on her head harmed, understand?"

As best as I could tell, Roy wasn't speaking, but he did nod, once Sam moved his finger away. Both men turned and went their separate ways.

Sam never spoke of his conversation with Roy, and I didn't let on that I'd overheard them. That evening, I made chicken potpie and baked a big chocolate cake for my man, my protector, my hero.

CHAPTER THIRTY-FIVE

Mom Is With Us

The second week of October arrived, and though I didn't mention it to Sam, I was dreading the 31st. I thought too often as the date grew close of the night Roy had terrified me, and—knowing Halloween was his favorite holiday—I imagine he'd have something wicked up his sleeve.

I needn't have worried. As Sam and I headed to our sauna one evening, Roy came down the hill carrying his Army duffle. He never looked at me, but he did address Sam.

"Going home for the winter."

That's all he said, and hardly glancing Sam's way, he loped down the beach toward his canoe, and he was off.

It was probably the most relaxing sauna I'd taken in a month or more. Roy was gone! I practically melted in the steam, and if Sam hadn't finally nudged me to don my robe and head back to the cabin, I'd likely still be in that sauna today.

I pulled my old, fuzzy, blue robe around me and sank onto a chair by the fire. Sam turned on the radio, just in time for the seven o'clock news. Warm and toasty, I towel-dried my hair by the stove as the North Wind Messages came on.

"To Sam and Bonnie on Caribou Island," the announcer said.

I turned toward Sam and grinned, the towel still bunched against my head.

"Bonnie, it's time to come home," the announcer continued. "Call me collect as soon as you can. Love, Dad."

My smile melted, and I froze. Sam reached for me, and I crumpled into his arms, sobbing. "Sam, it's Mom! It's Mom. I know it's Mom!" I cried into his shoulder, and when I finally pulled away, Sam was crying, too.

Sam held me and rocked me on the couch, both of us crying, until I finally regained some self-control. "We have to go, Sam."

"I know," he said.

"No, we have to go *now*."

He held me by the shoulders and stared into my eyes. "I know." He released me and stood. "Go get dressed, and let's head across the lake and call your dad."

I turned toward the picture window. It was full dark now, and Sam and I never took the boat across the lake in the darkness. It was just too dangerous. Still, I wasn't going to protest. I rushed up the stairs, flung my bathrobe over a chair, and I quickly pulled on my clothes. As we headed down the beach, my nose began to run in the cold from crying, and without caring, I wiped my nose on my sleeve. I fought not to cry again. I wanted desperately to speak to my father, but I feared what he'd tell me.

With Sam at the helm, we crossed the choppy lake in the dark. I should have been concerned over the dangerous journey, but I could focus on nothing but my mother.

Safely on the other side of the lake, we quickly docked and hopped into the Jeep, and Sam rushed us to Sterling. When we reached town, we stopped at the very first phone booth we saw, and we called my dad.

When he picked up the phone on the first ring, a sob clogged my throat, and I couldn't speak.

"Bonnie?" He somehow knew it was me. "Your mother is dying, Bonnie. You need to come home now."

I wanted to be strong for my father, but I burst into sobs.

My father cried softly on the other end of the phone, and when he spoke again, his voice sounded strangled by his tears. "She's in hospice. We almost lost her the other night. Bonnie . . ." A sob hung in his throat. "We don't expect her to live long."

After I again gathered enough restraint to talk, I told my father through my tears that I'd get a plane ticket tomorrow and be there as soon as possible.

As soon as I landed in Minneapolis, Dad picked me up and we went straight to the hospice hospital. Uncle Bob met us in the lobby, and each tried to prepare me for what I'd see. The director of nursing saw them talking with me and came to my side. "Your mother has come close to passing twice in the last twenty-four hours." She took my hand and held it in both of hers and offered me a sorrowful smile. "Bonnie, she won't last long after seeing you. She's been holding on for your visit. It won't be long, now."

Her words were logical, of course, but a big part of me wouldn't accept it. What did this woman know? She had no clue how strong my mother was, how many years she'd fought and continued to win her battle against emphysema.

When I entered my mother's room a few minutes later, despite what everyone had told me, I was completely unprepared for what I saw. My mother had shrunk—she had melted away, her small body now nothing more than skin stretched thinly and tightly over sharp-edged bones. Her head was turned away from me, and I put my hands over my face, stifling back a sob.

I swallowed the ache constricting my throat. "Mom," I finally managed.

Slowly and with great effort, my mother turned her head to face me. Her sunken eyes appeared cloudy, but the second she recognized me, they sparkled. She gave me a beatific smile that—in spite of her weakened condition—still managed to light up the gloomy room.

Seeing her lovely face filled me with strength, and I returned her smile with a heart that spilled over with love for her. I rushed to her side. "Oh, Mom!" I hugged her frail body close to me as gently as I could. I carefully lowered her back to the bed, fearful of hurting her. Though she still smiled, her eyes closed, and she sank onto the pillow and immediately slept.

Dad stood behind me and put his hands on my shoulders. "She sleeps a lot now, Bonnie."

I sat by the bed for hours. I watched my mother's labored breathing, which seemed to grow more difficult each time she slept. During her waking hours, she'd sometimes moan softly from the pain, and she'd turn her head away from us, and her beautiful face would grimace. She never wanted us to see her pain, so when she'd turn back to us, she'd be smiling.

I scooted my chair to her bedside, and I'd hold her hands in mine for hours at a time. The nurse told me she'd wanted her fingernails cleaned and trimmed before I arrived, and so when she awoke again, I remarked on how lovely they looked, bringing out another smile from her.

"I love you, Mother. I love you so much," I'd say each time she awakened.

"I love you, too, sweet Bonnie." We said this same thing to each other time and time again. Sometimes we wouldn't speak, but we'd stare into one another's eyes, unable to find the words for all we wanted to say. How do you say goodbye forever to someone you love so much?

As she suffered through a particularly rough bout of pain, she turned to me and again tried to smile. "Tell me about the wilderness," she said. "Take my mind off this."

I began talking. I told her about the hunting, about the fishing, about building cabins, and about how much we loved our sauna. I talked about the northern lights, about canning all that salmon, and about panning for gold with Dad and Uncle Bob.

As I spoke, I thought of how my parents had unselfishly let Sam and me go, allowing us to follow our wish for Alaskan living. Even though it meant us being thousands of miles away from them, they believed we could succeed, and they embraced our dream and were happy for us, never once making us feel guilty for leaving them behind.

I spoke of Alaska and Caribou Island in glowing terms. I talked about everything that was pleasant, and I left out everything that was not. I wanted my mother to feel completely at peace and not worry about her daughter living in the often-harsh wilderness.

I talked for hours, and eventually, Mom's eyes grew heavy again.

"Bonnie," she said, her thumb stroking my hand as I held hers. "You have to write your story."

What's the use, Mom? You won't be here to read it. I held back a sob, but I couldn't stop my eyes from puddling.

"Promise me," Mom said. She'd been the one to encourage me to write and submit stories to the *Farmington Independent*. She believed that my stories would make others happy.

I pressed my lips together to keep from crying, and I managed to nod. "Thank you, Mom. I will. Thank you for everything you have ever done for us." Even as I said the words, they sounded weak and generic.

I tried again. I put a hand over my heart. "Mom, you will always live right here, right inside my heart. You'll be here every day for the rest of my life. I have so many, many wonderful memories, and I will always cherish them."

My mother smiled at me, her eyes bright with unshed tears. "I love you, Bonnie."

"I love you, too, Mom."

My mother slept.

The night before I left Minnesota after laying my mother to rest, I drove my sister Connie home. We talked quietly about Mom and about how much we missed her. We traveled a long straight-stretch leading up a rise, and as we topped the knoll, we both caught our breath. The northern lights danced in the sky before us. Though seeing the *aurora borealis* wasn't unheard of in Minnesota, it was indeed rare. Nature's lightshow seemed to be a beautiful message straight from God, a heavenly celebration of my mother's arrival.

Connie reached across the seat and took my hand. "Mom is with us," she said.

"Yes. She sure is." I squeezed my sister's hand. "She always will be."

CHAPTER THIRTY-SIX

Grieving

Returning to Caribou Island after my mother's funeral was hard. I knew when I'd left that, even though my father, my sisters, and the rest of my family would always welcome me back to Minnesota, a homecoming would never be the same without my mother's smile to greet me.

The day after I returned, Sam said it was time to go trapping. He'd already set some while I was away, and while I'm sure he could have finished on his own, he must have sensed that I should not be cooped up in the house alone all day. Perhaps he saw that I was headed toward depression, and with winter isolation soon at hand, he encouraged me to help him set more traps. "More pelts equal more money," he said, and I couldn't argue with that.

We crossed the short distance across the mild waves to the southern mainland by boat. Once on foot, we traipsed miles and miles of Sam's favorite places, setting many traps. He gently asked about my trip, about how my father was doing, and about my time with my mother.

It took everything within me to answer Sam's questions. I didn't want to talk. I didn't want to think. I felt lost, and everything around me seemed bleak. "I've never been so sad in my life," I managed, trying not to break down yet again.

Sam pulled me closer as we walked. He rubbed my back and settled his arm at my waist. I didn't want to push him out of what I was feeling, but I didn't think he could relate, not truly, not deeply. He loved my mother, of course, but she was *my* mother.

"You're supposed to feel sad," he said. "It's okay to feel sad."

I took in a deep, body-shuddering breath, and huffed it back out. Maybe Sam was right. Maybe what I was feeling— that sense of utter aloneness in the world—was normal at this point. "I just—I just wish she were here."

Sam looked around, as if searching for something. "She is here." He waved his arm in a wide arc. "She's everywhere. She will always be wherever you are."

I thought of the northern lights Connie and I had seen in Minnesota, and I told Sam how we felt it was a sign from heaven. I thought he might think it foolish, but his reaction was quite the opposite.

"I'm sure it was," he said. "I think signs like that are all around us. We just have to be open to seeing them."

In that moment, quite possibly, I may have loved my husband more than ever before. My chest still felt empty, but somehow, it was as if that deep hole filled just a little. A teaspoon full of hope. I wondered if that's how it would be, if it would take that long—one tiny spoonful at a time—to fill the hollowness inside of me.

"Look for the signs, Bonnie. You'll see them."

We continued our long walk, setting more traps here and there, in places where we saw signs of muskrat or mink, but I saw nothing special that I could consider a sign from above.

God, I prayed, *if you really send us signs from heaven, open my eyes and let me see one.*

I searched around me, gazing at the sky, peering into the trees, trying to make myself open to seeing, as Sam had said, and yet nothing seemed like the message from above I so desperately needed.

When we returned to the lake, heading toward our boat, I looked out over the water, and I saw what appeared to be a huge, white island rolling across the water.

"Whaaaa—" I'd never seen anything like it. As suddenly as it had appeared, it was gone. I stared at the spot, wondering if I'd imagined it, hoping to see whatever it was again, and then there it was—a gigantic, bright-white, glistening mass growing larger by the second. Then, just as quickly, it rolled away, leaving soft waves in its wake.

"A Beluga whale," Sam said. "It's awfully late in the year for one to be this far up from the ocean."

There it was. The sign I'd so desperately needed, just when I needed it the most.

Throughout November, Sam and I continued to work the traps, and on the days the weather was too harsh for trapping, we gathered and chopped firewood. Though it was hard work, this season, I enjoyed hefting the stove-box-sized chunks of logs Sam had cut, dropping them into the trailer we pulled behind Mojo. Sam sensed that I needed to stay busier than usual, and the two of us worked each day until we were exhausted, ensuring I'd sleep through the night instead of lying awake crying, as I'd done for so many days after my mother had passed.

We had a brief visit from Clark and Mary in late November, and Mary tried a few times during our girl-chat over raisin bars and coffee to get me to talk about my mother. I thought of my friend Susan, and how she talked about the murder of her mother in Washington State. She shared intimate details of the crime, of her relationship with her mother, and of her heartache afterward. I wondered often after my mother's passing how Susan found the courage to share her grief. I pushed away Mary's questions, quickly changing the subject to meaningless topics, until Mary finally gave up.

I suppose we each grieve differently.

In December, I sank into despair. Sam and I were isolated by unsafe lake conditions, and each day seemed to take a week to pass. I became snappish with the man I loved. I'd never felt so unhappy. I wavered from not wanting to get out of bed (and when I did, I wouldn't change out of my fuzzy old bathrobe) to not wanting to get into it. My motivation was gone.

One afternoon while Sam was chopping wood, I turned on the radio, hoping for news of a weather break. But no. More news of the williwaws. More news of seventy-mile-per-hour winds. Which meant more days of isolation. And then when the news went off, the stupid, ridiculous, hateful Christmas carols came on. It was more than I could take.

"Shut up!" I raged. I jumped up from the couch as "Joy to the World" came on, and I rushed across the room and flung back my leg, ready to kick that radio into a billion pieces. A thud on the porch stopped me, as Sam deposited another load of firewood.

Then, I thought of my sweet mother and felt great shame, because this radio was a precious, well-used gift from both my parents when Sam and I first came to Alaska. It was our only link to the news and North Wind Messages. What was I thinking? I smacked the *off* button. "There's nothing joyful about this world, God," I said. "How can You expect me to be joyful when my mother was laid to rest a month and a half ago? It's not fair!"

I went back to the couch and plopped down on my back, hugged a pillow to my chest, and cried. My beautiful mother was dead, and she was only fifty-two years old.

Sam's footsteps again thumped on the porch, and I quickly dried my face on my sleeve. I knew my behavior wasn't fair to him. He tried so hard to make me happy, to pull me out of my misery, but I'd grown from sad to angry, and I could swing back and forth between the two emotions as easily as a metronome.

I sat up as Sam came in the door.

"Say, Bonnie, are you going to hunt for a Christmas tree? If not, I'm going to put the axe in the shed."

Christmas tree? Was he kidding? "No. I'm not celebrating Christmas this year."

Sam shrugged and shut the door. He had never given a hoot about a Christmas tree, and I'm sure he didn't care this year, either. If I wanted to ignore the holiday, he wouldn't mind one whit. I forcefully peeled myself off the couch and started dinner. Even Scrooges must eat.

The next day as I did laundry in the sauna, I couldn't get Christmas out of my mind. I thought of every Christmas I'd ever spent with my mother, and again I'd swing from crying to being angry. I climbed the steps to our bedroom to put away stacks of freshly folded clothes, and my feet felt like concrete blocks as I lifted them.

In our bedroom, I slammed drawers as I put the clothes away. I looked toward the knotty-pine ceiling. "Look, God, I need something to get me out of this slump. Not for my sake, because clearly You don't care about what I'm feeling. It's for Sam's sake." I wanted to dig a big hole and bury myself in it, but I didn't care enough to put forth the effort. Tears slid down my face, and I sank onto the bed. "We need Christmas, God. It's Your Son's birthday. Help me make Christmas for Sam."

I sat up and blew my nose, but my diatribe wasn't over. "If you love me, God, then send me some company for Christmas." I'd just asked for a miracle. Between the winds and the storms and the heavy snows, there would be no way we'd have Christmas company. Besides, who'd come to a frigid, remote island on a holiday? Christmas was for families.

"While You're at it, why don't you send a woman to spend Christmas with us? Would that be too much to ask? Anytime we've had company for Christmas, it's always been a man." I harrumphed and huffed, and I stomped down the stairs, my face burning with shame as much as with anger. What gave me the right to talk to God like that?

CHAPTER THIRTY-SEVEN

Christmas Miracle

Two nights later, as the wind continued to wage war outside our door, Sam and I sat by the woodstove reading our books. Sam put his bookmark into place, stood, and turned on the radio. "It's message time," he said.

Part way into North Wind Messages, we were surprised with mention of our names.

"To Sam and Bonnie on Caribou," the announcer read, "Can you pick up my friend at the landing tomorrow at 3:00 p.m.? Thanks, Derik." The announcer paused, then spoke again. "I suppose that means tomorrow, Sam. Hope you didn't have other plans."

Sam grinned at me. We loved how the announcer ad-libbed his messages, adding his own personal notes. We'd never met him, yet since we'd invited him into our home via radio every night for years, we felt like he was an old friend.

Sam shook his head. "Fat chance that'll ever happen. Listen to that wind."

As if on cue, the wind let out a long, loud whistle. I thought of my prayer—or my rant—two days earlier. The one chance of company at Christmas was going to be ruined by the wind. And even if a miracle really happened, Derik's friend wouldn't be a woman. No woman in her right mind would come to Caribou in this weather, especially at Christmas.

The next day, the wind raged on. Sam and I sat at the table in mid-afternoon, watching the waves lift higher and higher. "No chance of getting across that mess," Sam said, and I agreed. Sam could cross the lake in windy conditions, but never in williwaw conditions. We knew Derik's friend would understand as soon as he reached the other side of the lake and saw those waves.

I stood to take the sugar cookies out of the oven, and as I returned to the table with a plate of cookies and the coffee pot, Sam held up a finger and cocked his head. "Listen," he said.

I stopped with the coffee pot in midair, listening. "What?" I whispered.

He pointed out the window. "No wind."

I stared where his finger pointed, amazed to see that the whitecaps had turned to lapping froth. "Are you kidding me?"

Sam grinned and stood, then pointed to the clock. It read *2:33*. "Better put mine in a Thermos. I'm off to get Derik's buddy!" He quickly pulled on his coat and boots, and as I handed him a full Thermos of coffee, he scooped up a handful of cookies, shoving one into his mouth. "Better make another batch," he said, talking with his mouth full.

"I can take a hint," I said, and for the first time in days, I smiled.

While Sam was gone, I quickly straightened the house. I could hardly believe that, after weeks of being storm-stranded, a mere half-hour before pick-up time, Skilak laid herself down and rested, giving Sam a free pass to pick up Derik's friend. I bustled about, whipping up another batch of cookie dough, lighting the propane lanterns in the kitchen and living room (the overcast skies made our cabin a little dark, which was something I hadn't cared to correct until now), and I added more logs to the fire.

I'd just put the pan of cookies into the oven when I heard Sam's boat motor. I stood by the window, watching Sam and the other man get out of the boat, and—oddly enough—Sam carried the man's luggage toward the house. Since when had he become a concierge, I wondered. I noticed something else; the wind had picked up again and the lake was getting rougher.

When the two entered the cabin, I stood from the table to greet them, and the tall, thin man pulled off his wool hat. Imagine my surprise when out tumbled a headful of bleached-blonde curls! *He* was a *she!*

Sam grinned at what must have been my bulging eyes and gaping mouth. "Bonnie, meet Kat, Derik's friend. Kat, this is my wife, Bonnie." Sam's brow raised a notch. "I think Kat was meant to come here." He jerked a thumb toward the lake. "Can you believe it? Waves are kicking up again."

I thought of my prayer to God asking him to send me a woman for Christmas. *Oh, yes, I could believe it.*

"W-w-welcome!" I offered to take her coat, and I hung it on the peg by the door. "You must be freezing," I said, noticing that her clothes weren't nearly heavy enough for Alaskan weather. "Have a seat. We'll have you warmed up soon enough." I motioned toward the kitchen table. "I'll pour a cup of coffee for you."

When I passed Sam on the way to the kitchen, he shrugged. Who knew Derik's buddy was a female?

After Sam joined us at the table, Kat told us her story as we gobbled up two whole platters of warm sugar cookies. She'd driven all the way from Vegas, where she'd been a card dealer, stopping only to fuel up on the journey.

"I took all the cash I had, which didn't amount to much, and I jumped in my old Cadillac and headed north."

My eyes followed her long, red-tipped fingernails that tipped ring-laden fingers as they reached for another sugar cookie. I realized she must not have eaten much, if at all, on her journey.

"I met Derik at a restaurant in Cooper Landing," she said between bites.

"Ah," I said. "Gwin's Restaurant and Lodge. Have you known Derik long?"

"Nope. Just met him." She smiled and dipped her head. "I was down to my last quarter and couldn't even pay for my coffee. Didn't know where to go or what to do at that point. I was almost out of gas, too. Derik walked in and sat down beside me. He asked how I was, and that was probably just a friendly gesture, but I hadn't talked to anyone in days, so I unloaded on him.

"We talked a long time. When he learned what dire straits I was in, he offered to let me stay in his cabin here on Caribou. Said I'm welcome to stay in it as long as I want." She shrugged. "I got no other place to go, so I took him up on his offer. Here I am."

I smiled and shook my head, amazed. I mean, what are the chances that a pretty woman from Las Vegas would end up in the Alaskan wilderness? Especially during a storm, in *December!* This, I thought, is the stuff books are made of!

As she talked, I took in her clothes—thin blouse, thin jeans, boots with a slight heel, and those pretty nails—nothing that would keep her warm or be useful on the island. And then I thought of her in Derik's cabin.

I couldn't imagine what Derik must have been thinking when he saw her at Gwin's and offered her refuge in his cabin—his *shack*. He'd refused to replace the stovepipe, meaning it would be nearly impossible to keep a fire going, and to my knowledge, he still hadn't patched the cracks between the boards. This poor, forty-something, orphaned woman would freeze!

I offered to let her stay the night in our cabin, but she insisted that she wanted to "settle in" to her new, if temporary, home.

Sam shrugged, and he carried her luggage out to load it onto Mojo's trailer. "I'll unload her things, and then I'll be back to eat," he said.

While he was gone, I tried to think of what I could make for supper. It was obvious by the way she devoured those cookies that she hadn't eaten well in quite some time. *She needs me.* The words popped into my head, and they wouldn't leave.

I decided to pull out all the stops for Kat. *She needs me.* I took down some home-canned chicken and decided to make a huge pot of chicken and dumplings—real comfort food to welcome her to Caribou. I pulled out jars of blueberry and cranberry jam, and I made plenty of dough for extra biscuits. *She needs me.*

When Sam returned, he sniffed deeply. "I don't know what you're cooking," he said, "but it smells amazing!"

I rolled out the red carpet for Kat—as best as I could in a wilderness cabin—and made sure her plate never emptied. She ate more than I'd have ever imagined a thin woman could. By the time she'd filled her belly, her eyelids were growing heavy. Soon she yawned deeply.

"I'm so sorry!" she said. "Please don't think me rude. Your company is wonderful and welcoming. I'm just . . . I'm exhausted."

I prepared her a Thermos of hot chocolate to warm her once she'd settled in Derik's cabin, and she and Sam were off.

When Sam returned, he came in shaking his head. "I don't think Derik's cabin was quite what she was expecting. She looked disappointed."

"Who can blame her? Sam, I'm afraid she'll freeze."

"Ah, she'll be okay. I got a fire started. Don't know how long it'll last with that rotten stovepipe, but she should be okay overnight."

All night, the wind gusted and whistled. All night, I worried about Kat. *She needs me.*

First thing the next morning, I shoved Sam out of the bed. "You have to go get Kat. I'm really worried that she had a rough night in that cabin. She's probably cold, and—heck—she might not even know how to keep a fire burning! She doesn't have any food, and Sam, you can see the daylight between the boards, and—"

"Whoa!" Sam held up his hands. "Don't worry! I'll go get her!" He pulled on his quilted flannel shirt. "I wasn't planning to leave her down there."

And it was a good thing he didn't. Kat had spent an absolutely miserable night in the cabin. When he arrived, she was trying to start a fire, unsuccessfully. Her hands were trembling from the cold. Sam said she'd hung blankets on the walls to block the wind. She was thrilled he'd come to rescue her.

As she warmed by the woodstove in our cabin, I pulled Sam aside. "We have to get her out of there! Can we put her up in the guest cabin we built? It's solid. She'll at least be warm and comfy there. What do you think, Sam? She won't make it long at Derik's cabin."

"Of course she can. After breakfast, I'll carry some wood up there, and you can take her up to check it out and see what she needs."

Over the course of the day, Kat and I spruced up her little cabin. I gave her some curtains, some kitchen utensils, a coffee pot, and coffee. It was as if we two grown women were playing house, and we had a great time making the snug little cabin look homey and cozy. I considered my prayer—my rant—to God some days earlier, and I had to turn away and swipe away the puddles in my eyes. Yes, Kat needed me, but perhaps I needed her more.

Sam came in through the door with another armload of wood, bringing me out of my reverie. "You two are making this hunting cabin look all girly," he playfully scolded. He changed his tune, however, deciding that "girly" might be all right when Kat served him coffee. She'd added cinnamon to the coffee pot, and we all took a break and sipped the steaming brew around the woodstove.

I appraised our work as we rested. "You know what this cabin needs?"

Sam's eyebrows rose. "What? Ruffles?"

I ignored his silly jab. "It needs a Christmas tree. In fact, both of our cabins need Christmas trees." I turned to my husband, and for the first time when I'd brought up a Christmas tree, he smiled.

"Christmas trees," he said. He reached out and squeezed my knee. "I think that's a fine idea."

As Kat and I made popcorn strings, paper chains, and my now-signature aluminum-foil-wrapped Christmas ornaments, a few times I had to turn my head to blink away tears. I thanked God for bringing this woman into my life when I most needed a female friend. I considered Kat my Heavenly Father's direct answer to my prayers.

When Kat, Sam, and I sat down together for Christmas morning breakfast, I couldn't hide the tears that puddled in my eyes when Kat reached for both Sam's and my hands.

"Thank you, Bonnie, Sam," she said, looking at each of us in turn. "I couldn't ask for a better Christmas. You two were an answer to my prayer."

I swallowed against the tightness in my throat. "And you, Kat, are an answer to mine."

Kat stayed with us for a full month, when one day in early January—during a lull between storms—the three of us were thrilled to get back to the mainland. For Sam and me, it was just a visit—time to send and receive mail, and stock up on some supplies, but for Kat, it was goodbye. I knew I would greatly miss her—when she arrived, she needed me, and as I was battling depression of my own, I needed her to need me—but she and I were now in better places emotionally, and she was ready to get a fresh start and begin putting her life back together.

CHAPTER THIRTY-EIGHT

The Bonnie Lass

The remaining winter turned out to be as strange as we probably should've expected. We had freezing temps and the lake would start to freeze. Then the wind would start with milder temperatures, and the ice would break up. This was a *constant*—ice would start to form and wind would break it up...ice would start to form and wind would break it up, and it made trapping that winter virtually impossible. The lake didn't freeze completely over until the beginning of March, and even then it was never really safe to travel with the Jeep.

But, finally, the warmer months arrived, and with them, a beehive of activity. After being cooped up during the long, dark winter, Alaskans work hard and play hard during the long summer days, trying to accomplish everything needed to endure the next winter ahead.

With each passing year, we welcomed more and more visitors to the island—it seems our home had become the gateway to the great outdoors—a magnet for adventure seekers, hunters, and, of course, our dear friends—or maybe it was Sam's charismatic personality and my great coffee that attracted them. Whatever the reason, it did not matter—especially after the extended period of isolation during the long winter months—we always welcomed them with open arms.

With more visitors came more ferrying—not to mention some of the "weekend warriors" depending on Sam to ferry them across the lake—for them it was the convenience of being able to leave their boats at home and still get a ride to the island, or they could leave them on the island and not have to haul them home. Also, Sam knew the lake and how to navigate it in rough weather, and folks felt safer with him in the pilot seat—*I know I certainly did!* With this ever-growing responsibility, Sam often complained that he needed a bigger and better boat. Who knew that an opportunity would present itself one day in early May.

Sam was working on our dock when he heard the loud hum of a boat motor, and looked up to see a boat fast approaching. The pilot—a middle aged man and the only occupant in the boat, slowed down as he neared the dock.

"Hello there!" The friendly man waved.

"Good morning!" Sam reached out and grabbed the bow of the boat to steady it, then tied it to the dock. "What brings you out to Skilak?" It wasn't the man as much as the boat that got Sam's attention. It was welded together with heavy gauge aluminum—not your typical assembly line production—custom built by someone who knew what they were doing.

"Out for a test drive in my new boat. I was going by when I noticed you on the beach and thought I'd pull in and say hi." The man extended his hand toward Sam. "The name's Jim."

Sam introduced himself and the two men shook hands.

"That's a well-built boat you've got there, Jim! I need a boat like that for Skilak Lake. If you don't mind my asking, where did you get it?"

Jim fondly patted the side of his boat. "A friend of mine, Darrel Aleckson—owner of Aleckson Fabrication—built it for me."

"Do you think he'd build one for me?" Sam's eyes roved the entire length of the boat before settling on Jim.

"I'm sure he would . . . for the right price. He works out of his garage in Soldotna—tell him Jim sent you."

"I'll definitely do that. Thanks!"

Sam got right on it. During our next trip to town, he paid Darrel a visit, and after introductions, the two men discussed Sam's boat specifications. Sam wanted another bow-picker—only the cabin on the new boat would be *welded* together instead of *pop-riveted* like our current boat. But best of all, it would be welded together with a much thicker gauge aluminum. The new boat would be bigger, stouter and more sea-worthy; the sidewalls and floor were going to be double-walled with air-tight chambers—a boat that could stay afloat no matter what kind of stormy brew Skilak threw at her.

Darrel agreed to build the boat, and as luck would have it, he was free to get started on it right away. Two months later we would launch *The Bonnie Lass*, in Skilak Lake—our fifth boat since moving to Caribou Island. Each boat was always an improvement from the last, but *The Bonnie Lass* would prove to be the boat of all boats—the best we'd ever own, and the perfect boat for Skilak Lake.

*Sam is happy with our newest lake boat, a custom-built bowpicker that
can handle whatever Skilak throws at her.*

*We love our new lake boat with the huge roomy cabin and a deck built
for hauling just about anything anybody needs hauled across the lake.*

You name it, and our new boat The Bonnie Lass *could haul it!*

Of all the visitors Sam and I had over the summer, none were more welcome than my father and his neighbor and dear friend, Connie. They arrived in mid-July, ready to do some serious fishing.

Connie took well to Skilak and Caribou, and after seeing the sadness in my father's eyes and hearing the heaviness in his voice in our phone calls since my mother had passed, it was nice to again see him smiling and happy. I'd known Connie for as long as I could remember, as she lived only two houses down from my parents. She'd been widowed for several years, and she'd become a wonderful, understanding companion for my father. I had always liked her, but as I watched her caring emotionally for my father during their visit—the way she'd tenderly touch his hand or his elbow, or lower her eyes in deference as he spoke of Mom, or even speak fondly of my mother, herself—I came to love her.

During their visit, we often grilled the fresh salmon we'd caught, and Connie enjoyed her nightly saunas. She'd come out of the sauna, her hair swirled atop her head, her body steaming, and she'd fling her arms skyward. "This place is heaven on earth!"

Dad, of course, wanted to spend most of his time on the water. We often took the boat down to the outlet of Skilak Lake, where it empties into the Kenai River. One day, as we were returning to the island, something flashed on the surface of the glittering lake.

"What's that?" Connie and I said in unison.

Sam pulled the boat closer and closer as the metallic object bobbed on the lake. "It's a beer can!" We guessed it must have fallen from a fisherman's cooler somewhere on the upper Kenai River above the lake and drifted down.

Sam cut the motor and drifted up to the beer can, reached down and scooped it up. "It's full, too. And ice cold!" He popped the top, tilted back the can, and emptied its entire contents into his mouth, downing the whole thing. He wiped his mouth on his sleeve. "Ahhhhhh!"

My dad roared with laughter, and soon we were all giggling. Dad laughed until tears streamed from his eyes. "Leave it to Sam to find the only can of ice cold beer ever to have sailed Skilak Lake." He chuckled. "Special delivery for Mr. Ward!"

After another week of fishing and fun, it was time for Dad and Connie to leave. Sam and I took them into Soldotna, where the four of us stayed at a hotel the night before their flight back to Minnesota. It seemed a luxury, at first, to stay in a nice hotel with tiny soaps and little bottles of shampoo, and we enjoyed hamburgers and fries together at the restaurant/bar that butted up against our room. The luxury—at least for me—didn't last long. The bar grew rowdier as the night grew darker, and I didn't sleep a minute that entire night. The sounds of Skilak soothed me to sleep, but the sounds of so-called civilization kept me awake.

One early evening in late summer, I stood at the stove stir-frying moose teriyaki while a pot of rice simmered on the back burner. At the sound of a boat motor, I looked out the kitchen window expecting to see Sam returning from taking Warner and his oldest son, Josh, back across the lake. They had spent the day visiting with us. But it wasn't Sam's boat—I didn't recognize the inflatable boat pulling into our beach.

I turned off the flame under my frying pan and headed outside just as a young couple stepped out of their boat and onto the shore. A tall, slender woman with waist length black hair waved as the man pulled the boat completely out of the water and higher up the beach.

"Hello!" I waved as they approached the cabin.

The man, who stood a few inches shorter than the woman, raised his hand. "Hello, is this Sam Ward's place?"

"Yes, it is—I'm his wife, Bonnie."

The man had curly strawberry blond hair and a grin that made his eyes sparkle. "I'm Perch, and this is my girlfriend, Sally." I had to look up at Sally, because she stood about six inches taller than me. Sally and I exchanged smiles.

"I worked with Sam up on the slope," Perch said. "And he told me if I ever made it out to Skilak Lake, to look him up." He swept out both arms. "Well, here I am." He looked at Sally and back to me. "I mean, here *we* are. Hope we aren't intruding—"

"Of course not. Please, come in." I waved them inside. "Sam will be back in a short while." I headed to the stove. "Can I get you some coffee?"

"Sounds great!" Sally sniffed the air. "What smells so good?"

"Moose teriyaki!" I set two mugs of hot coffee on the table. "Please, have a seat. Are you hungry?"

"Yes." Sally slid into one of the kitchen chairs. "Starving!"

I chuckled inwardly at her boldness and honesty. Sally wasn't one bit shy. I liked her already!

"We've actually been camping on the lake for the last two days." Perch took a sip of coffee and set his mug on the table. "Heading back to Fairbanks tomorrow."

"You're a long way from home." I got up from the table and stirred the rice to fluff it up. "You're welcome to stay in our guest cabin tonight, if you'd like."

"Ohhh," Sally slumped like a deflated balloon melting down into the chair with her head thrown back. "That would be heavenly." This time, I couldn't suppress a chuckle. I think Sally had about all the camping she could handle right now.

Even Perch had to chuckle at Sally's dramatics. "Honestly, Sally, it hasn't been that bad."

Sally gawked at Perch, her mouth gaped open and eyes unblinking. After a long pause, her mouth started working again. "Re-e-a-l-l-y?" She sat straight up in her chair and ticked off on her fingers. "One, I'm hungry. Two, I'm cold. Three, I'm filthy." As if suddenly struck with an idea, she looked at me, her eyes opened wide. "Do you have a sauna?" At my nod, she smiled—*big*, then turned back to Perch. "Four, I have a gazillion mosquito bites, and—"

Perch raised his hands in defeat. "Okay, okay, point taken—the lady doesn't like camping!"

Just then I heard Sam's boat motor and jumped up from the table. "Sam's here!"

Sam hurried in and joined what was quickly turning into a party. We ate and Sally helped me clean the kitchen. Then we settled in to enjoy having company.

"Hey, Bonnie," Perch said. "Did Sam ever tell you about the day he pranked his ol' boss Mike up on the slope?"

Sam pulling a joke on his boss was news to me. "No! Tell me about it." I turned to look at Sam, who grinned sheepishly and ducked his head, suddenly interested in examining his hands.

"It was real funny." Perch chuckled. "It was the prank of all pranks." He leaned forward and jerked a thumb toward Sally and me. "C'mon, Sam, tell these girls what you did to your boss."

"Yes, c'mon, Sam," I pleaded. "We want to hear it—I—." I turned to Sally for affirmation, and she nodded vigorously, then I turned back to Sam. "*We* insist."

"Well." Sam sighed. "Since you ladies insist." He set down his mug and looked thoughtfully toward the ceiling. "It was a dark and stormy night—"

Perch coughed out a laugh.

"Oh, wait," Sam said. "Wrong story." He pushed back his chair a few inches, leaned forward, and propped an elbow on his knee. "Back then—" He looked over at Sally. "I had a full-length beard, and my hair and mustache were long, too—"

"Ladies," Perch interrupted. "He was rough looking—I don't mind telling you."

"Hey," Sam objected. "What do you expect from a guy straight out of the wilderness? *Anyway*, I guess I was in my third week of work," he continued, "and I started rooming with ol' Davie, my mining foreman. Well, we're sitting around one night, and Davie decides to cut his hair. Now he has never cut his own hair before, and I'd bet my last dollar that he'll never cut it again, either." Sam chuckled at the memory. "Davie does a butcher-shop job of his hair and decides it's too ugly to be seen in public, so he asks me to shave it for him."

"Sam must have done a bang-up job," Perch said, "because Davie preened."

"Afterwards," Sam continued, "Davie turns to me and says, 'Why'n tarnation don't you cut that ugly mop offa your head while you're at it?'"

"'Okay, why not?' I told him, and he starts whacking on me with the scissors. He don't stop at my head, though. He whacks my beard and mustache, too."

"Both of them boys looked like they'd gotten tangled up with a weed-eater." Perch laughed.

"That next morning," Sam continued, "I climb into the truck with the straw boss, just as I've always done. Well, ol' straw boss turns to me and yells, 'Who the hell are you? Get outta my truck! This truck is for me and Sam Ward only!'

"I looked at him and said, 'Hey, it's me! Sam!'

"Well the two of us have a big ol' laugh, and the straw boss gets a big idea. 'Looky here, Sam. Let's pull a good one on ol' Mike when we get to camp. When they're all lined up in the hallway, bullshitting like they do, I'll tell him we're expecting a new tie-in boss today. Then you come in, and I'll make like you're him!'"

I make my eyes big toward Sam, surprised that he'd trick his boss by pretending to be a boss, especially after only a few weeks on a new job.

"'Sure,' I tell him, 'it'll be fun!' Well, that ol' straw boss gives me one of the half-dozen fitter hats he keeps piled up in the truck and tells me, 'Here, put this on.'

"So I did, and I pull it down real low over my head just so." Sam mimes a low-slung hat over his eyes.

"We get to the camp, and the straw boss walks into the hall first and has everyone believing the new tie-in boss is on his way in. They're all standing real upright and stuff, ready to make a good impression. I walk in, and the straw boss waves me over to where our boss, Mike, is standing with his men—Mike had several other bosses who worked under him—and he says, 'Mike, this here's our new tie-in boss.'

"Now what we didn't know at the time, was that the real tie-in boss was supposed to have shown up a day earlier, but he didn't show. So Mike was already mad at him for being a day late."

"Now, Sam is really into character," Perch said. "He's got that fitter hat pulled down so low his ears are sticking out like Dumbo ready to take flight. He looked like one big ol' dork, and he sticks out his hand real rigid-like, offering to shake."

"I grabbed Mike's hand with both of mine," Sam said, mimicking, "and with as much Oklahoma accent I can muster, I said to him, 'Pleased to meet you, Mr. Shrewsbury,' and I start jacking Mike's hand up and down as if it were a pump handle. I wouldn't let go of his hand, just kept on talking. 'I hear you're from Oklahoma, Mr. Shrewsbury,' I say. 'Well, I am, too. We're gonna get along real good, Mr. Shrewsbury.' And I got this big, dumb grin on my face, and he's trying to extricate his hand from this crazy, big-eared goofball, and I just keep on pumping my hand up and down." Sam demonstrated for our entertainment.

I started laughing, and then Sally hooted out a laugh so loud that I thought coffee might come out her nose—and that made me laugh even harder.

"Mike finally recognized me," Sam continued. "He jerked his hand loose and pointed at me, and said, 'Damn your hide, boy! Your eyes gave you away. I was about ready to smack that goofy grin off your face and send you packing back to Oklahoma, and then I recognized your eyes.'"

All of us erupted in laughter as Sally and I wiped tears from our eyes.

"All of us guys gave Mike a hard time after that," Perch chuckled. "All because of this one right here." He pointed at Sam. "Men were trying to shake his hand, men pulling down their fitter hats when Mike would walk by, making their ears stick out." Perch laughed at the memory.

"Yep," Sam said, still chuckling. "I had him going there for a while."

Perch shook his head, then picked up his coffee mug and winked at Sam before draining the cup.

I was still laughing when I reached for Perch's cup to get him a refill.

"Hey!" Perch said when I took his cup from his hand. "Officer, I'd like to report a mugging!"

Sam grimaced and palmed his face. "Worst joke ever."

"Oh, he's got more," Sally warned.

"Hey, Bonnie," Perch said, ignoring his girlfriend. "Why are men like coffee?"

I took a deep breath before answering, because by now I didn't know what might come out of Perch's mouth when he told a joke. "I don't know, Perch. Why are men like coffee?"

"Because the best ones are rich, hot, and can keep you up all night."

And that's how the rest of our evening went—listening to more of Perch's jokes—punctuated by Sally's entertaining and colorful banter—and then we took turns in the sauna and turned in for the night.

The next morning, as I prepared breakfast and the coffee perked, Sally readied the coffee mugs. She leaned toward me and whispered, almost conspiratorially, "I could do this all my life."

"Huh?" I said.

A genuine smile lit her brown eyes. "Sit around that stove in your cozy little cabin, telling stories with you and Sam and Perch." She tucked a strand of her long hair behind an ear. "Do you know how lucky you are? You and Sam live in a wilderness paradise."

I returned her smile and nodded. Indeed, I knew we were blessed, but it surprised me to hear such honest, heartfelt words come out of Sally's flamboyant mouth—Sally who doesn't like camping. "Thank you," I finally managed.

CHAPTER THIRTY-NINE

Close Calls

Our fun-filled summer vanished all too quickly, leaving nothing but memories in its wake, as the winds of autumn—in all her magnificence, breathed color into the landscape and ushered in—*hunting season!*

Loni was the first of Sam's hunting buddies to show up. He flew in and landed on the lake in front of our cabin, and, on the promise of delivering Sam to some of the best hunting grounds in the state, he whisked my Sam away within the hour.

I had forewarned him he might regret it.

"Sam," I hissed, trying to keep my voice low while Loni sat downstairs drinking a cup of coffee. "Do I have to remind you what happened the last time you went bear hunting with Loni?" Loni had prematurely shot the bolt action rifle he'd borrowed from Sam, damaging Sam's ear enough to cause him severe pain and bleeding. Sam had lost a significant amount of hearing in that ear.

"Aw, Bonnie." Sam grabbed a pair of wool long-johns and a couple extra pair of wool socks out of the dresser and shoved them into his backpack. "You don't need to worry."

Humph! Easy for you to say!

"Besides—" He stopped packing long enough to look at me. "How often do I get an opportunity like this?" He scanned the bedroom to see if he'd missed anything.

In spite of my worry, I couldn't help but smile at his almost child-like enthusiasm. He was right about the opportunity to go where the men were headed. They were going to follow the coastline down to Homer, head across Cook Inlet, and then on to King Salmon, which is located on the northern Alaska Peninsula—and roughly two-hundred-fifty miles from Skilak Lake, as the crow flies. Sam's opportunity to travel to the Alaska Peninsula depended entirely on the generosity of his pilot friends, as you cannot drive there. So I understood his desire to jump at this chance for a trip across the inlet.

"I think I got everything." Sam looked around the room one last time, then turned to me and smiled. "I love you, Bonnie." He wrapped his arms around me and squeezed, lifting me off my feet, then set me back down and kissed me. "You take care of you." He tapped me on the nose. "For me, ya hear?" He winked. "And don't worry about me, I'll be okay!"

"You better be, mister!" I poked him in the chest.

Loni must have finished his coffee and left, because just then we heard his plane engine turn over.

"That's my cue to leave." Sam hefted the pack over his shoulder, paused to smile at me, then headed down the stairs, grabbing his Holland and Holland .375 Sako on the way out the door.

I poured a cup of coffee and sat at the kitchen table and watched as Loni's floats lifted off the water—then the little plane banked and headed southeast. I held my mug in both hands as though I needed something to hang on to. My eyes followed the little plane until it flew out of my line of vision. *He's in your hands, dear Lord,* I prayed. *Bring your son home to me, safe and sound.*

I tried not to worry, but I couldn't help it. The last time Sam flew across the inlet, it was with a couple friends from Kenai, and they'd had a near-death experience. The men had flown all the way to King Salmon, where they stopped to refuel. Afterward, they took off and were heading to the pilot friend's favorite hunting ground to look for caribou. About twenty minutes into the flight, the engine started sputtering, and to the men's horror, it quit. Shocked, the pilot announced his fuel gauge registered on empty. To his credit, the pilot remained calm and tilted the plane in an attempt to gravity feed any remaining fuel to the engine. To the men's relief, the engine started again. But a moment later, it died a second time. The pilot turned to the men, his eye's wide with fear, and told them to start praying—*and all three did!* The plane was loaded down with hunting gear, three men, and floats, so it was heavy and losing altitude in a hurry.

Sam told me later, "We openly prayed as we watched the cottonwood trees beneath us growing bigger by the second. We were only a few feet away from crashing into them when the pilot got the engine started again—just in the nick of time. He pulled back on the stick and we climbed in altitude and then he turned the plane back toward King Salmon. Unfortunately, the engine quit again, but we were close enough to the airport that the pilot was able to glide the plane in on a dead stick!"

To say they were relieved would be an understatement. All three men knew they had survived what could have been a tragic and possibly fatal crash. All three gave thanks to God for delivering them out of the sky safe and sound.

Come to find out, when the pilot had refueled his plane earlier, he'd neglected to put the gas cap back on the tank, and when they took off in flight, the gas spewed out of the tank like an aerosol spray can. It didn't take long to empty the tank.

Three days later, I was packing firewood into the house when I heard the drone of an airplane overhead.

They're back!

I dropped my armload of wood and brushed pieces of bark and wood chips off my jacket and ran down to the beach just as Loni's plane landed and taxied into shore. I waved as Sam stepped out.

He threw his hand up and smiled, then reached back inside to get his backpack, which he tossed onto the shore. He reached in again and pulled out his gun, said something to Loni—that I couldn't hear from shore—shut the door and tapped on it a couple times.

I ran into Sam's arms, almost knocking him down as he stepped off the floats and waded through the water to shore.

"Oh, it's so good to see you." I beamed. "How was your trip?"

Sam rolled his eyes, but before he could answer, Loni backed the plane out into deeper water, and Sam and I watched as he turned the little plane and revved the engine into a full throttle take off. We threw our arms up and waved goodbye. Once he took flight, Sam shouldered his gun and picked up his pack, and arm-in-arm, we walked to the cabin.

"To answer your question," Sam said and shook his head, "From the day we left, we had nothing but trouble—never did get to do any hunting."

I had noticed that he didn't return with any game, but didn't say anything. "Oh, no! What happened?"

"I'll tell you about it in a little bit." Sam let out a long breath as we entered the cabin. He dropped his pack to the floor and set his gun in the corner. "Sure is good to be home." He sighed. "But right now, I'm plum tuckered!"

"Awww, I'll bet you're hungry too, aren't you?"

"I'm starving. Haven't had anything to eat since yesterday afternoon." Sam grinned. "Got anything good to eat for an ol' bear like me?"

"You betcha." I chuckled. "How about some creamed bear for the ol' bear?"

A short while later, as I cleared away the supper dishes from the table, Sam lit a Camel and eased back in his chair. "That sure hit the spot, Bonnie!" He grinned. "Haven't had creamed bear that good since the last time you made it."

"You're silly!" I laughed and waved his comment away as I sat down at the table. "Okay." I crossed my arms and stared hard at my husband. "So what happened?"

Sam leaned forward and rested his elbows on the table. "Everything was going fine, but then about half-way across Cook Inlet, the engine quit in Loni's plane—"

"What! Again?" I gasped. "Oh, my God!"

"Loni says, 'Oh, shit! My magneto quit working!' He turned a switch on his control panel—said it was to the other magneto, and a few seconds later the engine started again."

"My, God!" I stared at Sam in horror. "That's the second time you've flown with somebody that the engine quit mid-flight!" I reached out and placed my hand over his, this man that I love more than life itself, and silently prayed, *Thank you, Jesus, for bringing him home safe and sound.*

"Fortunately," Sam continued, "we didn't have any more engine problems after that. We made it to King Salmon, and after landing at the airport, Loni taxied the plane to a hangar, where we found a mechanic."

"To fix his magneto?" I asked, as I refilled our coffee cups.

"Yeah. But the bad news—" Sam took a swig of coffee then set his cup down. "The mechanic told us he couldn't get the part until tomorrow." He shook his head. "Which meant we were stuck there till then—"

"What'd you do?" I placed a plate of raisin tarts on the table.

"Nothing we *could* do—but wait!" Sam picked up a raisin tart. "To kill time, we decided to walk around town—not much of a town really, just a few hundred residents, if that, a few businesses and the airstrip." Sam shoved half the tart in his mouth and chewed, then swallowed it down with a swill of his coffee.

"Sounds rather boring." My tea kettle whistled and I jumped up to retrieve it from the stove.

Sam nodded, his eyes following me.

"Oh—" He raised his brows, as though struck with an afterthought. "There's a road that connects King Salmon to the little town of Naknek, which sits, oh, about fifteen miles down the Naknek River from King Salmon. So, we got the bright idea that we'd walk there to kill time." Sam chuckled at the memory. "Anyway, we must have walked about five miles or so and found a little burger joint. We were starved by that time, so we bought ourselves a hamburger, scarfed it down and then walked back to the hangar."

I poured steaming hot water from my kettle into the washbasin and turned to Sam as I placed the kettle back on the stove. "That's ten miles you guys walked! You must have been worn out."

Sam nodded as he finished eating his tart. "You know what was really sad though?" His face was suddenly somber. "On our walk, we passed several local natives passed out in the ditches alongside the road. Beer and wine bottles littered the area." Sam waved his hand. "This is in the middle of nowhere—in the middle of brown bear country—not to mention the wolves." Sam shook his head. "They were so vulnerable lying there in the ditch." Sam took his time sweeping a crumb off the table with his thumb, and without looking up, he added, "I wonder how many have died there?"

It was a sad thought indeed. I resumed washing the plate in my hand.

Sam jerked his head up, took a deep breath, and continued. "So we get back to the hangar. It's almost dark, and Loni notices something is wrong with his plane—"

"What?" I dipped the plate in the pan that held the rinse water, swirled it a couple times, and then set it in the dish drainer.

"The elevator—"

I scrunched my face. "Huh?"

Sam laughed. "That's what I said when Loni told me. Anyway, it's the flap on the tail that controls the plane's pitch. So, it was another thing we had to get fixed before we could fly anywhere. If it wasn't one thing," Sam huffed, "it was another during this whole trip." He grabbed another tart and held it up. "These are delicious!"

"Thanks!" I smiled.

323

"Anyway," Sam continued, "come to find out, we learned from the mechanic the next morning, that while we were on our walk, the blast from a jet of one of the airlines that flies in and out of King Salmon caused the damage."

"How could it do that?" I was finished washing our dinner plates and now turned and leaned against the counter, drying my hands on a dishtowel.

"When the jet taxied around to take off, Loni's plane was parked in the line of fire of the jet's engine—the blast was enough to break the elevator."

"Goodness! So, where'd you guys sleep?"

"We pitched the tent on the tarmac near the hangar. Believe it or not, that would be a good night's sleep compared to the next night. Anyway, I'm getting ahead of myself. We waited around most of the following morning for the mechanic to replace the magneto and fix the elevator, and finally flew out of there shortly after noon. Loni flew us to this really nice lodge—said the hunting should be good there." Sam's eye's opened wide. "He wasn't kidding!"

"What do you mean?" I joined Sam at the table and picked up a tart.

"We ended up pitching a tent a short distance from the lodge, under the wing of Loni's plane—and if you didn't already know that you were in the thick of bear country, all you had to do is look at the front door of that lodge—it was built out of thick solid boards and there wasn't a spot on that door that didn't have a nail spike sticking out of it—enough to put a porcupine to shame—"

"Wow!" I shook my head in disbelief. "There must be a *lot* of bears there!"

"Oh, yeah!" Sam said. "They wanted to make sure no bear could knock down the door."

When I thought of the safety of the lodge with its bear-proof door compared to the pup tent with thin nylon walls where Sam and Loni would sleep, a shudder ran through me that had nothing to do with the cold.

"Anyway," Sam continued, "by the time we finished putting up the tent and rolling out our sleeping bags, it was dark and the weather turned real nasty. Cold wind and rain pelted the tent all night. I was so exhausted, I didn't care. I went right to sleep, but I woke at intervals throughout the night, and every time I did, I saw Loni sitting at the tent opening puffing nervously on one cigarette after another and watching for bears.

"The next morning when I got up, I didn't see my rifle lying next to me where I'd left it the night before. I asked Loni—who was looking pretty haggard by now—where it was, and he tells me that he had to leave the tent during the night to relieve himself and he took my rifle for protection in case he ran into a bear. After he told me this, I went outside to look for it. I found it all right, and I was mad as hell. It was lying in the mud—the barrel was full of mud and water! That's when Loni suddenly remembered he had leant it against the plane the night before." Sam rolled his eyes and shook his head.

"Needless to say, our hunting trip was over! We were both ready to pack it in. We gathered our gear and headed home." Sam looked at me. "I couldn't get home soon enough to suit me—but unfortunately, Mother Nature wasn't so obliging. Loni flew us home by way of Lake Clark Pass, and all was good until we cleared the mountains and started over Cook Inlet. Then—" Sam shook his head, and let out a gust of air. "That wind raging down Cook Inlet lambasted us so hard the plane shook like a rag doll. All we could do was hang on tight, and the whole time I was wondering if I needed to kiss my ass goodbye!"

"Oh, Sam!" I clasped my hands to my chest. "How frightening!"

"All of Cook Inlet Ocean, as far as we could see, was a churning, frothing violent mess. We even saw water funnels." Sam's eyes opened wide. "*Big* water funnels—it was that rough. And then I looked out my window and happened to spot a huge ship far below us getting tossed around by massive waves—I could see a dozen or more men scrambling around on the deck. But at the distance between us, they looked no bigger than ants. Then, all of a sudden, all the ant-sized men ran to the sides of the boat and hung on for dear life as a huge wave crashed over the deck. When the water cleared the deck, the men scrambled back to whatever chores they were doing, but they only had seconds before they had to stop again and run to the sides of the ship and hang on as another wave crashed over them. But, as bad as they had it, we didn't have it much better. We were bucking against some strong wind in that little plane, getting jostled about. Gotta hand it to Loni. He had his hands full, and I think he did a great job. We couldn't make any headway, so Loni climbed us to nine-thousand feet, hoping to escape the turbulence." Sam shook his head. "However, it wasn't much better up there. So, Loni turned the plane and headed down Cook Inlet, going with the wind, and that helped a little. We finally reached the Kenai Peninsula side of Cook Inlet, and the going was much easier after that."

Sam shrugged. "And here I am!"

I rose from the table and walked over to my husband and wrapped my arms around him. "And here you are! Thank

God!" I leaned over and kissed the top of my husband's head and just held him tight. "I love you, Mr. Ward!"

"I love you too, Mrs. Ward!"

CHAPTER FORTY

Bully Trapper

The months whizzed by in a blur of activity, and before we knew it, we were in the thick of winter and one of the best trapping seasons we'd ever had on Skilak Lake. Early one morning in February, Sam and I had risen long before daylight, ate a quick breakfast, then bundled up warm and headed to the south shore on our snowmobile. On the mainland, we covered numerous miles on foot checking the traps, as there are no trails wide enough to take the snowmobile through the forest and thick vegetation.

Later that afternoon, as we headed home with our days bounty, it dawned on me that it was Valentine's Day. I wanted to do something special for Sam—*but what?* We sell most of our fur pelts, but I also set aside some to make hats, mittens, and crafts. I had already made Sam a beaver fur hat that he wore on a regular basis. And then it hit me—*I'll make him a mink hat!* We had a surplus of mink pelts, and now that I had a treadle sewing machine, I could make this hat in a day. Satisfied with my decision, I smiled and wrapped my arms around my husband and squeezed him tight, as the cold wind whipped past.

"Bonnie, look!" Sam pointed at something far out on the lake. I squinted against the glare bouncing off the fresh, sparkling snow, but I could only see specks from this distance. Oh, if my mother could see me now, she'd scold me for not wearing my glasses today—*sorry, Mom!*

"What is it?" I yelled above the roar of the snowmobile.

"Wolves!"

"How many?"

"Looks like four or five."

When the lake froze over, we often saw wolves, coyotes, moose and caribou traveling on the lake. The view from our kitchen picture window provided much better entertainment than any television show ever could.

A few minutes later we pulled into our yard, and I hopped off the snowmobile, ready to bound for the cabin and warm up, but Sam had other plans.

"I'm gonna head across the lake and get the battery out of our Jeep. I shouldn't be too long." We'd had our battery stolen a few times in the past, and besides, due to the deep cold, it would start better if we warmed it in our house before using it.

"Okay, but don't you want to have a cup of coffee and warm up first?" I rubbed my upper arms briskly in an attempt to warm up. "Aren't you cold?"

"I'm fine, but I'll take you up on that coffee as soon as I get back." Sam winked, and with a wave, he was off. I stood watching my well-bundled husband point the snowmobile back onto the snow-covered ice and head out. Though we'd usually take Mojo across the lake, at times like this when we had over four inches of snow on the ice, the snowmobile provided more reliable transportation for us. In spite of the below-zero temperatures, the cloudless sky shone a brilliant, deep blue.

A few minutes later, the stove was roaring and the coffee brewing. Sam's plans actually worked in my favor. Though Sam didn't cater much to holidays—they were far too commercialized to hold much sentimentality for him—I decided that, once he headed out across the lake, I'd make a nice Valentine's Day dessert for him. I could surprise him with a cake much sooner than I could surprise him with a mink hat. That would have to come later.

At my kitchen table, I arranged ingredients to make a chocolate cake, while watching Sam grow smaller in the distance. Love filled my heart, perhaps because of the holiday and the romantic task at hand, but more likely because of my genuine admiration for the hard-working man who zipped across the lake, disappearing from sight as he rounded Frying Pan Island for the last two-mile-leg of his journey.

Soon enough, my cake was in the oven, and the decadent scent of chocolate filled the air. I next put together a biscuit-topped moose casserole—one of Sam's favorites—and placed it in the oven with the cake, so it would be hot upon Sam's return. After I'd tidied the kitchen, I made a cup of coffee and sank into my chair by the fire, cutting out the shape of a heart from a sheet of waxed paper.

When the timer went off in the kitchen, I made the chocolate glaze, drizzled it between layers, stacked them, and then poured on more glaze. When the glaze had set, I placed the waxed paper with the cut-out over the top of the cake and dusted it with confectioner's sugar. When I removed the waxed paper, I was quite pleased with the heart on top of the cake, and believing it would also please Sam, I smiled at my creation.

Just as I was setting the table, I saw the speck on the lake in the distance growing larger. Again, my heart filled with gratitude. My Valentine's Day dinner was coming together, and with perfect timing, my husband was on his way home.

Sam's boots stomped on the porch as he stamped off the snow, and he flung open the door to find me standing with two cups of coffee in my hands. "Welcome back!" I said.

And then I saw his face.

Something had happened. "What's wrong?" I asked.

Sam attempted a sideways smile that failed. "Ah, nothing much." He shrugged out of his coat. "Ran into a trapper. Had an . . . altercation."

"An alter—what happened!"

Sam crossed the floor, took the coffee I held for him, and pulled a long swallow. "Ahhh, that's good."

"Sam! What happened?"

He nodded toward the kitchen table, where steam curled from the biscuits sitting atop the moose casserole, and he sheepishly smiled. "Mind if we eat while I tell you?"

Bonnie! I scolded myself. *Whatever it is, your husband has just returned home, cold and hungry, so let him eat!* Though I was anxious to find out what kind of "altercation" Sam had experienced, I sat down at the table opposite him and scooped out a large helping of casserole onto his plate. I struggled to remain patient as Sam shoveled in two or three bites and chewed. He again drank from his coffee mug, and I was nearly ready to explode with a litany of questions when he sat the mug down and spoke.

"See, Tony was at the landing, loading his snowmobile onto his truck when I got there," Sam said.

I let out a soft sigh, relieved to have the story underway. Tony was a young man from Sterling we'd met, and we immediately liked him. He was young and ambitious, and he'd asked Sam many questions about trapping.

"You remember that Tony had asked me awhile back if it was okay with me if he did some trapping at the lower end of Skilak Lake? Of course, I didn't mind . . . I planned to trap farther on up the lake.

"Anyway, today I asked him if he'd had any luck, and he just shook his head. Said, 'I'm done, Sam. It's over for me. I quit.'"

I shook my head. "Why? He was all gung-ho about trapping. Why would he let one unsuccessful trip cause him to quit?"

"That's what I wondered at first, but I could tell something else was wrong. Tony was strung as tight as a guitar string, all nervous-acting." Sam took another big bite of biscuit and chewed slowly, and I knew I had no choice but to wait out hearing the entire saga as Sam ate.

"Tony leans toward me, and even though we're the only two on the landing, he drops his voice to a whisper," Sam said. "He motioned toward the lower end of the lake and said, 'There's another trapper over there. He's been on my trail all morning, and he ain't friendly.'"

I put down my fork. "Did he know who it was?"

Sam's face darkened and he shook his head. "Said the man had sprung and pulled all of Tony's traps—all of 'em!—put 'em in a big pile on the beach, and stomped out a message in the snow." Sam drank the last from his mug and turned toward the coffee pot.

I hopped up to get him a refill, not wanting to slow the story any longer than necessary. "What did the message say?"

"Said, '*My line keep off.*' Tony was torn up about it. He told me that a man like that'll kill a person, and there won't be a soul out here to find the body.'"

"Oh, no! What did you say to him?"

"Nothing to say. Ol' Tony jumped in his truck, said, 'It's good seeing you, Sam, but I'm out of here!' He peeled out of there, flinging snow everywhere. That boy was spooked, I tell you."

"What a shame!" I hated to hear that Tony was going to give up on trapping, but I was relieved that Sam's "altercation" was nothing more than a disappointing encounter with Tony.

But then Sam continued. "So I raised the hood of the Jeep, and I see a figure out on the lake heading my way."

I tensed, realizing the true altercation hadn't yet happened.

"He was far away, coming from the mouth of the river, so I kept working to get the battery out of the Jeep, but I wondered if it might be that trapper."

"Was it?"

"'Fraid so. Man was wearing snowshoes, and I could hear him coming. Snow crunched with every step."

My thoughts raced ahead, and in my mind, I could hear the ominous crunching of snowshoes on snow growing louder. The muscles in my neck grew tight.

"He was a big man. Tall. I'd say an easy six-four, maybe six-five. He never broke his quick stride. I put the battery onto the snowmobile and was just tying it down when he crossed over to me. I raised up to say, 'Howdy,' and he started cussing me out."

"Whaaaat?" Who acted like that?

"Yep. He said, 'What the heck are you doing on my trap line? I left you messages to get the heck off! You hard of hearin', ol' man?' Except he didn't use the word 'heck'."

"No, he didn't!" I said.

Sam's lips mashed into a hard line. "Then he shoved me."

I put down my fork and leaned toward my husband, aghast.

"Caught me off balance as I was turning, and I did a backflip over the snowmobile, landed on the other side."

I gasped.

"He comes around it, calling me every name in the book, ready to pound me into the ground, but as I hopped up, I slid my hand into my Carhartts and pulled out the crescent wrench I'd just used to take out the Jeep battery. That big ol' trapper reached for me with both hands, and before he could take hold, I clobbered him across the side of his forehead with that wrench."

"Oh, Sam!" My hands trembled, and I gripped the edge of the table to steady them.

"That slowed him down," Sam said. "He staggered backward, and blood ran down the side of his face. I heard more snow crunch behind me, and for a second I worried he might have a partner, but I saw that a truck had pulled down to the landing.

"A man jumped out and ran to where the trapper was sitting on the ground, holding his head. The man must have known the trapper—was probably coming to pick him up at a pre-arranged time, which is why the trapper was coming to the landing while I was there.

"Anyway, the man yelled at me. Said, 'What's going on here?' I told him I was just taking the battery out of my Jeep to take home, and this here fellow comes up and shoves me over my snowmobile, accusing me of running his trap line.

"'I ain't running nobody's trap line!'" Sam's face reddened as he spoke. "That trapper's holding a handkerchief to his forehead, and he looks up at me, says, 'Yes, you are! I followed your snowmobile tracks.'

"Well, I pointed to my tracks, which went straight across the lake, and I told them, 'I live on Caribou Island, and that's where my tracks show I came from. That's the opposite direction from where you came from.' I pointed toward my battery. 'Like I told you, I came to get my battery.'"

"You didn't tell them the tracks were Tony's, did you?" I asked.

"Of course not. None of his business whose tracks—or whose traps—those were. He don't own Alaska. Tony can trap wherever he wants to trap."

"What happened next?"

"The guy from the truck helped the trapper up. The trapper, he's still holding the handkerchief to his forehead, but he apologizes. Says, 'I'm sorry. I thought you were the one running my trap line.' He looks at my battery on the snowmobile, and he says, 'But I can see you're not.' Then he holds the handkerchief out for me to see all the blood that's on it, and blood's still trickling down his head.

"I reckon he wanted an apology in return." Sam grimaced. "He didn't get it."

I reached across the table for Sam's hand, and he took mine and squeezed.

"Don't worry, Bonnie. It's all right." He released my hand and picked up his mug. "I don't expect we'll ever see that man again."

And we didn't.

CHAPTER FORTY-ONE

Somersaulting Super Cub

One mid-March morning as I kneaded sprouted-wheat bread dough at my kitchen counter, Sam brought in a load of wood and stacked it by the stove. He straightened, stretched his back, and then stood there for a moment, as if in deep thought.

Just when I opened my mouth to ask if he'd strained his back, he spoke. "Bonnie, I know what I want to do."

I sprinkled more flour over the surface of my countertop and continued to knead the dough before placing it in a large bowl to rise. "What do you mean?"

"I want to start a commercial fishing venture. Probably on Prince William Sound." He nodded slowly, as if agreeing with himself after saying the words aloud the first time. "We might even decide to live on one of the islands out there, possibly on Latouche Island—I hear there's property for sale out there.

"We'll need a good commercial fishing boat, first. I'll ask Darrell to build it. He did such a great job on our bowpicker." Sam stroked his chin. "Probably take him a good while, maybe a year, but I figure we can be ready to move this time next spring."

Move? *Move?* I had a brief flashback of the moment so many years earlier in Ohio, when Sam walked in the door of our newly remodeled home, told me he'd quit his job, and that we were moving to Alaska.

"But . . . but the island. The cabins. This is our home, Sam."

Sam turned to me, his eyes bright with hope. "Don't you think it'd be a great adventure?"

"Well—I guess so." And just like that, my fears melted like snow in the spring. I smiled. "Perhaps it would be a fantastic adventure. I love fishing!"

Sam grinned, but just as quickly, the grin faded, replaced by a look of surprise as the sound of a plane's engine reached us, growing louder by the second.

"Sam!" I said, my heartbeat picking up speed. "Who could that be?" I grabbed a towel to clean my hands as both of us ran toward the front door.

Outside, we stared skyward at the little Piper Super Cub that lowered from the air toward the lake. The airplane had tundra tires, and it was the same bright yellow as our friend Al's plane, but this wasn't Al.

We walked down to the beach just as two men stepped out. It was Kenny, the man who'd bought Winston's cabin, and his son-in-law Jake. Kenny and Jake hadn't been out with their families since last summer. This was a nice surprise!

Kenny reached into the Super Cub and retrieved a box before heading toward us. "Halloooo!" he called.

"Howdy!" Sam said, and I waved and smiled.

"Brought a care package for you," Kenny said as he drew near.

It wasn't uncommon for friends with bush planes to fly out occasionally—especially in the winter months—to air-drop care packages to us when we were stranded on the island, knowing we can't get to the mainland. These packages often included staples like coffee, flour, and sometimes treats like candy.

I hugged Jake and Kenny before retrieving the box from Kenny's arms, and the men shook hands.

Kenny nodded toward the box. "Little something special in there."

I peered into the box. Ice cream!

"Oh, Kenny! Jake! Thank you so much!" I tilted the box toward Sam, and he looked inside.

"Candy bars and ice cream! That's a care package, all right!" Sam beamed like a little boy at Christmas.

We often made snow-cream with freshly fallen snow, sugar, and vanilla, but *real* ice cream—that was quite a treat!

We invited the men in for coffee, and though they insisted they couldn't stay, they stuck around for a few cups each, and we enjoyed a lovely chat with our friends before walking them back down to their plane.

Jake stood at the shore and warily eyed the lake. "I don't quite trust that ice. I believe I'm going to take off on the beach."

Sam looked at me, then Kenny, then Jake. "I—I don't believe I'd do that. The beach is rocky," Sam said, waving his arm toward the shoreline, our small 12-foot aluminum boat, and the dock. "And as you can see, there's not much room between the dock and everything else there on the beach." He rubbed the back of his neck, as he often did when he was concerned. "Besides, the ice along the shoreline is still mighty solid. It'll be safe to taxi onto the ice along the shore."

Jake smiled and clapped a hand on Sam's back. "Ah, there's plenty of room on the beach." He thrust his hand toward Sam, and the two shook, and he headed toward the Super Cub as we said our goodbyes to Kenny.

Sam and I walked partway back to the house, then turned and watched as the little yellow plane's engine revved for a full-throttle takeoff. We raised our arms, waving goodbye to our friends as the Super Cub roared down the beach at full speed. The plane bounced up and down, jostling the men inside as the tundra tires hit the rocks along the beach.

I lowered my arms, and my hands found my cheeks as I watched in growing horror as the plane failed to lift off. "Come on, come on, come on!" I pleaded.

"Get up! Get up!" Sam said.

The tundra tires began to skim the surface of the beach, then finally lifted off, and just when I thought I could breathe, I realized the tires were too low to miss our aluminum boat.

I cringed at the crunching sound as the wheels hit the boat, and the speeding plane and boat both flipped through the air. "Sam! Oh, my God! They crashed!"

The yellow Super Cub somersaulted and landed upside down, it's propeller still turning, beating at the ground, throwing rocks. My heart thudded in my chest, knowing the men had to be gravely injured. "Oh, no!" I screamed, and my weak knees finally grew strong enough for me to move again. I lurched toward the little plane, but Sam reached out and grabbed my hood, yanking me backward as large rocks peppered the ground ahead of us.

"You're going to get yourself killed! Wait here until the engine stops."

I breathed in short, shallow gasps until the engine finally slowed and stopped, and I assumed Jake must have been conscious enough to shut it off. When the propellers finally quit turning, Sam and I hurried to the plane, albeit cautiously, just as the doors slowly creaked open. Amazingly, both men, while hanging upside down, managed to unhook their seatbelts and half-fall, half-slide, out of the airplane. "Oh, thank God!" I said, my voice trembling. I could hardly believe that, after their terrible crash and flip, both men were not only alive, but weren't mortally wounded.

"Are you okay?" I asked Kenny as I neared him.

He gripped the side of the door to steady himself, and he looked at me wild-eyed and nodded. "I'm okay."

I gave him the once-over, and other than a growing, pale-blue lump above his right eye and a somewhat rumpled appearance, he looked fine. Jake was similarly bruised and banged up, but neither man was badly hurt. "Thank God," I muttered again, shaking my head. I could hardly believe their good fortune.

The four of us surveyed the damage to the airplane. The little yellow Super Cub had taken the brunt of the tumble, and it was in much worse shape than its occupants.

"Looks like we're going to be here a while," Jake said, his face still pale from the scare of the crash.

"No worries," Sam said, already turning toward our cabin. "Let me get Mojo and a tow rope, and we'll upright this baby in no time."

I walked around the plane again, taking care not to step on its outstretched wings, hardly giving our crumpled boat a second glance. I felt heartsick for these two men who, out of the kindness of their hearts, came all the way from Anchorage to deliver a care package to Sam and me, and who now were stranded until their airplane was repaired.

True to Sam's word, Jake, Kenny, and he had the plane back on its wheels in under an hour. Sam attached a tow rope to the plane's tail, and while Kenny and Jake lifted and pushed, Mojo dug in his tires and pulled, and the plane flipped back over, tail over nose.

The nose and tail had taken most of the damage, but the propeller tips were also badly bent out of shape from chopping at the rocky ground. There was no way Jake could get his plane airborne again without quite a bit of work.

Sam towed the plane up to the tree line and tied it to a tree, the Super Cub's now-damaged nose pointing out toward the lake. Despite the damage to their plane—which would no doubt be expensive to repair—the men seemed to be in good spirits—likely because they'd survived the high-speed crash. Sam assured Jake that his plane would be kept safe until the ice went out, and they could then haul it across the lake, where they'd have it repaired on the mainland.

In the meantime, Kenny got on the radio and made arrangements with a pilot friend of his in Anchorage to fly in and pick them up. He shot a sheepish glance toward Sam when he gave instructions to the pilot. "Be sure to land on the ice, close to the shore. Stay off the beach."

Kenny followed Sam and I up to the cabin for a cup of coffee and to warm up inside, but poor Jake couldn't leave his sick Piper Super Cub. He walked in circles around it, touching it here and there, examining the wings and assessing the damage, and—no doubt—the cost it would take to repair it.

A few hours later, Kenny and Jake's friend swooped in for a smooth landing, and when they again went airborne with

Kenny and Jake on board, I'm sure we were all equally relieved with their smooth takeoff—on the ice.

The super cub flipped in take off after hitting our 12 foot aluminum boat (in the foreground).

The men tied one end of a rope to the tail of the plane and the other end to the Mojo, so Sam could flip the plane right side up.

Sam flipped the plane back into its upright position with the Mojo.

For the remainder of the long winter, Sam and I didn't leave Caribou Island. We didn't trust the ice, which easily broke into upright shards twelve or more inches long. *Pencil ice*—as we often referred to it—would give under the weight of a person, pulling them down to an icy death in a heartbeat. It didn't matter; we had plenty of work to keep us busy. It seemed we never ran out of projects or chores, and now we had a brand-new dream to focus on. We spent our stranded days (and some nights) making plans for our new adventure at Prince William Sound.

The ice finally went out in early April, and Kenny and Jake returned—via boat this time—along with the Walkers. Sam, Jake, Kenny, and Clark removed the wings from Jake's plane, lashed them down to Sam's boat, and then they hauled them across the water to the mainland. On a second trip across Skilak Lake, Sam hauled the main body of the plane. On the other side, Kenny and Jake transported Jake's Super Cub in pieces to a mechanic to repair the damaged plane.

Again, we'd seen how living in the Alaskan bush required the teamwork and support of friends and neighbors, and as Sam and I made plans for our newest adventure, we spoke often and with thankfulness of the friends we'd made who would, no doubt, support our latest dream.

CHAPTER FORTY-TWO

Latouche Island

Sam and I decided that—logically—it would be the spring of the following year before we could move to Prince William Sound. We'd need Darrell Aleckson to build the boat Sam was designing, and it could take him as long as a year to custom-build the kind of specialized watercraft we wanted. Sam wanted an airtight, double-hulled, aluminum boat, crafted to make an air chamber between the two walls. He'd designed our bow picker for the lake the same way, and the boat was incredibly buoyant and virtually impossible to sink.

Sam wanted our commercial fishing boat built in much the same fashion, but with an enclosed bow and a cabin complete with a kitchen booth (including a sink and a stove, which thrilled me!), a bedroom, and a work deck on the back. We spent many afternoons and evenings drawing out plans for our boat, and when we finished, we started an ever-growing list of all the gear we'd need to go into business. Shrimp pots—how many? Longline—how much? Ganglions and hooks—how many of each? The list grew and grew, and every time we thought we had thought of everything, something else would occur to one of us, and we'd keep the list going.

"Sam, how are we ever going to afford all of this?" I said one evening as we rolled up the plans for our new fishing boat. "It's not going to be cheap."

My husband frowned. "We have the money we made from selling the cabin next door. And if we need to . . ."

"Stop it! Don't say it! We're not going to sell this cabin, Sam! This is our home!"

"Not unless we have to. You have my word."

Never let it be said that Sam Ward wastes time when he has a dream. That man makes things happen! A few days after transporting Jake's plane across the lake, we made our first trip to town since the ice went out.

We first stopped at Darrell's home in Soldotna. Darrell led us into his garage workspace, where Sam rolled out his plans for the commercial fishing boat he wanted. I held my breath. Would it be too much work? Was it possible to build all the specialized features and tweaks Sam wanted?

Darrell studied the plans and frowned, tracing his finger across each of the pages. Then he looked up at Sam. "This is fine work, Sam. I couldn't have designed a boat any better myself."

Sam straightened and hooked his thumbs in his pockets. "Thanks. I appreciate that. But will you build it?"

A slow smile crept across Darrell's face, and he looked back at the plans, then at Sam. "It'll be my pleasure."

I beamed as the two shook hands.

"I've got a few other jobs to finish up first, but I should be able to knock her out, in, oh . . . say, ten or twelve months."

Our customized commercial fishing boat would be a reality within a year! I looked around the garage as the men chatted, but I'm not sure I saw much. My focus remained fixated on the adventure ahead of us.

After we left Darrell's garage, Sam surprised me by driving in a direction we'd never been before. "Where are we going?" I asked.

He'd only grin at me, that mischievous twinkle glistening in his eyes. "It's a surprise."

When we pulled into someone's driveway, I had no idea what he had in mind. I climbed out of the Jeep, and Sam rounded the front end and took my hand. "Come meet a legend," he said. "Wild Bill."

Sam introduced me to the man whom I'd heard about many times during our Alaskan homesteading. Wild Bill was a young—yet very well-respected—and ambitious pilot, loved by the people in inaccessible communities of Alaska. He'd become well known for flying propane tanks out to remote villages, and soon he was hauling wood, food, boat parts, or just about anything anyone living in the Alaskan bush wanted or needed. Turns out, he hauled people, too!

My dear, sweet, sneaky husband had already contracted Wild Bill to take us on a sight-seeing tour of Latouche Island out in the Prince William Sound. I bottled up my breath as I climbed aboard Wild Bill's airplane, though I couldn't contain my grin. When I exhaled, a little squeal came out, causing Sam to chuckle.

"I thought you might like this." He squeezed my knee as I hugged myself to keep from bursting with happiness. This would be my first look at Prince William Sound, and Sam could hardly wait to show it to me. Sam had been to the sound hunting with Clark. "Did you know there used to be a big copper mine on Latouche Island? It was founded in the 1890s. What history!" The cords in Sam's neck stood out as he talked. "At one point, there were nearly four thousand people on the island, and it's only twelve miles long."

My usually calm husband animatedly moved his hands in the small, confined space of the airplane as he talked. "You know that earthquake that hit Alaska back in '64? Latouche Island raised nine whole feet and moved about sixty feet southeast. When the island rose, they found stumps that had been submerged below sea level in prehistoric times. Can you imagine, Bonnie?" His eyes shined as he shook his head in amazement.

A shudder ripped through my body, and while Sam mistook it for excitement, it may well have been fear. If the island raised once, I wondered, couldn't it sink again?

I wanted to be as excited as Sam was . . . I wanted to be *thrilled.* And while I was excited about seeing Prince William Sound, I was nervous, even anxious, about Latouche. We'd homesteaded lovely Caribou Island, made lifelong friends in the process, and now he wanted to move to an island that had once partially sunk into the ocean? The plane felt stuffier as I thought about this, so I turned away from Sam and peered out the window in an effort to feel the larger world around us.

It worked. We neared steep mountains that, from our distance, may easily have been a lush, tropical jungle but for their snowcaps and rocky peaks.

As we descended from the maze of mountains and glaciers, Wild Bill spoke. "Below us is the small city of Seward, and we're getting ready to fly over Resurrection Bay."

I peered out to see dozens of fishing vessels in the bay. The vast, blue ocean below us seemed to glow from within, and it left me breathless.

Once we left Resurrection Bay, the Gulf of Alaska opened before us. Bill turned the plane in an easterly direction, and we skirted lush, green mountains with jagged cliffs and glaciers all the way to Prince William Sound.

"Hold on," Wild Bill said, turning to grin at us.

Just then, he banked the airplane hard, and I gripped the armrests as I slid toward the window. We were almost vertical as Wild Bill hugged the rocky precipice with his airplane.

Just as quickly, Wild Bill leveled off the plane, and we were floating. My ears popped, and for a moment, I wasn't sure if we were right side up or upside down. The glistening blue water below oriented me, and I let out the breath I'd been holding in a *whoosh*.

Sam chuckled.

Soon we were descending, and while I'd prepared myself for a bumpy jolt of a landing, Wild Bill slid that plane in as if he were spreading warm butter on hot toast. I knew then why everyone spoke so highly of him. "Thank you, Wild Bill!" I gushed. All was right again in my world.

"I hate to cut your visit short," Wild Bill said as he offered me a hand to step out of the plane, "but I have to make another flight out to a far-flung village before nightfall. Gotta deliver some freight." He pushed his sunglasses back on his face and accepted Sam's handshake. "Can you be back here in thirty minutes or so?"

"Sure enough," Sam said.

Sam led me around the island—or as much of the twelve-mile island as we could see in thirty minutes. We found some old buildings and other remnants of the vacant town that had been bulldozed over many years back. Some had moved off their foundations—*earthquake,* I thought—and the ones left were dilapidated. "Wish we had time to explore these," I said.

"Me, too." Sam took my hand and led me toward the forest, searching the ground for signs of animal life. He spotted black bear tracks and deer tracks, and of course there'd be plenty of fish in the sea. "We won't go hungry here," he said.

I nodded, unable to speak as I again thought of leaving Caribou Island behind. From the air, Latouche looked luxuriously green. Up close, it looked wild and unkempt. The ground beneath my feet was frozen hard, and I thought of how long it had taken to chop out my garden on Caribou and make it fertile and productive. We now had a lot of seasonal visitors on Caribou, but Latouche looked . . . well, lonely.

I squeezed Sam's hand, and he slipped an arm around my shoulder. "Time to head back to the plane. We don't want to keep Wild Bill waiting."

Our plane ride back to Sterling was even more enchanting. "Look, Bonnie," Sam said, pointing out the window.

We were skirting close to a rocky ledge on a steep mountain slope, and three mountain goats turned to watch us soar past. We were so close it seemed I could have reached out the window and touched them. "Oh, Sam," I said on a breath.

As we left the Sound, the Gulf of Alaska opened before us, and as far as I could see, there was nothing but ocean. It was positively captivating, and I'll admit, a part of me hated to leave it behind.

Still, I was happiest when we were back on Skilak Lake, heading home to Caribou Island.

Later that day, we arrived home to find a note on our door.

> *Sorry we missed you. We bought the house on the hill behind you from your old neighbor Roy. We stopped by twice, coming and going, and we'll stop by again when we get back from the mainland. Hope to see you then.*
>
> Your neighbors,
> *Mick and Mindy*

"Oh, Sam!" I said, after reading the note from him. "Another couple! I wonder what they're like?"

Sam kneaded my shoulder from behind. "Got to be better than what we had up there." He laughed, then picked up our bags and pushed past me through the door.

We'd just put away our supplies from town when we heard a boat nearing our beach. I looked out, and sure enough, it was a couple. I hoped they weren't good friends of Roy's or anything at all like him. I twisted the dishtowel I held as I watched them unload supplies onto the dock. They looked toward our cabin, and they must have seen me, as both threw up their hands and waved. Startled, I stepped back, then I stepped forward again and returned their wave.

The two left their supplies on the dock and walked toward the cabin, and as they drew nearer, I relaxed as I saw their smiles. I stopped strangling my dishtowel, and I pulled down coffee cups and loaded them onto a serving tray. Then I headed to the door, taking a deep breath before opening it.

They were a young couple. "Hi! You must be Mick and Mindy. Welcome! Come in." I held open the door, and Mick offered me his handshake, and Mindy gave me a little hug of a greeting. Already, I liked them.

Sam stepped on the porch behind them, and after introductions all around, they settled at the table for coffee.

The two bragged about our cabin, and Mindy's green eyes lit as she fingered the curtains I'd made.

"Such a cozy little haven you've made, Bonnie." She waved her hand toward the living room and kitchen. "I'd love to pick your brain about how you did all this." She leaned forward and whispered as the men carried on their own conversation about getting lumber from the sawmill on the mainland. "Our cabin needs some serious love. It's . . . well, a little creepy."

I couldn't help but laugh with relief. "Yes. Yes, it is."

"That fence!" Mindy said, and I nodded. "That fence is the first thing to go!"

"You'll tear it down?"

"Oh, absolutely! Who needs a fence out here, anyway?"

Yes, yes, yes. I liked this woman!

Over the weeks to come, Mick and Mindy made more trips back and forth, and Sam even ferried them a time or two, helping them carry lumber and other supplies for their cabin. He and I stayed busy as well, though we enjoyed the occasional visits from the couple as they came for shared meals and to pick our brains for living off the grid and survival over the long winters.

"So, you plan to stay here over the *winter?*" I asked.

"Winters. Plural," Mindy said. "We plan to live here full time."

I'm sure my mouth gaped open, and I turned to stare at Sam, wishing he could read my mind. *Figures! As soon as we have our first, full-time, year-round neighbors—and one's a* woman—*we're going to move away!*

I gathered my wits and reached across the table to squeeze Mindy's hand. "You'll love it here," I said, blinking hard to keep the tears at bay. With every fiber of my being, I meant those words.

CHAPTER FORTY-THREE

Farewell, Dear Friend

Sam and I stayed busy putting our plans into motion to start a commercial fishing venture. Mick and Mindy visited as often as they could, as they were also busy working on their home (which didn't look so much like an upright shoebox, anymore). Sam and I took his furs from trapping season into town to sell them, and we met up with Ted, and his wife Susan, for a nice, leisurely lunch.

Sam and I returned to the cabin with our boat loaded with fishing supplies. One entire corner of our cabin was piled with ganglion leaders and hooks. We had shrimp pots and large spools of longline stacked on our front porch. We spent the next few evenings tying halibut hooks onto the ganglions, and then we brought them in and hung them on rope that Sam had stretched from wall to wall in the corner behind the woodstove.

"Sam," I said, appraising the new appearance of our cabin. "This looks more like an ocean home than a lake home."

He chuckled. "Yeah. If only that big beluga will breach the lake again, we'll be ready for it."

As I waved away my husband's silliness, the sound of an approaching boat caused me to turn. "Who's that?"

I peered out to see, Joe, an old acquaintance and friend of Ted's from Soldotna, pulling his boat up to the dock. Sam looked over my shoulder. "That's odd," he said. "He's never been here before."

We walked down to meet him, and from the grim lines on his face, I knew he'd come bearing bad news. "It's Ted," Joe said. "He had a massive heart attack yesterday in his home." Joe swallowed audibly and lowered his head. He looked up at Sam from hooded eyes. "He's on life support. The doc told Susan there's nothing they can do. He's brain dead."

Sam sucked in a short, loud breath.

"But . . . but . . ." I stammered. "We just saw him a few days ago, and he was fine!"

Joe pursed his lips and nodded. "Yep." He sighed and shoved his hands into his pockets. "Susan says if you want to see him while—you know—you'd better come now."

We talked solemnly for another minute, and Sam invited Joe up to the cabin.

"Got to get back before dark." He looked toward the sky. "S'pposed to get windy tonight, so I need to go." Joe climbed back into his boat, and Sam waved him away. We stood watching him until he disappeared into the gloaming.

That night, Sam and I shed some tears as we thought of our poor friend Ted and his wife Susan. "And their children!" I said. "Poor kids!"

"He's so young," Sam said.

"How old is he?"

"Only thirty-six. His birthday's next month." Sam pressed a palm against his eye to rub away a tear. "Shoulda got that heart valve fixed."

I gaped at him. "What heart valve?"

"Ahhh, he told me when we were trapping that he needed to have a heart valve replaced. Doctors told him that almost a year ago, but he kept putting it off. I told him he needed to take care of it, he had a family to think of." Sam turned and stared at the wall, looking away from me.

I knew he was crying, and it broke my heart into more pieces.

The next day, we sat down with Susan at her kitchen table as their kids disappeared to their bedrooms. We tried to be as supportive as we could, offering touches and hugs and tissues liberally. Susan shared that Ted had just returned from work and was relaxing in his chair as she cooked dinner, and he suddenly clutched his chest and moaned, then he stood and fell hard to the floor.

"I ran to him, and he wasn't breathing. I started CPR, and then—" a sob broke from her chest. When she regained composure, she spoke in a strangled voice. "Then I had to stop to go call for help. I wonder if I hadn't have stopped when I did . . ."

Sam pulled her close. "Now, now. Don't say that. There was nothing you could have done."

She sniffled and nodded, pulling away to blow her nose. "That's what the doctor said, too."

Sam and I went to visit Ted a few days before they unplugged him from life support. The doctors stated that he'd remain in a vegetative state either way, as he had no brain activity at all. We agreed that Ted wouldn't want to live that way, tied to a machine for the rest of his life.

We hugged our friend goodbye one last time, and then we left.

A few days later, we received word on the island that Ted had passed away.

CHAPTER FORTY-FOUR

Paddle, Fritz! Paddle! Paddle! Paddle!

Our summer zoomed right past, though in August, Sam and I enjoyed another fun fishing week with Dad and Connie. This time Connie's brother, Fritz—who shared their same interests of the outdoors and fishing—joined them on their trip to Alaska.

One day we took the three of them to Darrel Aleckson's so they could see the beginning stages of construction on our commercial fishing boat. Dad and Fritz spied our dinghy pre-ordained for *The Bonnie Lass II.* They determined between themselves they'd like to take it out salmon fishing on the Kenai River the next morning, if that was okay with Sam. Though long afterward, neither would take ownership of the idea, and with good reason.

Shortly after daybreak, Sam took Dad and Fritz across the lake, and then drove them and the dinghy to the other side of the Kenai River Bridge in Soldotna. Sam would spend the day visiting his friend Warner at his home in Sterling, while Dad and Fritz fished. After determining a pick-up time, Sam pull-started the motor on the two-man dinghy, and set the two afloat. I can only imagine the sight—my dad, a medium-sized man in the front, and big ol' Fritz at the stern, steering from where he sat perched atop a cooler full of beer.

Later that evening, the three men returned to Caribou Island with nary a fish. As the five of us sat huddled around the campfire, they told us their tale, punctuated with gales of tear-producing laughter and dirty looks.

"We decided to head up the Kenai River," Fritz said, his eyes round in their pouches of puffy eyelids. "We motored quite a good distance, figured we could drift back downstream at our leisure, let the current bring us back."

"It would have been a good idea, too, except we didn't know how fast that current could get," my dad interrupted.

"And we didn't know about the rocks," Fritz said.

"Rocks!" Connie said. "Oh, my goodness! You could have capsized!"

Fritz nodded. "Yep. We thought more than once that we were goners." He looked toward my father, and inexplicably, the two men cracked up, laughing so hard it took them a minute to compose themselves before either could continue the story.

"See," my father finally said, wiping at his eyes, "we'd just cracked open a beer and settled back, decided we'd drink one before we dropped in our lines . . . figured we'd need both hands to reel in the big ones we'd catch . . . and then for no reason, the motor quit on us."

Sam leaned forward at this point, and I could tell he wondered if there was a mechanical issue—or if perhaps my father or Fritz had done something to preempt the motor's stall.

Fritz must have understood Sam's body language, because he shook his head. "We didn't do nothing to it—it just stopped running. I tried and tried to restart it, pulled and pulled, and pulled some more, and when my arm gave out, I just opened another beer and decided to give 'er a rest, and try again later."

"We were in a good spot at that point," my dad said.

Fritz nodded.

"Too bad that didn't last long," Dad said.

"What happened?" I asked. "Why didn't it last?"

"We were drifting along, sipping our beers, and your dad is dragging his line in the water, not really paying attention, and I just so happened to put my hand in the water, meaning to trail it, like you do when you're relaxing, and that's when the water shot right up my arm." Fritz marked the spot near his elbow. "We were not drifting so much as we were sailing right along at a pretty good clip."

"It was so peaceful," my dad said, "that we didn't notice the current had picked up."

Connie leaned closer to me, as if she were going to speak in a conspiratorial whisper, but she said her words loudly. "*Peaceful,* meaning *they'd caught a good beer buzz.*"

Dad chuckled. "There may have been that."

Fritz grinned, but just as quickly, his grin disappeared, and he looked at me and waved his hand in front of him. "Bonnie, I look up ahead of your dad, and I see downstream ahead of us this big rock. I'd say *boulder,* but it was too jagged for that. I yell at your dad, 'Look out!'"

"Now, wait a minute, Fritz," my dad said. "I'm the one who saw the rock first. Remember? I yelled at you to get your paddle."

"Yeah," Fritz conceded. "And you yelled long and hard about that paddle." Fritz leaned toward us and rocked side to side, animating the story as he told it. "I'm trying as hard as I can to get the paddle out, but I'm wedged in, and it's wedged in, and the dinghy is going faster and faster and faster—and if you hadn't noticed, I'm a big ol' boy—"

At this we all chuckled.

"—and I'm afraid I'm going overboard, and if I do," he motioned toward my father, "my partner here will have sailed clear to Timbuktu before I surface, and the whole time, he's yelling at me, 'Paddle, Fritz! Paddle! Paddle! Paddle!'"

His own laughter interrupted his story, and my father started laughing again, and before I know it, Sam and Connie and I are also laughing, though we're not exactly sure why.

"I think your little dinghy's gonna split right down the middle," my dad said, "and here's big ol' Fritz in the back of the boat, rocking us side to side, and I'm paddling as hard as I can paddle, and I'm not sure if we're going to capsize or bust headlong into that boulder!"

"Oh, no!" I said.

"And the whole time," Fritz said, "your dad is hollering at the top of his lungs, 'Paddle, Fritz! Paddle! Paddle! Paddle!' Don would take a breath, and yell it again. 'Paddle, Fritz! Paddle! Paddle! Paddle!'"

The two men erupt again into gales of laughter, as Connie and I look at one another, smiling, but confused.

"How did you get around the rock?" Connie asked.

Dad shrugged, and he and Sam spoke in unison, surprising me. "Current."

"Yep," Dad said. "Current took us right around it."

Sam nodded. "Usually will, but you can't be too sure. It's awfully dangerous."

Fritz held up his hands, palms facing, about a foot apart. "It was a narrow miss, sure. And there were more rocks again. A real rapids. We went right through it, though. Not a scratch on us."

"No thanks to you," my dad said, grinning at Fritz.

"Hey, I got my paddle loose in time for the second go-round."

"Second?" I asked, looking in turn at each of the two fisher-buddies.

"Oh, yeah," Fritz said. "We coasted along a little way, catching our breath, drinking another beer or two—"

"Or three," Connie said, and we laughed.

"And we were trailing our lines," Fritz continued, "and we're waving at people along the shore—you know, in them cabins along the river there—and they're waving back at us. And then, before you know it, we see 'em again."

"More rocks," Dad said.

"And more, 'Paddle, Fritz! Paddle! Paddle! Paddle!'" Fritz cracks up again, and my dad joins him. "Hey," Fritz manages, swiping at his eyes, "at least the second time I got my paddle loose and helped you."

"Yeah," Dad said. "These looked as treacherous as the first, and there were more of them. We could see the Kenai River Bridge ahead, and I yelled back at Fritz to paddle toward the shore."

"'Paddle, Fritz! Paddle! Paddle! Paddle!'" Fritz said, laughing again.

It seemed to get funnier each time he said it, and now we all laughed right along with the men.

"We paddled right to the shore this time," Dad said, "you know, since I had help this time," he shot a mock-scathing look toward Fritz, who continued to laugh.

"We dragged the dinghy up onto the shore, and we hiked about a mile to the nearest bar."

"Imagine that," Connie said, elbowing me.

"Hey," Dad said. "We needed something to calm our nerves after that experience." His face appeared perfectly somber as he said those words. "It was harrowing."

Fritz's lips twisted to one side, and he nodded. "Yes, it was." He cleared his throat. "Anyway, Sam had given us the number where we could reach him, so Don called him, and in about an hour, Sam picks us up, and we ride back to the dinghy."

"We're telling Sam here how the motor wouldn't start—" Dad said.

"Even though I pulled and pulled and pulled," Fritz said, mimicking the action now.

"—and don't you know it," Dad said, shaking his head, "Sam pulls the cord and that motor fires right up!"

Fritz laughs again. "Darndest thing I ever saw. But the funniest thing of the whole trip was—"

"Paddle, Fritz! Paddle! Paddle! Paddle!" the five of us chorused, and we fell into yet another fit of laughter.

That night, after the campfire had died down, and we'd all curled into our beds, an inexplicable giggle bubbled and escaped my throat.

"What?" Sam said, turning to me in the bed.

"Paddle, Fritz!" I whispered fiercely.

"Paddle! Paddle! Paddle!" Sam and I said in unison. We chuckled as he pulled me close, and we drifted into sleep, smiling.

CHAPTER FORTY-FIVE

The Great Alaska Cold

We grew closer with Mick and Mindy, and by fall it was just the four of us on the island. In November, I baked Mindy a cake for her birthday, and in December, she baked one for me. At Christmastime, we hiked through the deep snow to their now-lovely cabin, where Chef Mick prepared us an amazing feast of prime rib roast in mushroom-wine sauce.

January brought with it one of the coldest seasons our region of Alaska had ever recorded, with common temperatures twenty or thirty below zero. It was what would, in later years, be referred to as "The Great Alaska Cold." Gale force winds—which were commonplace this time of year—reached gusts of a hundred miles per hour, brutally pounding our cabin walls. Trapping was difficult and there were many days we couldn't travel across the lake to our trap lines.

We had to take extra precautions against the weather with our birds, too, so Sam added a kerosene heater to the coop to ensure our chickens stayed warm and their little feet didn't freeze.

Imagine my surprise, then, when I went out the following morning and discovered that my gorgeous, pure-white Silkies were neither gorgeous nor white! Soot from the kerosene heater had settled all over their fluffy white feathers, and they were now solid black! One of the hens turned her head sideways and blinked at me, as if to say, "Can you believe this mess!"

Sam and I laughed to the point of tears, and we continued chuckling as he took out the kerosene heater. "Well," Sam said, and shrugged. "At least we tried."

A few days later, with temperatures reaching thirteen below zero, we prepared for Derik's arrival. The winds had finally ceased long enough for the lake to freeze over. He'd sent a North Wind Message, letting us know he was flying down on Saturday. Sam checked the ice to make sure it was safe for his plane to land, and it was four to five inches thick between our island and Little Caribou Island. To guide their landing onto the thickest ice, Sam marked a runway for the pilot.

He cut spruce boughs, and then he chopped holes into the ice, "planting" the boughs upright, several paces apart in two parallel lines. The water quickly froze around the boughs, and soon it appeared as if perfect rows of trees had sprung up across the lake. He would do the same later on our ice road, as a trail marker.

The entire time Sam worked, the temperature never rose a single degree. A light wind blew, chilling the air around him even more. When he finally finished and came inside to warm, his earlobes were white.

"Sam! Your ears are frostbitten!" I ran toward him.

He cupped his hands around his ears. "Oops." It wasn't the first time one of us had been frostnipped, and it reminded me of the time the tip of my nose had turned white after crossing Skilak. Sam had placed his hand over my nose to warm it until my skin literally defrosted.

I returned the favor now by ushering my husband toward his chair in front of the stove, where I stood and alternately heated my hands over the stove, then cupped them around his ears.

In no time, his ears were again pink and alive.

By the end of January the ice in our water hole—we had to chop through the ice to reach the lake water below—was now over a foot thick. The frozen surface of Skilak was passable now, but we didn't have transportation to get to town for our mail. Our Jeep was stuck at the upper landing and wouldn't start, and even if it did the loop road was impassable. Sam had made numerous trips across the lake on the mojo to try and start it so he could drive it back to the island. The engine wouldn't budge! He brought the battery home each time to keep it charged.

We hadn't been to town for our mail since before the lake froze, and I knew our post office box would be over-flowing with mail from loved ones. Oh, how my heart yearned for that mail—our only link to family so far away, and the main reason for our *pull* to town. So, having given up on our Jeep for the time being, Sam called Warner on the CB radio, and the men made arrangements for Warner to pick Sam up the following morning—if the state road crew had plowed the road to the lower landing. Sometimes they did and sometimes they didn't. I was keeping my fingers crossed.

Sam dressed warmly and headed across the lake on the mojo the next morning. A few hours later when Sam hadn't returned, I did a little happy dance in my kitchen because I knew he must have made it to town by then. Sure enough, he returned late that afternoon with a large box stuffed full of mail, a package of small gifts from home, and a special treat—a chocolate bar—for me! To Mick and Mindy's delight, he had also picked up their mail for them, as they were in the same stranded situation as we were. Sam and I spent the evening in front of the fire pouring over letters, magazines, catalogues, and the box of goodies from my family.

That next morning, as the temperature dropped to fifteen below zero, we decided to stay indoors and do more of the same. Sam turned on the radio in time for the noon news—something we rarely did, but on this cabin-bound occasion, it was both a nice form of entertaining and a time-passing pleasure—and we settled into our chairs to re-read our mail and listen to the radio announcer.

I'd just been lulled into a peaceful reverie when a location and name I recognized came across the radio and startled me out of my musing.

". . . shooting this morning at Millie's Moose River Inn in Sterling. One dead and one still in critical condition at Central Peninsula ICU," said the newscaster. "Bob Stagler was pronounced dead on the scene, and the man transported to the hospital was shot several times and later identified as his brother, Stanley Stagler.

"Police have taken one suspect, John Hurn the third, into custody at this time." The announcer paused. "Our thoughts and prayers go out to this family and to our friends at Millie's."

Sam's arm moved beneath my hand, and I looked down, surprised to see that I'd reached out and gripped him when I'd heard the news. "Oh, my God! Oh, my God!" I said. It was a prayer as much as an exclamation. "Sam! That's Marion's brother Bob! The one who—"

"The one who delivered the logs to us for the cabin we built for the Rodgers," Sam said. "Yes, our Bob."

Our Bob. Funny how we'd claimed him—and indeed, we'd claimed him. Bob had been so kind when we'd first arrived on Caribou. He'd risked his boom rig—not to mention his life—by driving a full load of heavy logs across the frozen Skilak Lake to keep Sam and I from having to offload them and drag them a few at a time behind our Jeep to the island. Later, when we'd learned he was our dear friend Marion's brother, he'd gone from being a friend to feeling like family. Our Bob. Gone. We were heartbroken.

Sam called Warner on the CB and offered our sincere condolences. He learned that Bob's brother Stan had been shot twice in the abdomen and once in the thigh, and was in ICU fighting for his life. Warner said he'd call if there were any changes and to let us know when services were going to be held for Bob.

We went about our days' work without our usual enthusiasm. And all the while, the Great Alaska Cold just kept getting colder. A thick blanket of ice fog hovered over the lake all that day, thick and smothering. We couldn't see beyond our boat dock. I was thankful that Sam marked our ice roads with spruce branches, because it would be easy to get lost while traveling on the lake. That evening, our temperature dropped to twenty-three below zero.

The next morning we heard on the radio that it was forty below zero in Kenai, and seventy-five below in McGrath. That night, the mercury dipped so low that our propane lights quit working. We had to light candles until Sam went outside and took a blow-torch to the propane tank. It worked! Again, the next morning, we woke to thirty below zero, and I couldn't use my propane stove. By noon it *warmed up* to twenty-five below, and the propane worked.

The next day, Sam traveled to the mainland to attend Bob's funeral. I had to stay behind to keep the home fires burning so our canned goods would not freeze. Sam walked arm-in-arm with Marion to the casket to view his friend's lifeless body. After he returned home, Sam told me that Marion had told him about the murder, and how her brother Stan was still fighting for his life in ICU. She'd unbuttoned the flannel shirt Bob wore in the casket and showed Sam the bullet holes.

"It was the saddest thing I've seen," Sam said, his eyes misty and distant with memory. "Just like that, his life ended."

I pulled my husband close, and he held to me tightly.

A few days later, we had a "warm up" where the high reached four degrees. Sam and I used this heat wave to cut and haul firewood in Mojo. As we were unloading our trailer, we both grabbed our ears as a deafening, sonic-boom-type sound exploded around us. The ear-shattering sound lasted a good ten seconds or so.

"What in the world!" I said, when I could finally uncover my ears and be heard.

"Ice," Sam said. "The lake cracked open."

I ran into the house and grabbed our binoculars. Sam and I hustled to our perch on the other side of the island that faces the upper end of the lake, and, sure enough, we saw it. A huge, jagged crack ran all the way from the upper end of Skilak Lake to the lower end. I was reminded of the time the same thing happened during our first winter on Skilak. Only that time,

Sam was walking across the lake when it happened. At the time, I thought it sounded like a huge seven-forty-seven commercial airliner must have crashed on the lake ice.

We largely spent the rest of the winter and much of the spring hibernating. The Jeep finally started for Sam in mid-February, and he drove it across the ice and brought it home. By the time mid-March arrived, we were more than ready to go check on the status of our boat. Now that we had our Jeep, Sam and I headed to Darrell's, and though we completely understood that the frigid weather had kept Darrell's work to a minimum, we were nonetheless a bit disappointed to see that our boat was still in the early stages of being built.

To help things along, Sam and I rolled up our sleeves and got to work. "We've got to find a way to get out here more often," Sam said. "Otherwise, we won't get this thing finished before the next winter comes."

I thought about that as we worked, but I had no idea how we'd pull off getting to Darrell's more often. Between rotten ice, waiting for the breakup, and Skilak's moody late-spring and early-summer uprisings, I couldn't foresee us making it across the lake more than a couple of times, if that.

Sam must have been thinking about it, too, because on the way back from Darrell's, Sam pulled into the Naptown Trading Post in Sterling.

"What are you doing?" I asked. We'd already picked up some supplies on the way to Darrell's house.

"I spotted something earlier, and I want to check it out."

I figured he'd seen some kind of fishing supply, or maybe a new axe, or some kind of tool. Nope! Sam had seen a camper.

"A camper?" I said. "What on earth for?"

"Something to stay in while we build our boat!"

By the time we left the trading post, we were owners of an 18-foot camper. Sam called Warner and Marion from the trading post phone, and they welcomed us to park the camper at their place.

"We need to put a motor on our boat, and we need to get that thing on the ocean. We can't do it sitting on the island, waiting for the ice to break up."

Sam was right, as usual. So on March 23, I took a temporary last look around the cabin and told it goodbye. "I'll be back," I whispered as I locked the door. We loaded the Jeep, and I squeezed in among our belongings.

As we headed across the lake, I couldn't help but laugh, thinking of *The Beverly Hillbillies*. There I sat, my feet propped on a stack of canned goods, a lawn chair crammed against my left shoulder, and a crate of five chickens behind my head, sitting upon a pile of boxes.

"What are you laughing about?" Sam glanced at me a couple of times as he navigated the Jeep across the ice.

I comically sang an impromptu version of "The Ballad of Jed Clampett," making up the words as I went along.

"Come and listen to a story 'bout a man named Sam. Poor fisherman barely kept his family fed. Then one day he was fishing for some foooooood—"

Sam laughed and finished the verse with his own made-up rhyme. "And up from the sea came a big be-luga. Whale, that is. Big and white. Plenty to eat."

The two of us broke into gales of laughter, and somehow Sam managed to stretch his arm across the pile of goods between us and squeeze my knee. "I love you, Bonnie Ward."

I beamed at my husband. "I love you, too, Sam Ward."

CHAPTER FORTY-SIX

Exxon Valdez Oil Spill

The next morning, Sam and I were still feeling elated about our new adventure when we pulled into a gas station in Sterling to fill up the Jeep with gas. An acquaintance of ours, known to us only by his nickname, Boomer, was pulling out, and he waved at us to stop and chat.

Sam pulled alongside Boomer's truck and lowered the window. "What's up, Boomer?"

"You ain't heard the news?" Boomer asked, his forehead creased with deep lines.

"What news?"

"The *Exxon Valdez* oil tanker hit Bligh Reef in Prince William Sound. She's dumped millions and millions of gallons of oil into the sound. Some say maybe ten million gallons or more."

I sucked in a breath and pressed my hand to my chest. This couldn't be! Sam turned to me, his eyes bulging.

"They say it's the worst oil spill in history. They're closing the sound to commercial fishing. Well . . . all fishing, I reckon. Damn shame." He shook his head. "I gotta run. Good to see you again, Sam, Bonnie. Take care."

And with that Boomer was gone. Sam and I sat there for a long few minutes, unable to speak. A car horn honked behind us, prompting us to move out of the way.

Hours later, we returned to our little camper, and the first thing we did was turn on the news. Warner had let us run electricity from their home to our camper, so we had a small television, and we plopped in front of it to learn more about the spill.

"The thick, black oil is covering everything," the news reporter said as he stood in a slicker with his back to the black-looking waves behind him. "We're told over a hundred bald eagles, a few hundred harbor seals, and perhaps more than a thousand sea otters have already been killed, in addition to hundreds of thousands of seabirds."

I held my hand over my mouth, as if I could contain the horror I felt.

"Commercial fishing has been suspended, and no one knows for how long," the man continued. "This could be devastating to the Alaskan economy; however, we're told that Exxon intends to offer the commercial fishermen reimbursement for their lost income, as well as paid opportunities to use their boats in the cleanup efforts."

Sam turned to me. "That's it, Bonnie. We need to get our boat finished as soon as possible." He reached for my hand and squeezed it. "If we can't fish, we can clean up the sound.

It'll be good money, and when it's all cleaned up, we'll be ready to fish."

My shoulders relaxed, and I breathed a bit easier. Sam always had a solution, and this one would see us through to our dream. Having a plan in place re-energized me, and I got to work unpacking and setting up our camper for the weeks ahead of us.

We spent as many days as possible helping Darrell on the boat. Darrell taught school, so we were limited to helping him with our boat on the weekends and occasional evenings. Though he had his own life, and we didn't want to tear him from his other responsibilities, Darrell understood our predicament, and he did all he could to speed up the process without sacrificing the quality of his work.

He showed us how to hook up the hydraulic hoses, which we could do on our own. Then, while he worked at school, Sam and I found an upholsterer to sew our cushion covers for the booth table, as well as our sleeper in the bow of the cabin. We also ordered and installed a captain's chair, fire extinguishers, a diesel cook-and-heat stove, and more. We'd already purchased an inflatable dinghy and a small outboard motor—the one dad and Fritz used on the river—so we could anchor in deeper water and still make it to shore as needed. Our list seemed endless, and we spent our days building and shopping and installing, anxious to get our boat on the water for the environmental cleanup.

One of our errands took us into Homer, Alaska. Automobile, boat, and even foot traffic was heavy, and the place crawled with workers getting ready to clean up any oil coming into Kachemak Bay. Big boats lined the dock, standing by for work.

I pointed out their location origins to Sam. "There's Texas, Louisiana, Oregon, and there's one from Washington. Sam, I thought the oil company was supposed to be hiring Alaskan boats for the cleanup."

Sam's mouth pulled to one side, and he put his arm around me. "Don't worry, Bonnie. We'll get on the cleanup. There's plenty of work to be done."

On June 22, *The Bonnie Lass II* was put out to water. We christened her with a bottle of sparkling cider and I became tearful when she bobbed buoyantly on the surface of the water. "Oh, Sam! She's beautiful!"

Four days later, we took her out for her maiden voyage. We sailed into Resurrection Bay, which I'd last seen from the air in Wild Bill's plane. We weren't out ten minutes when we saw a pod of orcas, also known as killer whales. Sam stopped the boat, and we stood on the deck and watched a male, a female, and their calf as they swam close to our boat, checking it out.

"Can you believe it, Bonnie?" Sam said as the orcas swam away. "Our very first cruise, and we've been approved by killer whales." His smile was cocky and he stood spread-legged, one fist on his hip. "That's gotta be a good omen."

Sam just launched the Bonnie Lass II

Bonnie on the deck of the Bonnie Lass II *getting ready for their first voyage.*

That evening, Sam signed our boat up with VECO Corporation—the oil pipeline company that Exxon had hired to clean up the spill—in Seward. They were discouraging, telling Sam that they'd hired enough boats for now.

Hearing that news didn't dissuade my husband. We simply took our boat into Whittier, over a six-hour trip away by boat, where Sam repeated the process by signing on for work with VECO Whittier. There he was told that he was fourth on the list for additional boats to be hired—if they needed more.

"They said they'll probably shut down the clean-up operations in September," Sam said, "so we may not get the opportunity." He shrugged. "Still, that's a little way off, so I'm hopeful."

That's my Sam; forever positive, forever hopeful. How I love him!

Sam was told to check back often, so each day, he'd go to the VECO office to see if they had work. Together we decided that it didn't make sense for me to stay on the boat with him in Whittier as he waited, so I returned to the camper, where I could help Warner and Marion with farm chores. It kept me busy, but as the week turned into a month, I missed my husband more each day.

Late one night toward the end of July, I sat at the little table in the camper, reading as my eyes grew heavier, when Sam burst through the door, scaring me half out of my wits.

"Pack your things, Bonnie. If the job won't come to us, we'll go to the job."

I dropped my book to the floor and leaped into his arms, yipping like a happy puppy.

Sam and I drove to Portage and took the train through the mountain tunnels to Whittier, where our boat was still docked. The next morning, a thick, soupy fog settled on the water, and the steady rain did nothing to wash it away. We decided we'd put off our trip to Knight Island, where a floating work camp, called a *floatel,* had been established in lower Herring Bay.

We put on our head-to-toe rain gear and ventured out on foot to watch the fishing boats come in. My friendly Sam quickly acquainted himself with the harbor master, who told him what, for fishermen, amounted to a horror story. The day before, one of the fishing boats came in bearing a hefty 56,000 pounds of salmon. The captain quickly went back out and returned with another load of the same size, only to learn that both catches were contaminated with oil.

If that wasn't heartbreaking enough to hear, at noon, the announcement was made that all fishing was closed in the Whittier district. It took some effort, but I managed not to cry.

"The floatel," Sam said, when we were back inside the warm cabin of our boat. He pushed up his wool sleeves. "That's where we'll find work. Weather permitting, we'll head out in the morning. We'll be fine."

And the weather permitted. After breakfast, we filled up with 111 gallons of gas, and we pulled out of the Whittier harbor, bound for Herring Bay on Knight Island. The trip was nearly four hours in fog that allowed only about five-hundred yards of visibility, but even so, I saw some thrilling sights. A sea lion popped its head above the water's surface, and it was so big that my breath caught. They look smaller on television, but this creature seemed massive! Sometime later, a pod of porpoises discovered our boat and decided to play with it, jumping out of the water, racing past us, doubling back, and racing past again. They must have played with us for a solid half hour, before heading on into the fog.

Finally, we arrived at the floatel, and though I thought I knew what it would be like, I was still surprised. A huge barge carried enormous work camp buildings that housed hundreds of workers, and boats were anchored all around. We anchored for the night at the back of the bay, and the next morning, we went to the floatel.

Sam asked around for someone in charge, and he was directed to a man named Clarence, who was number three in the operation's hierarchy.

The red-faced man pulled off his cap and scratched the back of his head as he talked. "Yeah. I might be able to get you two and your boat on. May take a few days. You hang around, I'll see what I can do."

In the meantime, the man told us we could hang out on the floatel, which was *huge!* We were invited to eat in their cafeteria—that looked much like a high-school cafeteria with rectangular tables and plastic trays and a food line. The meals looked quite good, which surprised me. There were hundreds of workers living on the floatel, which had bedrooms and hot showers for all. It amazed me to see those amenities right smack in the midst of such rugged landscape.

For three days, we anchored next to the floatel, watching more and more boats appear. Again, we deflated as we saw so many anchored that were from out of state, and some looked like they were hardly held together, much less able to float. As we met people and made acquaintances—including women and small children—we learned that many who were working the cleanup had never fished in their lives! And yet, the oil company continued to reiterate on the news channels that they were employing Alaskan fishermen whom the oil spill had put out of work.

After another two days with no work for us, Sam learned that they were moving the whole camp to Smith Island. Only those currently employed would be needed. Disheartened again, we pulled up anchor and headed back to Whittier.

We spent the night docked in Whittier, then got up the next morning, gassed up the boat, and made the ninety-mile, five-hour long trip to Valdez. The whole gray trip was foggy and rainy, but the fog lifted as we entered Perry Island, and visibility was great. We tied up in the Valdez harbor, and we decided to rest and sleep, prior to Sam and I going to the VECO office the next day to again ask for work.

We roused early that next morning, just after dawn, and in the bright light of day, the harbor was gorgeous. We sat at our table sipping coffee, enjoying the view of crystal-blue water dotted with bobbing vessels anchored in the harbor. In that moment, I understood completely why Sam wanted this life, and I realized that I wanted it, too.

I felt more hopeful as Sam and I walked into the VECO office shortly after eight that morning. We were directed to speak with a man named Tony, who was in charge of hiring on boats and employees. We entered to meet Tony and another man, who never looked up from his desk and didn't introduce himself. Sam cheerfully spoke, and he and I were both friendly, yet Tony never stopped frowning, and his words were terse and sharp. He impatiently tried to dismiss us, but Sam wasn't having it.

"Tony, sir, I've been trying to get on the oil spill cleanup all summer. My wife and I have a sturdy new boat, and we're hard workers. Surely you have some kind of job for us. We'll do whatever it is you need."

The man smacked a sheaf of papers against his hand and stepped toward Sam in a threatening manner. "Look, *son*, you don't have a snowball's chance in hell of getting your boat on this job. Stop wasting your time. *And mine.*"

I could almost see Sam's hackles rise when the man derogatorily called him "son."

Sam took a step forward, his face now only inches from Tony's. "Shame on you! Shame on you, and VECO, and Exxon, for hiring all these out-of-state people by the hundreds—people who were never affected by the oil spill you created—while the rest of us can't get work.

"My wife and I sank every cent we had into commercial fishing on Prince William Sound this summer, and for you to stand here all smug and rude and not give a rat's ass about whether people like us ever work again—well there's a special place in hell for you."

As Sam ranted, I slid behind him, gently tugging on the back of his shirt, hoping he'd just let it go.

"Thank you for nothing," Sam said, and we turned and left.

I couldn't remember seeing my husband so angry, except perhaps when I'd watched him argue with Roy from a distance on the beach. Amazingly, once we were out of Tony's office, Sam's whole demeanor changed. He gave a half-hearted shrug, and he lightly pressed his hand against the small of my back.

I looked up at him, and he briefly closed his eyes, then he looked at me. Then his lips twisted to one side. He licked a finger and stroked the air in front of us. "Bonnie, let's chalk this one up to experience."

I couldn't follow his meaning. "You—you mean we aren't going to try to get on the cleanup crew?"

His smile that followed was—and this still amazes me— truly genuine. "We've wasted enough of our time on these people this summer. Let's go have some fun!"

Breath whooshed out of me, along with the tension in my shoulders. I could hardly believe it! I guess Sam had gotten out his months of frustration in Tony's office when he'd unleashed all he'd been holding in. Whatever it was, my Sam was back.

He took my hand and led me out of the VECO building, his chest puffed out as he walked. It was behind us.

And, boy, did we have fun the rest of the summer! Sam and I took *The Bonnie Lass II* all over Prince William Sound. We explored some of the stunning beauty on the remote islands, few of which were inhabited by humans. We'd anchor offshore, then fire up the motor on our inflatable dingy and head to islands with names like *Squire* and *Mummy*. We saw bear, and deer, and sea otters, and whales. The water was so clear we could see a fathom deep, or so I imagined. Once we sailed over a submerged boulder the size of a small mountain, and we could pick out every crevice through the clear, emerald water. The scenery was what I'd always depicted in my mind that paradise would look like. And here we were, living in paradise!

Sam and I feasted well on the halibut we caught and on spot shrimp we pulled up in our shrimp pots. One day, we pulled up much more shrimp than we could ever have eaten in a week.

"Let's take them back to Sterling to sell," Sam said. "We can turn a tidy profit, that way."

It seemed like a fine idea, so we headed over to Mummy Bay on the southern end of Knight Island, where a huge ice boat remained anchored. Sam filled our lower storage hold with ice from the blower, and we went back and pulled up twelve pounds of shrimp.

We took our catch and headed toward Whittier, as the weather turned terrible. Waves quickly rose to six feet with whitecaps. By the time we went through Culross Pass, the waves had subsided to two feet, so we made it to Passage Canal and Whittier.

We were only a week away from the opening day of commercial halibut fishing! The "season" only lasted twenty-four hours, so you either hit it, or you missed it, meaning you'd have to wait until the next one, if you couldn't get out in time. Sam and I were anxious to get out there. This was what we'd come for, and here we were, six months later, ready to go!

Unfortunately, the weather kept us docked in Whittier for the next four days. The weather turned nasty, and the wind blew harder and harder each day. From August 31st to September 3rd, we suffered fifty-knot winds. Sam and I spent those days snuggled inside the warm cabin of our boat, waiting out the weather, as the waves rocked us in and out of sleep.

Then, on the morning of September 4—a day I'll never forget—the shrill blast of sirens startled me awake.

CHAPTER FORTY-SEVEN

Tsunami

I snapped into a sitting position as adrenaline surged through my veins, causing my heartbeat to race. I grabbed Sam's shoulder, stunned that the shrill blast of sirens hadn't awakened him. "Sam! Wake up! What is it? What are those sirens?"

He rolled over and stretched lazily, as if the wailing scream piercing the morning stillness equated to morning birdsong. "Town sirens," he said, and he closed his eyes.

I shook him more roughly than I should have. "What do they mean? What's happening!"

Sam rolled over and pulled the sleeping bag over his head. "It's a test. They have them every coupla weeks. Go back to sleep." He sounded like he spoke from beneath the seawater instead of floating atop it in our boat.

I let out a deep breath and snuggled up against him, willing my jangled nerves to stop jittering. The continuing sirens seemed to pierce my brain, and I covered my ears and tried to concentrate on the gentle rocking of the boat.

No use.

I rose on an elbow and peered through the door into the little cabin, half expecting something ominous to materialize. Every muscle in my body tensed, alert for anything—everything. Beside me, Sam's breathing had already settled into a slow, deep rhythm. How on earth could he sleep through the screaming? I cocked my head toward the VHF radio, expecting bad news at any moment, hoping I could hear it over the sirens.

Nothing.

Not even a squelch or static. Just silence.

Had we turned the radio off?

As the sirens continued to blare, I jumped from our berth in *The Bonnie Lass II* and pulled on my clothes. I checked the radio. The red light indicated *on,* so I checked the volume. It was turned up, but I cranked it as high as it would go, just in case.

There should at least be a broadcaster announcing that, "This is a test of our emergency broadcast system. This is only a test," right? And shouldn't the sirens have stopped by now? Were they broken? And how on *earth* could my husband sleep through this din?

I peered through the windows, searching the boat harbor for signs of life. No one moved about on the docks, and only a few seagulls competed for the scraps of fish someone had left behind. In the distance, the little town of Whittier still slept, curled snuggly around the Begich Towers—a former army barracks standing fourteen stories tall in which most of the townspeople lived. I couldn't see anyone stirring around from where I stood, but I couldn't imagine anyone—except Sam—could sleep through the constant screeching.

I went back into the berth and again shook my husband. "Wake up, Sam. Something isn't right with those sirens. If it's a test, why—"

"This is an emergency alert broadcast by the United States Coast Guard," the VHF radio announced.

I froze, head tilted toward the cabin, though the broadcaster's voice clearly reached me over the sirens' blast.

"The Alaska Tsunami Warning Center has issued a tsunami warning for the coastal areas of Alaska, due to a 6.9 magnitude earthquake in the Gulf of Alaska—"

"Sam! Listen! Did you hear—"

The sirens went silent, and the town's loudspeakers blared their own warning. "An earthquake off the Aleutian Islands has triggered a tsunami warning. Estimated arrival time for the tsunami is forty-five minutes. You must evacuate to higher ground *now*. Those with boats who want to head out of the harbor need to leave now. All remaining folks must head to the Begich Towers immediately."

"Sam!" A fresh rush of adrenaline kicked me into flight mode. "Hurry, Sam! Get *up!* A tsunami is coming!"

He slipped out of the sleeping bag. "I heard it." He slowly headed into the boat's cabin and put on his pants.

I remembered the folks staying in their boats across the dock, and how I hadn't seen any movement moments earlier. "Sam, I'm going to check on the neighbors, make sure they're getting out, in case they missed the alarm." I left Sam to dress as I head out and jumped onto the dock. I dashed past a few empty harbor slips to the first boat and rapped against its bow.

A middle-aged man stepped out of his cabin and raised a hand in greeting. His bright eyes belied the worry lines creasing his face. "We heard the radio, got the news. Thank you."

I nodded and ran toward another boat, where I'd seen people milling on the deck the night before. Before I reached it, I saw those folks rushing around, gathering belongings. I waved my arms, and a man threw up his hand, letting me know without words that they'd received the dire news. I wasted no time and ran as fast as I could back to our boat.

Sam glanced up as I hopped onto the deck. "Have you seen my hat?"

"What! Sam, what are we going to do? Are we taking the *Bonnie Lass* out of the harbor, or are we going to the Towers?" I sucked in a breath, not because I'd been running, but because at that moment it occurred to me how very long and narrow the Whittier Bay's Passage Canal is, and how Whittier sits at the far end of that canal, off Prince William Sound. It could take longer than forty-five minutes to get out of the canal and reach the deeper waters of Port Wells—and here we stood, wasting time. My knees went weak. "S-Sam."

He turned over a bucket, then shifted some of our materials around on the deck, calmly searching for his hat. "I don't think we have enough gas to make it out," he said, heading back into the cabin.

I followed him, watched in stunned amazement as he picked up a stack of paper charts from the table and set them back down.

"Are you *still* looking for your *hat?*" A tsunami was coming in a matter of minutes, and all he seemed to care about was a stupid hat! "Sam! What are we going to do?"

He shuffled more papers, picking up this thing and that, putting each one back in the same place he found it. "I think the safest thing for us to do is head to the Towers. There's not enough time to get gas and still make it out of the harbor."

I pressed a hand against the door to steady myself. My worst fear was coming true. I could imagine no place more dangerous to be than Whittier Bay during a tsunami. I'd even had nightmares about it after watching an old film of the 1964 earthquake known as the Good Friday Earthquake and the Great Alaskan Earthquake, shortly after moving to Alaska. The 9.2-magnitude quake lasted four minutes and thirty-eight seconds, and it was the most powerful earthquake ever recorded in North American history. Ground fissures, collapsing structures, and tsunamis resulting from the massive earthquake killed 139 people. Less than two-hundred people live here now, including Sam and me, and most of those live in the condominiums known as Begich Towers. The place where we *should* be heading at this very moment.

"Sam," I said again, quieter this time, as my voice didn't seem to want to work. "Let's go. We have to hurry." I took a deep breath, and miraculously, it seemed to work. My weak legs filled with a rush of energy and urgency, and suddenly I couldn't seem to stand still. I paced back and forth across the small cabin.

Sam knelt and looked under the table. "I'm not going anywhere without my hat." He huffed as he stood.

"Seriously! You've got to be kidding me!" I began throwing things around the cabin, frantically searching for the hat that anchored us to the boat. "Your hat could be the death of us!"

He smiled—actually *smiled*. "You need to stay calm, Bonnie. We're going to be okay." He lifted his Helly Hanson raincoat from his seat in the helm, then held up his trophy. "Here it is!" He waved the hat in the air, then tugged it onto his head and grinned. All seemed well in Sam's world, now that he had his hat. He held out an arm toward the door, inviting me to exit ahead of him.

Sam shut the door to our cabin, secured our boat, and as we jumped onto the dock, I prayed that we'd have a boat to come back to when all this was over.

Hand in hand, we hustled toward the Begich Towers. We paused only long enough to note that two large fishing vessels headed out of the harbor at full speed. All of the smaller boats remained in port. Sam squeezed my hand. I knew his thoughts, as if they were my own. *I hope we made the right decision.*

Only a scattering of us left the docks and caught up to the small number of folks leaving their homes and businesses in town, all of us hurrying toward the Towers on foot. I assumed everyone else in town was already there.

As we crossed the railroad tracks, our path merged with that of an older man on crutches, who almost out-walked us. I'd never seen anyone move so quickly with a damaged leg and crutches. When we neared him, he turned to look at us, and the fear on his face caused my mouth to go dry.

"You okay, sir?" Sam asked, and his grip tightened on my hand.

"I was here during the '64 quake," the man said. "It was bad. Real bad." As if spurred by his own words, the man's stride lengthened, and he quickly moved ahead of us, leaving his ominous words to repeat like a scratched record in my head.

It was bad. Real bad.

Whittier alone, as tiny as the town is and was, lost thirteen people in the waves that reached forty-three feet that day in 1964. The tsunami destroyed the railroad depot, two sawmills, many homes, and started a fire at the Union Oil Company tank farm. The devastation to the small community burned fresh in the minds of all who'd lived through it, and in spite of the magnitude of today's earthquake being smaller, I knew we were in grave danger. With every step, I prayed there would be no loss of life or property today.

I focused on the Begich Towers and Maynard Mountain that loomed up behind them. A thought struck me. "Sam, I'm not going to the Towers."

"What?" He glanced at me like I'd misspoken, but he never slowed his stride, and neither did I.

"I mean it."

"*What* do you mean? Yes, we are. We're going to the Towers, and we're heading to the top floor."

"I'm scared, Sam. I'm not going to the Towers." I pointed toward the huge, glacier-covered mountain standing far above and behind the Begich Towers, and Sam's gaze followed my finger. "I'm going to climb that mountain." I not only said those words; I *felt* them. I truly meant what I'd said, and I knew there'd be no stopping me. I couldn't get to high-enough ground to suit me, and though the fourteen-story Towers grew taller as we neared, they weren't nearly tall enough. In my mind, I saw again the film clip I'd watched showing the devastating effects of the tsunami following the '64 earthquake. The Towers weren't tall enough.

Sam, still holding my hand, tugged me in the direction of Begich Towers. "Bonnie," he said, his voice calmer than he possibly could have felt, "we'll be safe in the towers."

I shook my head and adamantly jutted my chin. "No. I am climbing that mountain!"

When he turned to me, Sam's face registered compassion. Compassion and love. As we walked, he released my hand and put his arm around me, pulling me close. "Okay," he said. "We'll go to the mountain." He dropped his arm, grabbed my hand again, and we picked up our pace.

"And climb it?" I asked, still unsure.

"Sure. We'll climb it." He smiled, and for the first time in minutes that seemed like hours, I believed we would be okay.

We hustled past the Towers, still holding hands, ignoring the worried looks and concerned glances sent our way by those who turned to go inside. We'd almost reached the mountain when we saw it—a broad, swift-running creek. From where we'd started, we had no way of seeing or knowing this water barrier stood between us and the mountain. We didn't know how deep it ran, or how quickly it might rise given the surge of a tsunami. I covered my hands with my mouth to keep from wailing then and there.

Sam turned to look at the Towers. "We're high enough here."

Despite the chill in the air, a cold sweat broke on my skin. I had been so determined to climb that mountain, but I turned to follow Sam's gaze, and he again took my hand.

A few stragglers ran toward the Towers. Beyond, our boat sat in the harbor, along with our hopes and dreams of commercial fishing. All our money was tied up in gear and that boat, which sat like a helpless duck, waiting to be washed away or smashed to smithereens by a tsunami.

Sam squeezed my hand, wordlessly assuring me that he was right there beside me, and that whatever might happen, we'd face it and get through it together.

My throat tightened, and before I ever said another prayer for our safety, I gave thanks to God for this man who stood beside me, holding my hand, as together we faced one of life's toughest storms.

Sam's grip on my hand caused my fingers to throb, but I didn't care. I didn't want him to loosen his grasp one bit. I continued to pray as we stood there, hand-in-hand, watching, waiting—waiting for the big wall of water that could wash away our whole future, everything we worked and planned so hard for. How big would the wave be? Would it reach us where we stood? I prayed. And prayed some more. *Save us, God! Save us, God! Please, save us, God!*

We waited for what seemed like hours, when in actuality, it was probably about twenty minutes, when a little red pickup came out of nowhere, moving slowly as it's driver half hung out of the window, an electric megaphone pressed to his mouth.

"What . . . is he . . . saying?" I gasped as we ran closer.

"Don't know," Sam said.

As we neared the pickup—or perhaps the pickup came nearer to us—we made out the man's announcement.

"No tsunami! There's no tsunami! . . . safe to return to your homes . . . tsunami! It's safe to return to your home, businesses, or boats. I repeat, there is no tsunami!"

Sam and I ground to a halt, and I doubled over with my hands on my knees, propping myself up as I tried to catch my breath. A sob broke out of me when Sam placed a hand on my back.

"Are you okay?"

I stood and wrapped my arms around him, and even though he must have felt as weak as I did, Sam lifted me off my feet.

Thank you, God!

When Sam placed me back on the ground, his face was lit with pure joy. "Let's get out of here, Bonnie. We've got some fishing to do."

CHAPTER FORTY-EIGHT

God, Please Let Me Faint

Because of the wicked weather, Sam and I had only three days left to get to Seward and get ready for the halibut opening. It would take great weather—nothing short of a miracle—to make that happen. We gassed up *The Bonnie Lass II,* purchased another 55-gallon steel drum of gasoline to sustain us, and we headed out of the long Passage Canal as fast as we could toward Prince William Sound.

The weather had indeed settled, and we had a lovely trip through Prince William Sound and the island passages, and I loved seeing the verdant mountains rising out of the blue-green water toward the brilliant sky.

Then, as we left Prince William Sound, things dramatically changed. It seemed that no sooner than the nose of our boat left the protection of the islands and protruded into the Gulf of Alaska, we hit harsh wind. It blew 35 knots coming into Port

Bainbridge, and within minutes, we were facing eight-foot waves.

"We can't handle this," Sam said. "We've got to turn back a bit."

Sam navigated the rough sea and took us into the safety of a small cove on Erlington Island, called Fox Farm Bay, where we docked and spent the night before heading out again the next morning.

We awoke to a drizzly day, though we were relieved to see the wind had died down. Hurriedly, we pulled up the anchor and ventured out again, anxious to get to Seward. Again, once we were out in the gulf, we hit nasty winds and waves. This time, Sam took us into North Twin Bay, which was a little closer. The day after that, we finally made it, but it had taken us an extra three days, and it was the evening before opening day. There was simply no way we could get to Sterling to get all our gear, bait our hooks, and return to Seward for opening.

"Well," Sam said, rubbing the back of his neck, "might as well learn a thing or three while we're here. Let's go talk to some fishermen."

We spent the day walking the docks, talking to and learning from fishermen who'd been at this for years—decades even. On opening day, we applauded as boats returned to the docks, loaded heavy with their catch, and then we headed to the cannery to watch the bellies of the boats open to unload thousands of pounds of fish. Enjoying the festive air of the fishermen, Sam and I were almost as excited as if the catches were our own. We could hardly wait until October, when the next opening day would occur.

"We'll be ready the next time, Bonnie," he said, squeezing my hand.

As the last of the boats came in, Sam and I decided we'd take the boat around to Homer, where we'd harbor it until the opening day next month.

After a hearty breakfast on September 15, we left Seward Harbor, heading for Homer. At fifteen knots, the wind would be manageable, so we headed toward Gore Point. Gore had a nasty reputation for sea conditions, due to the strong tides that flowed in and out of Cook Inlet and the Nuka Passage, and it had a rocky bottom that kicked up riptides in any kind of weather. Steep, rocky cliffs lined the western side of the point, so we knew we'd have to be cautious when we reached that area.

"Cautious" was a word that meant little, once we reached Gore Point. The big whitecaps became huge whitecaps as we neared the point, and the sea grew so rough that we couldn't walk upright. I would have to squat and duckwalk to move around, and at one point it got so rough that I knelt on the cushion in the kitchen booth, wedging myself against the table as I gripped the seat back, just to keep from being thrown around the cabin. Kneeling on the seat, instead of sitting, also allowed me to see out the window above the dash. That's where I spent most of my time during the harrowing trip, so that I could see what we were up against.

The waves became small mountains, and *The Bonnie Lass II* would climb up one wave, crest it going airborne, then fall down the other side as green water slammed against our window. It appeared as though we were underwater each time a wave hit.

I could hardly breathe. I think I squealed, but it could have been my imagination, as I could barely hear anything above the roar of the winds and the waves. My hands were so clammy that I'd lose my grip and start to slide as we were thrown up and down in the ocean. My stomach rolled with the boat.

God, please, let me faint.

That was my prayer, over and over. If I fainted, I reasoned, I wouldn't have to endure the gripping fear that made it hard to take in air, that made it impossible to stand, that made it difficult to think. *Just let me faint, please, God!*

And then I saw Sam.

My husband's knuckles were bone-white as he gripped the steering wheel, his face a mask of concentration and consternation as he sat at the helm, doing his best to keep us alive in the ocean's horrific conditions.

Shame burned my face. How could I pray to faint when Sam might need me? He couldn't leave his post even for a second, for to do so would surely cause us to capsize.

Please, God, don't let me faint! Don't let me faint! I'm so sorry! Sam might need me. Please don't let me faint!

And Sam did need me.

"Bonnie!" he yelled over the storm. "The gas drum! Get it away from the door and secure it." He glanced over his shoulder only once, then had to return his fierce attention to the massive wave we had to climb.

Again, we went straight up and back down. Again, a wall of green seawater slammed our cabin windows, making it seem as if we were underwater—and I guess we really were!

"I can't, Sam!"

"You have to," he said. "I can't leave the wheel. You can do it!"

Sam was right. I had no choice. If the 55-gallon drum fell across the doorway, we'd be trapped.

Move, Bonnie! I forced myself to turn loose of the seatback, and I duckwalked to the cabin door, my hands at my sides to keep myself upright. I pushed against the door, but it was no use. The drum of gasoline had slipped partway off the pallet and was blocking the door. I shoved to no avail. Finally, I sat and used my feet to push against the door, giving it everything I had, and moving it just enough so I could squeeze out.

On the deck, the roaring wind assaulted me. I sucked in a breath as I stared straight at giant walls of green water on both sides of the deck. I had to crane my neck to see the whitecaps at the tops of those waves. *Don't let me die, God. Sam needs me!*

I gripped the handles attached to the walls on each side of the door, knowing if I let go, I might be flung overboard. How in the world could I—a 105-pound woman—lift a 55-gallon drum of gasoline back up onto a wooden pallet? The barrel weighed close to 350 pounds! *350 pounds!*

I held tightly through another wave, closing my eyes to keep from seeing the walls of water surrounding us. *Think, Bonnie!*

Then I spied the bundle of rope within reach of my arm, if I stretched. I quickly undid the rope and tied one end to the handle, then lassoed the barrel and pulled the rope through the same handle. I'd use the waves as leverage!

When the boat fell down a mountain of water, I sat on the deck and pushed my feet against the cabin and pulled with all my might, letting gravity assist me. When we climbed the next wave, I held on for dear life so the barrel wouldn't again tip toward the door. One inch at a time, one wave at a time, the barrel finally righted itself back to where it needed to be. I quickly tied it to the same handle, securing it so it wouldn't tip again and block us in.

Weak, drenched, and half-sick with fright, I duckwalked back into the cabin, wedged myself again into the booth, and when Sam turned to glance at me, I gave him a thumbs up and tried to smile.

He grinned at me—actually *grinned*—in the middle of that storm! "I knew you could do it, Bonnie! Good job!" And then he turned his attention back to the sea.

Despite my fear, I felt a little surge of pride transfer from Sam into me. Yes, I'd been brave, and I'd done a good job. Weak ol' Bonnie had—in spite of her fears—transformed into a strong wilderness woman, and now she was a strong sea woman!

Some minutes later, the huge walls of water grew smaller. We'd made it through the worst!

Or so I thought.

I'd just made my way to Sam's side when I saw something crazy in front of us. I pointed. "What's that!" There was a churning wall of white water rising before us, making me think of a monstrous, sloshing, washing machine, our boat being the rubber ducky some child had tossed inside.

"Look at the chart," Sam said. "What does it read?"

I rolled the ocean chart open on the table. Between Sam's navigational equipment and the charts, even in unknown waters, we usually had a strong idea of where we were.

"We're approaching Dangerous Cape," I said. "The chart says tide rips."

"Can you see how deep it is?"

"Oh, no! Sam! In one place, it reads zero fathoms and four feet! And what does *RKS* mean?"

"It means rocks!" Sam shot me an incredulous look, as though I should have known that one.

"Rocks! But what about four feet of water? We'll crash!"

"Bonnie," he said, speaking softer, so to calm me, "that's the mean lower low water. The water's deeper than that. It's okay. I'll navigate through the rocks."

Navigate through—

"Are you kidding me! Sam, just go around!"

"Can't. It's too far. We have to go through it." In spite of the way Sam's muscles bulged from the strength it took to hold the wheel steady, and in spite of the sweat on his brow, Sam acted confident.

That made one of us.

So far, the trip had been the longest and roughest ride of my life, and I wanted nothing more than to get to a harbor, any harbor, safe and sound.

As we entered the riptides, pyramids of water seemingly rose out of the ocean all around us, on every side. Green water assaulted our windshield every few seconds, blinding us from what lay ahead. For fifteen solid minutes, *The Bonnie Lass II* was thrashed and pounded by waves as Sam and I struggled to hang on.

And then, it settled down.

My legs felt rubbery, and my knees threatened to give away as I made my way toward my husband. "That was the craziest, wickedest water ever! I don't ever want to go through anything like that again."

"Me, either," Sam said, but his voice had a doubtful tone I didn't like. And that's when I saw what he was staring at.

Just up ahead was another churning white wall of water, and this one looked worse than the last. "Oh, Sam!" My voice quavered as I spoke. I hurried as fast as I could manage back to the kitchen booth and again knelt on the cushion, wedging my rear against the table as I gripped the backrest. *Jesus, I prayed, please, please, please get us through this safely!*

I held on as tightly as I could, and I wonder to this day how my fingernails didn't leave claw marks in the aluminum dash. My mind flipped from terror to prayer, from terror to prayer, and from terror to prayer. This rip was much worse than the first, and though I'd try to twist to look at my husband, each time I'd almost go airborne, flung from the booth, and I'd have to turn back around to press in and hold on. A dull ache in my jaw built toward a sharp pain, and I realized I'd been clenching my teeth out of fear. Strength was being sapped from my body, and I wasn't sure if it was from the effort to hold on, or from sheer terror. Either way, I didn't think I could hang on another minute, as our boat was yanked and shoved and thrown in all directions by the battering waves.

Please, God! Please save us! Get us out of this!

Some long, terrifying minutes later, we came out on the other side of the rip, and the sea grew less violent the farther we went from it. We finally pulled into Seldovia's harbor— eight and a half hours after we'd started. That was eight and a half hours of pure torture! I can't explain how grateful I felt to step out of our boat onto the dock. I could have kissed the boards on which I walked!

We strolled slowly into town, my legs still feeling a bit rubbery, but I gave thanks to God with almost every step I took. We were once again on solid ground!

In town, Sam and I found a little restaurant and ate what seemed at the time like the best meal of our lives, though today I can't even tell you what it was. We knew we were fortunate and blessed, and we were both grateful to have lived through the life-threatening storm. We knew we could have died.

Sam and I spent the next couple of days in Seldovia before heading the fourteen miles up Kachemak Bay to Homer, where we planned to keep the boat until the next halibut season in October.

CHAPTER FORTY-NINE

Will Anyone Know?

Our trip back to Sterling in October was, thankfully, much less eventful. Sam purchased a reel for the boat's back deck so he could let out the line hydraulically. He let out about eight thousand feet of line, snapping on a ganglion with the baited hook about every fifteen or twenty feet. Our first catch was thrilling, and we were proud to return to the cannery with a few thousand dollars' worth of halibut. Finally, Sam and I were real commercial fishermen!

*Look at that smile! Captain Sam is a happy man
sitting at the helm of his commercial fishing boat.*

*Sam cutting bait for
the halibut hooks*

Letting out the longline

2

(left) Sam pulling in the long line with the hydraulic powered puller and davit.

(below) First mate Bonnie sitting in the captain's chair.

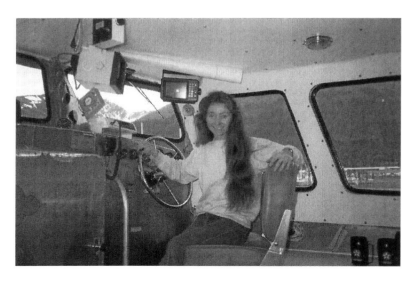

(left) Now that's a happy fisherwoman! Look at that halibut!

(Below) Bonnie loves her little diesel stove in the galley. Coffee, anyone?

(left) Sam blowing ice into the fish holding tank.

(below) No end to cutting enough bait for all those hooks!

Sam and I had indeed made a sustainable living as fishermen, but the *Exxon Valdez* oil spill had put a wrench in our plans. It no longer made sense to buy property on Latouche Island. We would occasionally return to Prince William Sound for what we called our "play time" vacations, but never to commercially fish. Still, we did a solid, steady business fishing the waters in and between Kachemak and Resurrection Bays.

Winter was no less frigid on the ocean than on the lake, so Sam and I headed back to Caribou Island to hole up until spring thaw. It felt so good to be back on the island where we could build a hot fire in the woodstove and snuggle in our warm bed.

Once the weather again broke, it was time to go back out to sea. We decided we'd spend the rest of our Alaskan years living in Sterling, where we had boat access to the ocean, and we could more easily acquire supplies as we needed them.

In the late summer of 1990, Sam and I said goodbye to our Skilak Lake home for the last time. We'd settled acres of land on the 159-acre island called Caribou; we'd cleared lots and cut roads and built cabin after cabin. And yet, despite the sometimes-painful birthing of our Caribou community, I realized we never really owned her. Like Skilak Lake owned herself, so did Caribou Island own her own self.

And when we lived there, *she owned us.*

As we sailed away, I stared at our cozy cabin home, and then at the island as it grew smaller in the distance, and I remembered how wild the land was the first time I stepped foot on it. I wondered if, a few hundred years from now, the rough wilderness that is Skilak and Caribou will reclaim their own; will anyone know we were ever there?

EPILOGUE

Sam and I lived in Alaska for fifteen years, leaving there in 1996. We purchased Sam's family homestead in West Virginia. No one had inhabited the property in over fifty years, so once again, we were wilderness homesteaders, of sorts. The two-story log cabin his mother had grown up in was now gone, and the land was completely grown over.

Together, Sam and I cleared the land, and he built us another beautiful cabin reminiscent of the homes he'd built on Caribou Island.

We live there still today, raising livestock and gardens, and we still cut and chop our own wood for heat. The mountainous West Virginia winters can, at times, be quite frigid, though none yet as brutal as those we lived through on Caribou Island. But when the wind begins to gust, and it roars down the mountainside to wail through the valley, I instinctively turn toward my picture window to check for whitecaps on Skilak Lake.

The End

ACKNOWLEDGMENTS

A book doesn't happen without the help of others, and my book is no exception. I owe many thanks to many people. For starters, I owe so much to my two favorite men for all their support, love and devotion, and for always being there for me—my heroes, my husband, Samuel Ward, and my dad, Donald Rose.

Sam, you had a dream! But, more than that, you had the guts and determination to pursue it, and in so doing, you led us on the greatest adventure of my life. Without you, there would be no story. What a ride it has been these 44 years together . . . and baby, it's not over yet! Every day you are in my life is my greatest blessing!

Dad, thank you for always being in my corner—for believing in me and cheering me on. I've said it before and I'll say it again—a daughter couldn't ask for a better father than you, and I thank God you are mine.

After finishing the manuscript for my first book, Winds of Skilak: A Tale of True Grit, True Love, and Survival in the Alaskan Wilderness, I searched diligently for a good editor to give it the professional edit and polish I knew it needed. After dozens of inquiries across the country, I finally found the perfect editor for me. Indeed, I struck gold, when my daunting search led me to Sandy Tritt, CEO of Inspiration for Writers, Inc. When it came time to edit my sequel, there was no hesitation on my part to whom I would turn. I made a beeline straight to Sandy and her wonderful team of editors at www.InspirationForWriters.com and never looked back!

Sandy, you are such a jewel, and I can't thank you enough for the thorough job and TLC you gave both my first book and this sequel. But, even more than that, thank you for putting up with millions of questions (okay, give or take five or ten). You were always there, always helpful, always guiding me in the right direction, right to the very end! I am forever indebted to you, and I look forward to working with you and your team again in the future.

I also want to thank Mae Phillips from coverfreshdesigns.com for the great job she did in designing the front and back cover for this book. Mae is amazingly talented and skilled at her job. She also creates all the designs for my promotional materials, such as posters, banners, bookmarks, etc. Anytime I need something done, she is quick to answer and create!

I also want to shout out a big thank you to Kristin Hankins for proofreading my manuscript. Kristin, you have an incredibly keen eye for spotting those errors, and I'm very grateful to you!

And finally, to all of my readers. I am forever grateful for your love, support and words of encouragement that have given me endless joy. Many of you have stated that our story inspired you—but, oh, what an inspiration you have been to me. You will always hold a special place in my heart.

God bless you all.

A NOTE TO OUR READERS

Thanks for continuing the journey with us. We hope you enjoyed it! We'd love to hear from you. Please visit us at:

Email: bonnieroseward@gmail.com

Website: www.windsofskilak.com

Blog: https://bonnieroseward.wordpress.com/

Other books by Bonnie Rose Ward:

Winds of Skilak: A Tale of True Grit, True Love and Survival in the Alaskan Wilderness

Printed in Great Britain
by Amazon